Annie Swynnerton
Painting Light and Hope

Katie JT Herrington
and Rebecca Milner

Manchester Art Gallery

Published by Manchester Art Gallery in
conjunction with the exhibition
Annie Swynnerton: Painting Light and Hope
Manchester Art Gallery
23 February 2018 – 6 January 2019

First published 2018. Reprinted 2018

ISBN 978-0-901673-96-1

Manchester Art Gallery
Mosley Street
Manchester M2 3JL
manchesterartgallery.org

Editorial project management: Lindsay Porter
Design: axisgraphicdesign.co.uk
Print: Cambrian Press

Front cover: Annie Swynnerton *The Sense of Sight* 1895. Courtesy National Museums Liverpool
Back cover: Unknown photographer *Annie Swynnerton in her studio,* 1931 © Royal Academy of Arts, London
Inner cover: Annie Swynnerton *Italian Landscape* c.1900s (detail) © Manchester Art Gallery

RA250 Royal Academy of Arts 1768-2018 with Art Fund_

FARROW&BALL
CRAFTSMEN IN PAINT AND PAPER

MANCHESTER CITY COUNCIL

Picture Credits

© Aberdeen Art Gallery & Museums Collections: p. 74

By permission of the British Library: p. 11 General Reference Collection HS.74/1099, p. 50 General Reference Collection HIU.LD52

Bradford Art Galleries and Museums, West Yorkshire, UK/Bridgeman Images: p. 87

Collection: Dublin City Gallery The Hugh Lane: p. 63

Courtesy of the Library of Congress LC-DIG-ppmsc-06623: p. 60

Courtesy National Museums Liverpool: front cover, p. 95

© Museum of London: pp. 98–99, 107, 108, 109, 110

Milan, Gallery of Modern Art (Museo dell'ottocento). © 2018. Photo Scala Florence: p. 26

By permission of Nottingham City Museums & Galleries: p. 43

Permission of Gallery Oldham: pp. 78–79, 83

© The Print Collector/Alamy stock photo: p. 55

© RMN – Grand Palais/Patrice Schmidt/Musée d'Orsay, Paris: p. 27 © RMN – Grand Palais/ Musée d'Orsay, Paris: p. 81

© Royal Academy of Arts, London: back cover, p. 47, 128, 129

Royal Holloway, University of London: p. 121

Salford Museum and Art Gallery: pp. 30–31, 45

Sotheby's Picture Library: p. 19, 92

© Tate, London 2015: p. 67, 85, 91, 97, 105, 117, 123

Richard Taylor Fine Art: p. 37, 118

© Anna Watson: p. 49, 73, 75, 106, 113

All other images © Manchester Art Gallery

Contents

'I have known love and the light of the sun.'

Annie Swynnerton, 1933

Foreword

Alistair Hudson
Director, Manchester Art Gallery

2018 marks the 250th anniversary of the Royal Academy of Arts (RA) in London and 100 years since British women over 30 were first granted the right to vote. To commemorate these significant events, the gallery is staging the first exhibition, in almost 100 years, of the work of Manchester-born Victorian painter Annie Louisa Swynnerton. Swynnerton was active in the women's movement throughout her life and in 1922 became the first elected female member of the RA since its founding in 1768. Achieving this accolade was ground breaking, but it came late in her life and, apart from an exhibition at Manchester Art Gallery in 1923, her work has rarely been seen in exhibitions since.

Swynnerton is not alone amongst late 19th- and early 20th-century female artists to have fallen into obscurity. There are many factors to blame for this, including the dominance of male artists, administrators and historians in the art world and prejudices that deemed women incapable of creative thought and vision equal to men. Swynnerton fought this in her own lifetime, but bias, convention and tradition have meant that studying and evaluating the work of female artists like her is difficult. Often, only limited examples of their work exist in the public domain and, in many cases, fewer documentary sources, which help to build biography and understand their ideas, have survived.

It has long been acknowledged that female artists have often been overlooked, or even supressed, by art history and now public institutions are starting to redress the gender imbalance of their collections. This has led to growing scholarship on female artists and an increasing and overdue number of exhibitions. Fortunately, and mostly due to her attaining Associate Royal Academician status, over 30 of Swynnerton's paintings survive in public collections in the UK. Manchester Art Gallery owns 16 of these but for many years only a few examples have ever been shown. *Painting Light and Hope* is therefore a unique opportunity to bring together many of the Manchester works with key public and private loans so that Swynnerton's art can be better understood and appreciated today.

The exhibition and accompanying catalogue reveal an artist who is firmly embedded in the rich artistic heritage of Manchester. Manchester's Victorian art scene was lively, with a successful art school, academy and our predecessor the Royal Manchester Institution (RMI), which held huge annual exhibitions. It was also a radical city, with many social reformers and political campaigners, including those involved in the women's movement, such as Lydia Becker and the Pankhursts. Given this radical and culturally rich past, it is entirely appropriate for the gallery where Swynnerton first exhibited her paintings to be honouring a woman who shook up male-dominated institutions through her activism and art. Her determination in art and life was hopeful, bolstered as it was by the joy and solace she found in painting out of doors. For anyone struggling to realise their creative ambitions today, hers is an inspirational story.

Introduction

Katie JT Herrington and Rebecca Milner

Manchester-born artist Annie Louisa Swynnerton (1844–1933) was a pioneering woman who challenged convention in art and life. At a time when women were not permitted to study art on equal terms to men, she found alternative routes to obtain rigorous training, enabling her to become a professional painter in oils. Working simultaneously within various traditional genres, she produced over two hundred paintings: portraits, subject pictures inspired by history, literature, mythology or her imagination, landscapes and nudes. She exhibited her work extensively throughout her career at venues such as the Manchester Academy of Fine Arts, the Royal Academy of Arts and the New Gallery in London, to mention but a few.

By the 1890s, Swynnerton had achieved an international reputation. In 1922 she became the first woman Associate Member of the Royal Academy since its foundation in 1768. Today, her work is represented in more than ten British public collections – including Tate, the Royal Academy, Gallery Oldham and Glasgow Museums – and four international ones, including the Musée d'Orsay, Paris. Yet, very few exhibitions or publications have given any attention to her work. *Painting Light and Hope* is the first exhibition of Swynnerton's art for almost a century. It presents work from across her career and, together with this accompanying catalogue, offers a critical perspective.

Exploring Swynnerton's work in detail reveals her as a significant artist amongst her male and female peers and highlights what makes her work unique. She comes into focus as an inventive artist who engaged with a range of established and emerging British and Continental European methods and styles of painting. The training that she received in Manchester and the familiar and social relationships that she developed during her formative years there are shown to be pivotal in enabling her career. Equally so are her periods spent studying in Rome and Paris.

Once established, she displayed knowledge of Symbolist, Pre-Raphaelite, Aesthetic, French and British Impressionist and Rural Naturalist movements, yet developed her own independent artistic identity. Her mature signature style was also shaped by her experience of the light effects and vibrant colours of Italy,

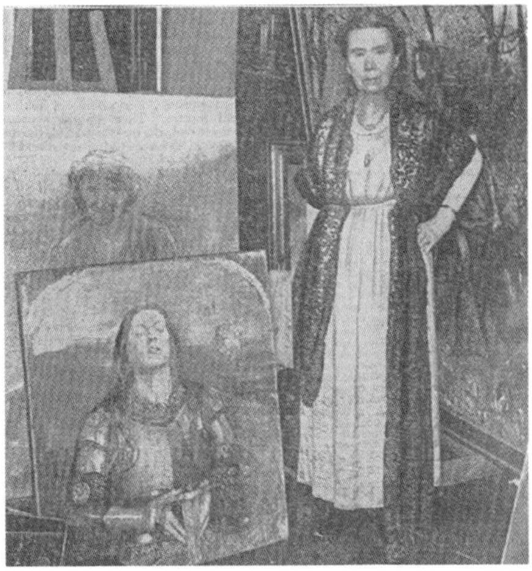

Annie Swynnerton in her studio (*The Times*, 25 November, 1922)

where she lived for extended periods throughout her life. Her passion for painting outdoors in the light of the sun and belief that it facilitated the 'perfection of drawing and modelling' underpin her mature paintings, and the light and bright palette of this period reveals her outstanding ability as a colourist.

However, her shimmering nudes, winged figures and portraits of suffragists are about more than aesthetics. Her distinctive approach to applying paint to canvas was closely aligned with a commitment to feminist politics throughout her career. Such politics, which respected women's agency and individuality, are reflected in the many representations of women in *Painting Light and Hope*. She painted women sensitively, portraying all ages and walks of life and celebrating female presence in the world while resisting traditional portrayals of beauty. As a result, her paintings visualised women's power, hope and potential at a time when many women, including Swynnerton, were fighting for professional, social and political rights.

In addition to unlocking the key themes and motivations in Swynnerton's work, *Painting Light and Hope* identifies some of her female fellow artists, sitters and patrons. This sheds light on the significant role of networks between women, which enabled them to travel, become independent artists and make a living in the late 19th and early 20th centuries. Mutual female support and the encouragement of a number of male artists created crucial opportunities for Swynnerton, which aided her career in spite of the constraints posed by a conservative and male-dominated art world. That she shared this struggle with other women surely fuelled her determination to overcome inequality and be respected for her creative vision.

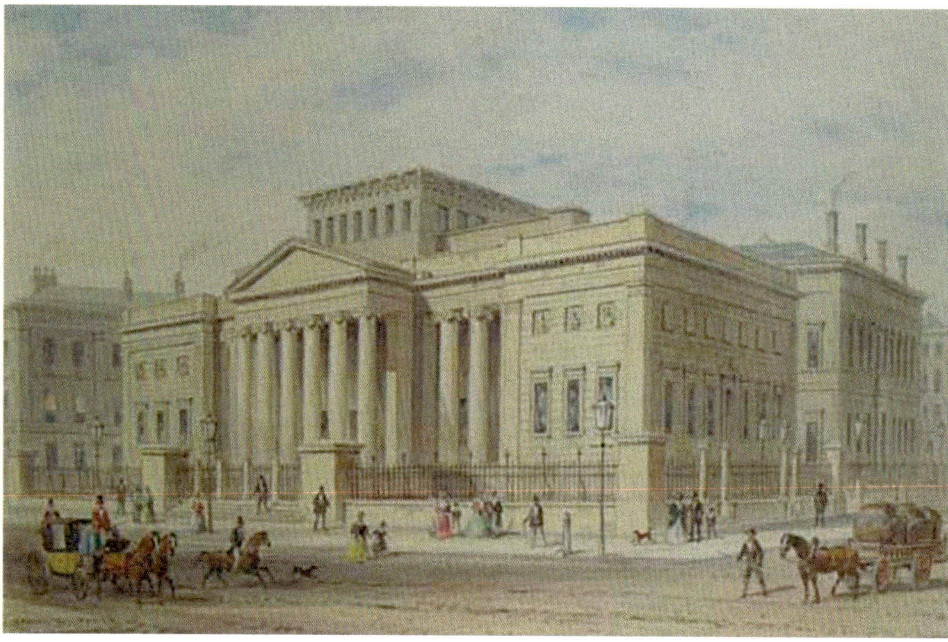

Thomas Hosmer Shepherd *The Royal Manchester Institution* c.1830,
now Manchester Art Gallery

Opportunity, Struggle and Activism: Swynnerton's Early Years in Manchester

Rebecca Milner

Annie Louisa Robinson, later Swynnerton, spent the first three decades of her life living, training and working mostly in Manchester, the city of her birth. It was in Manchester that she made her first ventures into the art world and where her strong political engagement emerged. She benefitted from, but was also constrained by, its arts institutions, and campaigned in reaction to the limited opportunities for women artists. She gave something back to the city, too; her campaigning spirit opened up opportunities that were previously barred to women artists and she was recognised for her contributions in an Honour Roll of Manchester Women.[1]

Born in 1844 in Hulme, Manchester, then a rapidly expanding working-class area, Swynnerton grew up in a large and aspiring middle-class family, and by the age of 17 was living with her parents and six sisters in a large house in Prestwich Park, north of the city. Her solicitor father, who was of reasonable but not extravagant means and counted Charles Dickens amongst his clients, was initially able to finance her education. As was the norm amongst her female contemporaries, Swynnerton was home-schooled. This traditionally included lessons in drawing and watercolour, then considered appropriate artistic accomplishments for young women. Her early artistic education also came from the study of 'her father's splendid library'.[2]

Swynnerton's family fell on hard times in 1869. Her father's firm was declared bankrupt in February and he moved with his wife to Cheetham Hill. Later that year, aged 25, and with her younger sisters Emily (b. 1845) and Julia (b. 1846), Swynnerton attended classes at the Manchester School of Art (MSA), located in the Royal Manchester Institution (RMI) on Mosley Street, now Manchester Art Gallery.[3] This was, as far as we know, the first time she engaged in formal arts training and it marks the beginning of her professional practice. Art school

---

1 This was compiled in the mid-20th century by the National Council of Women, Manchester and Salford Branch. Information held by Manchester Central Library Archive.

2 Anon. *Manchester Guardian*, 25 October, 1933.

3 The Royal Manchester Institution's building and collection were given to the city in 1882 and it became Manchester City Art Gallery. From 2002 it has been Manchester Art Gallery.

was a recognised route for women to work in education or the decorative arts, suggesting that Swynnerton and her sisters needed to earn a living following their father's bankcruptcy. They 'painted for a livelihood small watercolour drawings illustrating scenes from Dickens'.[4] This no doubt helped fund their passage through art school and lodging outside the family home close to the centre of Manchester. Swynnerton lived and worked together with her sisters throughout the 1870s and these relationships were the first, and perhaps the most formative, of the strong bonds she formed with fellow women artists and activists.

When Swynnerton enrolled at the MSA it was thriving, having converted from a school of design in 1849. Students flocked there, including large numbers of women from a wide range of backgrounds. The majority of these female students became governesses and art teachers, rather than artists. Some were also affluent young women who were traditionally tutored privately, for the purpose of accomplishment rather than to prepare them for work, and who stopped taking classes when they married. Swynnerton trained at the MSA for five years, which suggests she aspired to more than just genteel accomplishments.

Study of the nude had long been considered an essential part of a (male) artist's training. At the MSA, due to moral codes that prevented female students from studying from the nude, Swynnerton had access only to draped models. This inequality was a barrier to women aspiring to a career as an artist. Swynnerton would have to struggle to overcome these constraints but it did not prevent her from demonstrating considerable ambition and skill at the MSA, achieving medals for a monochrome painting from the antique in 1870 and a painting in oil from life in 1871. Then, in 1873, she won one of only two National Art School Competition Princess of Wales Scholarships for a group in oil and a chalk drawing, which consisted of a medal and an £11 cash prize; this money aided her first trip to study in Rome in 1874. This was a prestigious award and it was customary for it to be given personally to recipients by the Princess of Wales.

---

4 These works are untraced. Swynnerton refers to them in Anon. *Manchester Guardian*, 25 October, 1933.

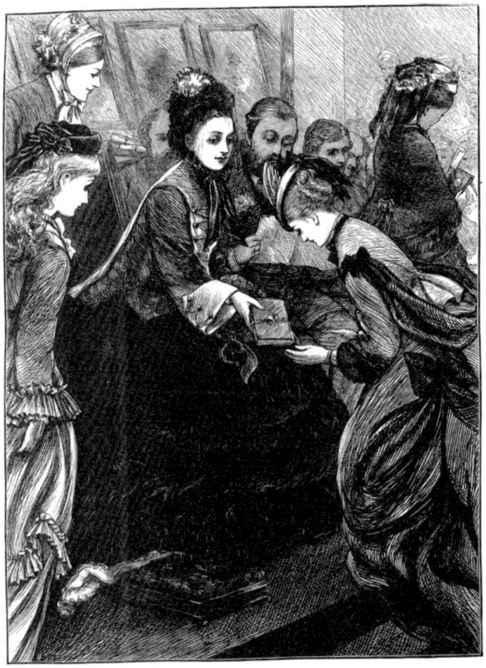

Illustration from *The Graphic* magazine 1873
showing the Princess of Wales Scholarships presentation ceremony

Swynnerton's first trip to Italy proved pivotal to her artistic development and was facilitated by her friendship with fellow MSA student Susan Isabel Dacre (1844–1933), whose portrait she would paint in 1880 (see Catalogue No. 4). Dacre was almost exactly the same age as Swynnerton, but by the time she became an art student in Manchester she had already lived and worked in Paris as a governess and studied art in the Louvre. She was a more worldly traveller and therefore a helpful companion to Swynnerton. At this early stage in their careers, their mutual concerns – to be taken seriously as professionals and have the same rights and opportunities as male artists – and a passion for art and travel provided the foundations for a life-long friendship and working relationship. The pair's artistic practice was bound up with their political engagement. Swynnerton became a member of the Manchester Society of Women's Suffrage in 1880–1 and Dacre sat on its executive committee from 1885–95.

From 1871, Swynnerton, her sisters and Dacre all began to exhibit work at the Autumn Exhibition at the RMI, the most important annual art event in the city. It showcased painting, sculpture and architecture by national and international artists and comprised upwards of 750 works, most of which were for sale. It also presented an opportunity for new artists to start building their reputation and earn money from their work. That Swynnerton began to exhibit during her training was a statement of her intent to establish herself as a professional artist. Many of her early RMI exhibits were portraits and, in 1872, she received her first critical review for a portrait of *Nellie Beswick* (untraced), one of two portraits of the daughters of a local industrialist. With the increasing wealth of Manchester, the clientele for art grew rapidly in the 19th century and local industrialists and merchants were keen to immortalise their families and furnish their large homes with paintings. Swynnerton practised her portrait skills on her own family members and she became an accomplished and sought-after portrait painter as her career progressed.

The following year, in 1872, Swynnerton and her sisters shared a studio in 5 York Street, very near the RMI, putting them at the heart of Manchester's art scene. As well as exhibiting opportunities, the RMI exhibitions allowed aspiring artists to see the work of other artists, past and present. The exhibitions consisted mainly of conventional portraiture, landscape, still life or genre painting, but with some works that may have inspired and challenged an ambitious young artist. Local artists including MSA headmaster William Jabez Muckley, Frederic Shields and Henry Clarence Whaite, and artists associated with a second-wave of Pre-Raphaelitism, such as John Roddam Spencer Stanhope, all exhibited regularly. Swynnerton would also have seen works by leading contemporary artists such as Briton Riviere, Edward Poynter, James Abbott McNeill Whistler and George Frederic Watts.[5] Watts was one of the few artists to show mythological paintings at the RMI, and his work had a formative influence on Swynnerton, who aspired to paint nudes and classical subjects. From 1875 her RMI exhibits show how she was extending her range, tackling not just portraits but also subjects such as *Offering to Bacchus* and *Amor and Psyche* (both untraced).

---

5 In 1874 Watts won a prize at the RMI for *Love and Death*, and he exhibited regularly in Manchester. Whistler exhibited two landscapes at the RMI in 1869, *Wind and Sea* and *Sea and Rain*.

After 1875, Swynnerton had the opportunity to exhibit at the annual exhibitions of another arts organisation based in the RMI, the Manchester Academy of Fine Arts (MAFA). Established in 1858, this was the association for professional artists in Manchester, offering a centre for classes, meetings and exhibitions. MAFA membership was exclusively male, although there was nothing in its founding constitution expressly excluding women: its classes, and the professional status of member or associate, had been closed to aspiring female artists, because attending life classes and studying from the nude model, especially in mixed classes with men, were deemed inappropriate for women. In 1874, Swynnerton was one of a group of nine female artists who petitioned MAFA to admit women for the first time.

Swynnerton and her female cohorts from the MSA had become increasingly frustrated with only being allowed to study from a draped figure and the barriers to membership of MAFA, where attendance at classes was a prerequisite. The matter was discussed by MAFA in 1869 and was eventually resolved in 1874 by setting up a ladies-only class and a category of membership known as 'Lady Exhibitors', which was a vital step forward. Swynnerton submitted pictures to MAFA exhibitions regularly from then onwards for over a decade, including portraits, images of contemporary women and Italian subjects, which received favourable reviews. Her representation of a mother and child, *Through the Orchard* exhibited in 1885 (very likely the same work as *The Young Mother*, see Catalogue No. 15) was considered 'a picture of great merit' and 'probably the best example of her art' that she had so far shown there.[6]

Despite more exhibiting opportunities and critical success, Swynnerton's campaigning was far from over. She channelled her ongoing discontent into establishing the Manchester Society of Women Painters (MSWP) with Dacre in 1879, encouraged by the rise in women's activism in the city from the late 1860s onwards and led in the early years by Manchester-born suffragist Lydia Becker (see Catalogue No. 29), who became a friend of both Swynnerton and

---

6 See Anon., *City News*, [day and month unknown] 1885.

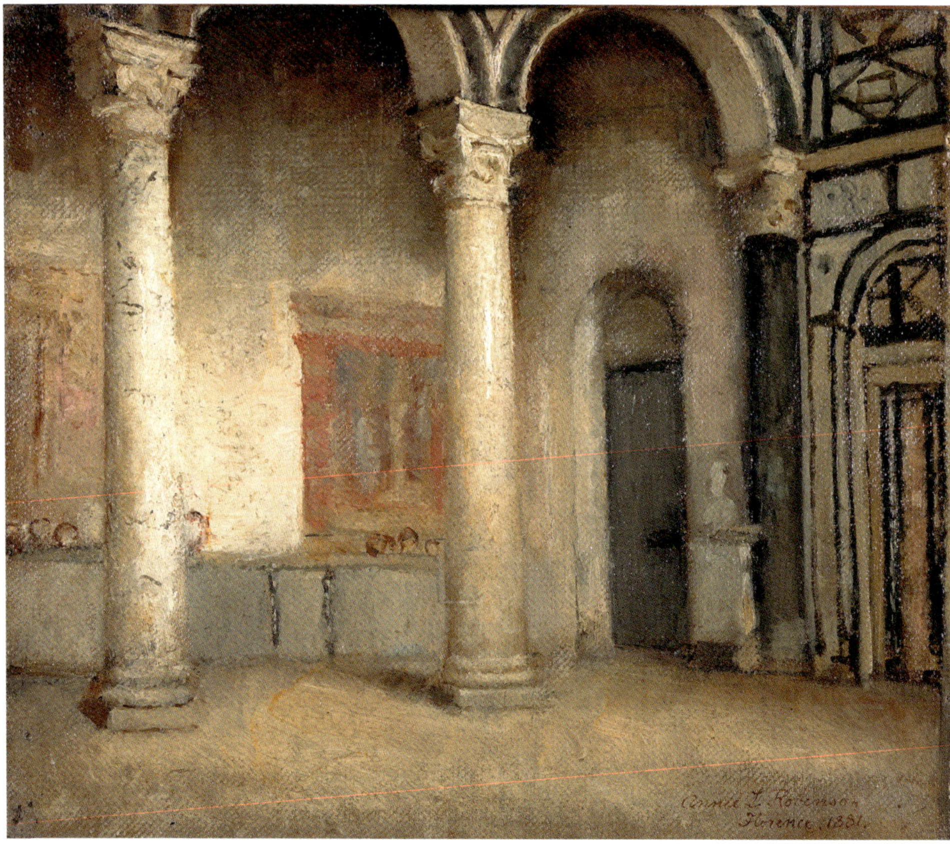

Annie Swynnerton *Interior of San Miniato, Florence* 1881,
shown at the 1882 Manchester Society of Women Painters exhibition

Dacre. The key issue for the movement was the right to vote, but activists also campaigned for education reform and equality in access to work and training in many professional spheres. Becker, for instance, championed the inclusion of women on school boards and was one of four women elected to the Manchester School Board in 1870.

With Dacre as president and Swynnerton as secretary, the MSWP committee set out to support women art students 'desirous of more thorough training, wider experience, and a higher culture'.[7] Classes in 'Elementary Drawing', 'Drawing from the Antique' and 'Drawing and Painting the Living Model' were organised and advertised in local and national publications by the society, which provided both practice and a modest income for the committee members.[8] From 1880–83 the society also held three exhibitions at city centre locations (see Catalogue No. 11) at which all members and associates exhibited. The work of Dacre and Swynnerton featured most prominently and commanded the highest prices, however, for Swynnerton, this was an opportunity to show off her developing range of subjects, which caught the attention of local reviewers. In addition to portraits, she showed imaginative subject pictures, contemporary women, classical subjects and Italian views. The positive reception of the MSWP exhibitions must have put further pressure on the MAFA committee to admit women on an equal footing with men as members and associates, which they finally did in 1884. The MSWP then disbanded, having achieved its aims, and in light of Swynnerton and Dacre's move to London, which may have made it more difficult for the group to keep going.

Prior to leaving for London in 1879, Swynnerton was invited to undertake a portrait of the Unitarian minister, and widower of novelist Elizabeth Gaskell, the Reverend William Gaskell for the Portico Library (see Catalogue No. 3). At the same time, her future husband, sculptor Joseph Swynnerton (1846–1910), was commissioned to produce a portrait bust of Gaskell. Swynnerton may have

---

7 See copy of MSWP subscriptions notice, MAFA cuttings book year 1878–83, Manchester Art Gallery Archive.

8 See MSWP announcement of art classes, *Manchester Guardian*, 3 September, 1879.

met Joseph in Rome where he was based, but he, too, exhibited and worked in Manchester in the 1870s and they certainly knew of each other's practice by the final year of that decade. Both artists had already benefitted from wealthy Mancunian patrons, but until this date Swynnerton had mostly painted their wives and children, while Joseph undertook a number of commissions for busts of eminent male citizens for public buildings.[9] The Gaskell portrait was therefore Swynnerton's most high-profile commission to date, when it was still rare for female artists to be asked to do official portraits of male public figures.

Gaskell would have been a sympathetic and well-connected sitter for the progressively minded Swynnerton. As minister of the Cross Street Chapel, he was at the heart of a circle of influential Mancunians that included radical politicians and reformers. Also, with his wife at their home in Plymouth Grove, he entertained eminent visitors that included artists, writers and intellectuals such as John Ruskin and Charles Dickens. It is not known whether Swynnerton had ever met Elizabeth Gaskell (who died in 1865) but the Gaskells' daughters Meta and Julia knew of her work by 1879, as they recommended that she paint their father's portrait. Their support and social connections, particularly Meta's, were significant in helping to further Swynnerton's career. Meta Gaskell, also an artist, facilitated an introduction to the artist Edward Burne-Jones whom Swynnerton met in the early 1880s in London.[10]

Ultimately, like many artists, Swynnerton found that she was limited by Manchester's arts institutions and was drawn to London and the Continent. London and Paris offered a wider range of art education, professional bodies, exhibitions and patrons. Swynnerton, with Dacre and a number of other Manchester-born women artists of their generation, such as Louise Jopling, sought training in the Parisian studio system where women could

---

9 Swynnerton painted portraits for the brewer Henry Boddington, possibly of his wife and his daughters (untraced). Two are listed in the catalogue for the 1880 MSWP exhibition. By then Boddington also owned Italian views and subjects by Swynnerton and Dacre. Boddington bought Swynnerton's *The Tryst* for Salford Museum and Art Gallery in 1880.

10 See exhibition catalogue *Paintings by Mrs. Swynnerton, A.R.A.* July 1923, City of Manchester Art Gallery, p.6, for discussion of Swynnerton's introduction to Burne-Jones by Miss Gaskell.

draw and paint the nude. For Swynnerton, presence in London in the early 1880s facilitated her growing artistic and social network and gave her more opportunities to show her work, whether at the Royal Academy of Arts or new avant-garde alternatives like the Grosvenor Gallery.

From 1883, Swynnerton with her husband began to split her time between London and Rome, and visited and exhibited less frequently in Manchester, although her work was still appreciated there and her absence from exhibitions mourned.[11] In 1910, the Manchester City Art Gallery (MCAG; from 2002 Manchester Art Gallery), which had superseded the RMI in 1882, showed 13 of Swynnerton's paintings in an exhibition that departed from the usual annual Autumn Exhibition and instead reviewed 'each part of modern painting'.[12] This was the largest number of her paintings to be shown at the same time in the city since the MSWP exhibitions of the early 1880s and she received equal weighting with many of her male contemporaries. In 1912 she showed her portrait *Evelyn* (private collection), depicting the daughter of Vernon Bellhouse, the managing director of a Manchester cotton-spinning firm who lived in Alderley Edge, which was described by the local press as 'one of the best pieces of face portraiture in the whole exhibition'.

It is not, however, until 1922, after her election as the first female Associate Member of the Royal Academy of Arts (ARA), that her connection to her native city was rekindled more seriously, following an invitation from the chairman of the Art Galleries Committee to stage an exhibition dedicated solely to her work the following year. She replied that she would 'certainly dearly love to show some work in Manchester', although she was ambivalent about all the belated attention following her ARA election. MCAG had yet to purchase a work from the artist, who was already represented in the collections of Tate, London and the Musée d'Orsay, Paris, as well as more locally in the galleries of Oldham and Salford. Nevertheless, Swynnerton appreciated the significance

---

[11] See Anon. *City News*, 15 October, 1910 and Anon. *Manchester Guardian*, Summer 1912.

[12] See MCAG catalogue *Autumn Exhibition of Pictures, Drawings and Prints*, 1910.

of her first retrospective and the recognition that was afforded her by the arts establishment, fellow artists and the public in Manchester.[13] Both the chairman and the curator, Lawrence Haward, were gracious in admitting that the city should never have left it so late to honour 'one of her most famous artists'.[14]

The local reviews of the 1923 MCAG Swynnerton exhibition praised the power, brilliance and vitality of her painting and highlighted its sculptural quality. One writer also located the key to her work in its combination of English and Italian artistic characteristics: 'The love of landscape under changing lights is thoroughly English; the large sense of space and the firm grasp of form have been learnt from Italy.'[15] There were many influences at work in Swynnerton's art, not least a powerful determination towards personal expression and a reforming spirit that are characteristic of her generation and city of birth.

Swynnerton's artistic vision was both shaped by and liberated in Manchester and her achievements in empowering female artists there were significant. By the time she left in the early 1880s, she had enriched and diversified the city's art scene through her relationships, activism and art. Aware to the last that she was not alone in struggling to become an artist, in her will, as well as artworks to MCAG, she left a bequest of £500 to be used for 'the advancement of art'. This was allocated by the Art Galleries Committee in 1938 (five years after her death) to buying the work of male and female artists from MAFA, and to supporting a young artist, Freda H Clough. She had just finished her studies in Manchester, and the grant would enable her to study painting at the Slade School of Art in London and in Paris for a period of 12 months. It was an entirely appropriate legacy, embodying Swynnerton's belief that 'Encouragement does not make artists, but opportunity helps.'[16]

[13] See Letter, 1923 Exhibition files, Manchester Art Gallery Archive, dated 6 December, 1923, Swynnerton to Haward: 'I shall never forget my visit to Manchester, and the great kindness I received from you all.'

[14] See Letter, 1923 Exhibition files, Manchester Art Gallery Archive, 21 December, 1923, Haward to Swynnerton regarding the purchase of *The Southing of the Sun*.

[15] See Anon. *Manchester Guardian*, 7 July, 1923.

[16] See copy of newspaper article (publication unknown), 25 November, 1922, Manchester Art Gallery Archive.

Annie Swynnerton *Joan of Arc* c.early 1900s (detail)

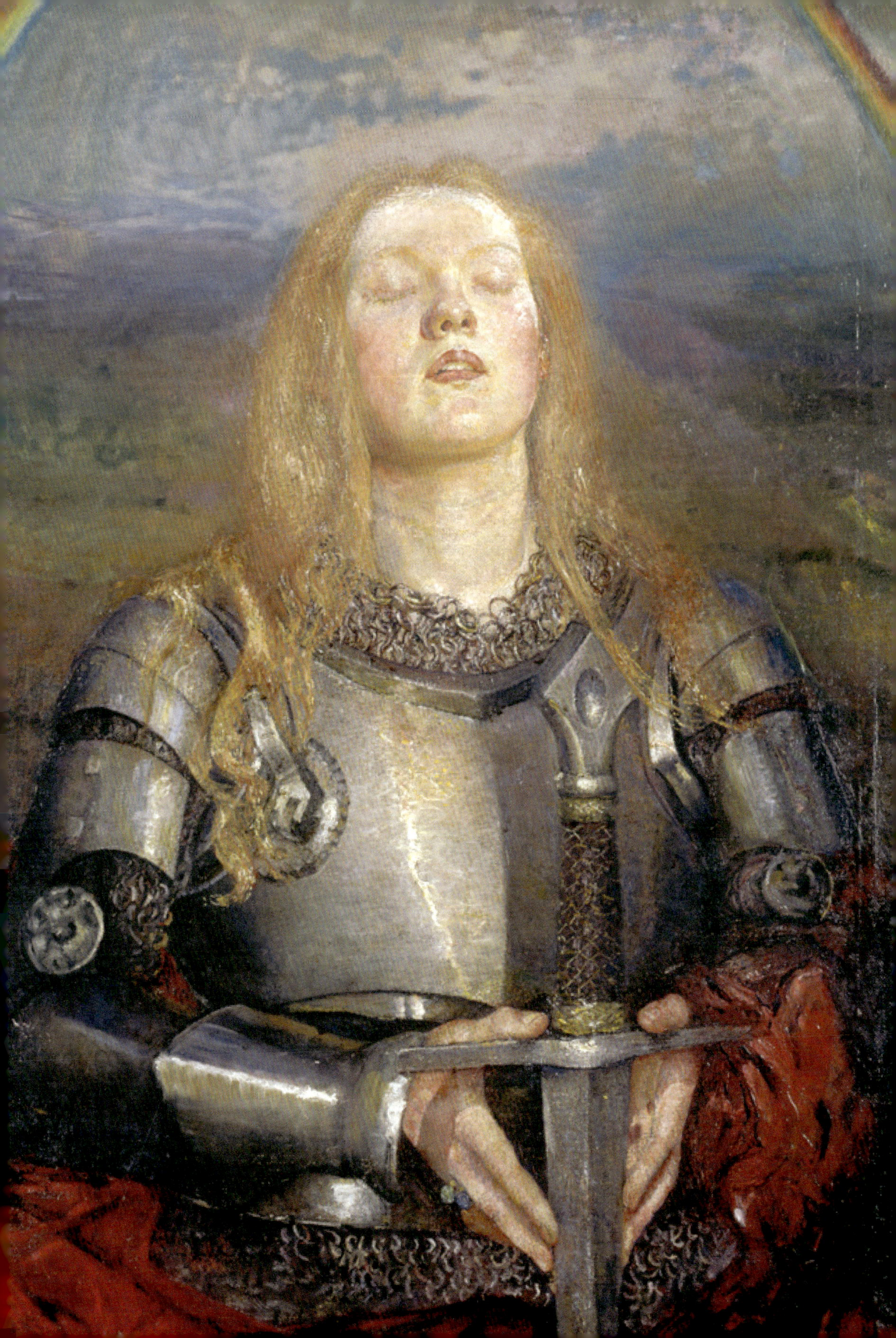

A Distinctive and Individual Approach to Painting: Swynnerton Amidst her Contemporaries

Katie JT Herrington

Swynnerton's works reveal a decisive change in her approach to painting by the early 1880s, namely from dark grounds punctuated by stark lighting to sunlit landscape backdrops produced outdoors. This, together with the significant diversity and innovation seen in her subject matter throughout her career, makes her collective work seem perplexingly eclectic at first glance. The effect is compounded by her simultaneous work in a number of traditional genres of painting: portraiture, subject pictures, landscape, and the nude, and, in her mature career, imaginative works, which do not fit neatly into such categories. It was not unusual for artists to work in multiple genres – leading male artists did – but it was ambitious and, as a result, Swynnerton's practice does not exhibit a straight path of stylistic development. There is, nevertheless, a consistent sense of purpose in her unique handling of paint – what is termed an artist's facture – that can be observed in her paintings from the outset of her career. The distinctive brushwork that she developed by her mature career is what makes Swynnerton's paintings of that period so immediately recognisable. At the heart of her experimentation with paint is a focus on light effects, through which she aimed to represent well-modelled forms and, in her mature works, to depict the natural world in vivid colours. It was through her individual approach to painting that Swynnerton negotiated a position for herself within the British and international art world amidst, and in thoughtful relation to, established and emerging artistic styles and art movements.[1]

Although she spent extended periods in Italy each year from her marriage in 1883 until the death of her husband, Joseph Swynnerton, in 1910, Swynnerton maintained a studio in London and exhibited work there throughout her career, beginning at the Royal Academy in 1879. She was an integral part of a circle of London-based artists of both sexes, who worked in a range of artistic styles. This included John Everett Millais, founding member of the, by then disbanded,

---

1 In the early 21st century art historians have come to appreciate that some 19th- and early 20th-century artists worked between art movements, combining artistic ideas and styles in useful ways, see: Elizabeth Prettejohn, *Art for Arts Sake: Aestheticism in British Painting* (New Haven, CT and London: Paul Mellon Centre for Studies in British Art and Yale University Press, 2007) and David Peters Corbett, *The World in Paint: Modern Art and Visuality in England, 1848-1914* (Manchester and New York: Manchester University Press, 2004).

Pre-Raphaelite Brotherhood, whose studio was close to the one Swynnerton occupied from 1879 near Langham Place in London's West End. By the 1890s, both Edward Burne-Jones and George Frederic Watts, chief exponents of the Symbolist movement in British painting, came to be her friends and share a deep admiration for her work. By that decade, Swynnerton had also formed a close friendship with portraitist John Singer Sargent, who was associated with the British Impressionist movement. It was probably through him that she met British Rural Naturalist painter George Clausen, with whom she also forged an artistic relationship. Like Watts, she was also connected to the informal group of artists who were based around Holland Park, although less intimately and not exclusively. As well as those artists already mentioned, this group included James Abbott McNeill Whistler, chief exponent of the Aesthetic movement.

Swynnerton's cosmopolitan lifestyle and the diversity of stylistic approaches evident among her artist friends serve to demonstrate that she was not part of a specific artistic movement. Indeed, she pursued her own concepts and visual approach in painting with a relentless independent drive. However, across her oeuvre, the visual appearance of her work involves the assimilation of traditional Academic modes of painting and aspects of contemporary 19th-century styles.

A key example of Swynnerton's approach can be seen in her subject pictures, nudes and imaginative paintings. There she combined ideas rooted in the Academic tradition of allegorical painting, which had held a considerable currency in the earlier 19th century, and in the emerging Symbolist movement in contemporary British painting. Dialogues between allegory and Symbolism can be seen in *The Dreamer*, *The Convalescent*, *Cupid and Psyche*, *Oreads*, *Oceanid*, *Illusions*, *The Sense of Sight* and *New Risen Hope* (Catalogue Nos 16, 17 and 23–28).[2] This blending was not an unfamiliar strategy – George Frederic Watts's Symbolist paintings drew on established allegories – but in Swynnerton's work it enabled her to address specific agendas. Allegorical painting traditionally involved the representation of

[2] Swynnerton also engaged with allegorical subject matter in earlier paintings but only one, *Oleander* (1883, Driehaus Collection, Chicago) is extant.

an abstract quality or idea through the depiction of figures, which are identified as specific mythological or literary characters by the inclusion of symbolic objects in the work. It therefore allowed her to display extensive knowledge of art and literature, past and present. Symbolist painting, on the other hand, was more allusive, representing aspects of the human condition and involving a wealth of imagery, rather than a single concept.[3] Symbolist painters believed universal and subjective ideas and feelings could be expressed in art through colour and line and both the *femme fatale* and eroticism were central themes of the movement. These beliefs are important, given that Swynnerton emphasised paint surface and colour, and represented women extensively, although in ways rooted in her commitment to the women's movement. Her exploration of Symbolist concepts in art enabled her to engage deeply with the visual articulation of aspects of the human condition that reflected her politics. She paid particular attention to the psychological states, hopes and ambitions of women from various backgrounds, each of whom she treated sympathetically and with individuality.

Swynnerton's paintings are, furthermore, characterised by ambiguous meanings in terms of subject matter and stylistic associations, which goes some way towards explaining why her oeuvre has not been the subject of sustained study until now. In 1911, Sargent wrote to his patron, Viscountess Nancy Astor (née Langhorne), who, in 1919, would become the first British woman member of Parliament to take her seat:[4]

> *... you want to know what I think of Mrs Swynnerton as a painter – further concealment is useless. I think she is a genius or words to that effect – really I am not exaggerating ... It is difficult to describe her style if you have never seen anything of hers, it is very powerful and rich, and sometimes rather like Watts only more intense.*[5]

---

3 From the 1850s onwards, Spiritualism and experimental psychologies had brought a renewed interrogation of the human psyche through art and a deep subjectivity to British painting; Andrew Wilton has recognised these tendencies as a Symbolist turn in British painting in *The Age of Rossetti, Watts and Burne-Jones: Symbolism in Britain, 1860–1910*. exh. cat. (London: Tate, 1997), 11.

4 Countess Constance Markiewicz was the first but she did not take up her seat.

5 Letter from John Singer Sargent to Nancy Astor, 13 May, 1911, Special Collections Folder 1416/1/4, University of Reading Library; quoted in Stanley Olson, *John Singer Sargent: His Portrait* (New York: St Martins Griffin, 2001), 187-88.

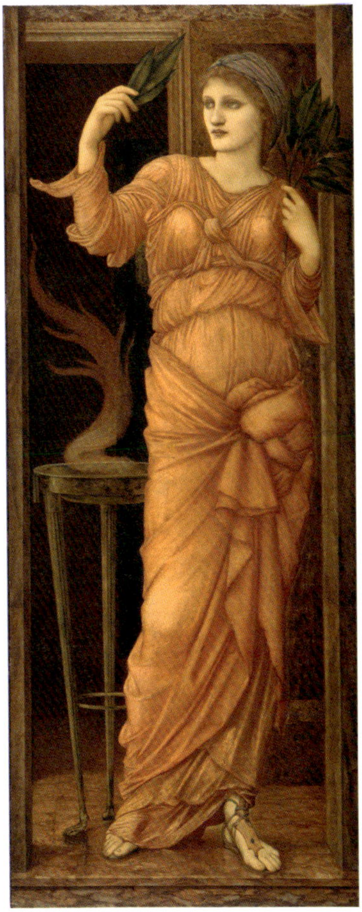

Edward Burne-Jones *Sibylla Delphica*
c.1886

Sargent recognised commonalities between Swynnerton and Watts's visual styles but there are also important differences between the pair's versions of Symbolism.[6] Both artists transformed straightforward allegorical painting through a Symbolist dimension. However, rather than any similarity in their approach to paint, its application or colouring, what united Swynnerton with Watts, broadly speaking, was their shared impetus to represent, through symbolic means, ambiguous ideas relating to the complexities of human experience. In Swynnerton's case, women's hopeful visions represented in the context of the aspirations of the 19th- and early 20th-century women's movement (see 'Hope Imagined').

A distinction between Swynnerton's canvases and those produced by Watts or Burne-Jones is apparent in their handling of paint and the resultant brushwork. This reinforces the fact that she was not a follower but a fellow artist amidst her male, and female, peers. In her subject pictures and nudes from the 1890s onwards, Swynnerton employed a comparatively bright, vivid palette and a number of different painting techniques within the same canvases. These techniques range from small areas of minute, delicate brushstrokes, akin to early Pre-Raphaelite painting, to more extensively employed thick and broad moulded layers of paint: see, for example *Cupid and Psyche* (Catalogue No. 23). Her more expressive brushwork had more in common with experimental painting techniques employed by contemporary

---

6 Alison Smith previously recognised commonalities between their work when she called Swynnerton's *New Risen Hope* (Catalogue No. 28) a 'Wattsian allegory'; Smith, *Exposed: The Victorian Nude*, exh. cat. (London, Tate, 2001), 228.

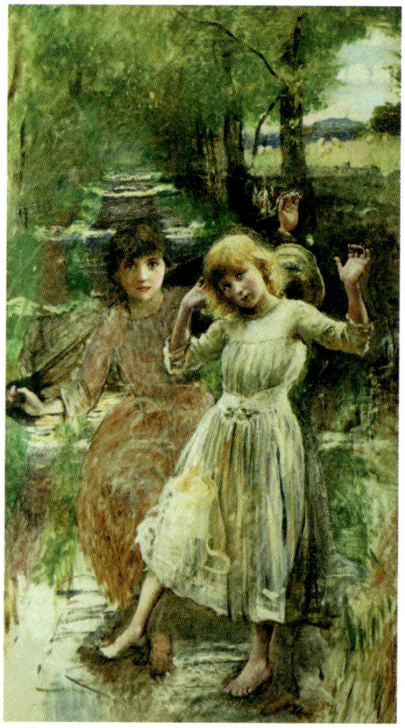

Annie Swynnerton *Crossing the Stream* date unknown

British and Continental European artists, although Swynnerton's paint has the added dimension of standing proud of the picture plane, creating a painterly relief in places. Watts's canvases of the same period, including his *Hope* series (See 'Hope Imagined'), on the other hand, have emphatic, encrusted, dry, chalk-like surfaces and a subdued palette, suggesting an air of fragility, and even decay, while Burne-Jones's application of paint in *Sibylla Delphica* (c.1886, Manchester Art Gallery), for example, is much flatter and smoother than Swynnerton's or Watts's. Burne-Jones's canvases also often contain passages of transparent paint washes, embellishments and warm, earthy palettes, accented by patches of bright, jewel-like hues, suggestive of his involvement in the decorative arts and pursuit of Aesthetic beauty.

In a letter to Frances Horner in 1893 that advised her frankly on a prospective commission, Burne-Jones expressed great respect for Swynnerton's work, albeit with a hint of sexism:

> *I think [Swynnerton] far and away the ablest woman who paints – indeed I think most highly of her work – strong, powerful and beautiful in colour.*[7]

---

[7] Letter from Burne-Jones to Frances Horner, 18 January, 1893, Edward Burne-Jones Archive, Fitzwilliam Museum, Cambridge.

He seems to notice that Swynnerton's strength and power lie in the aesthetics of her paint. By the mid-1880s she had adopted a white canvas primer, such as the Pre-Raphaelites were known for, which can be seen clearly in her unfinished work *Crossing the Stream* (date unknown, Manchester Art Gallery), and, also, a recipe for mixing paint with a medium that enhances its qualities recommended by William Holman Hunt. Her aim was to ensure the intensity of her colours and make them last. She did not, however, adopt the comprehensive application of minute brushwork seen in Pre-Raphaelite paintings.

Although she did not share a specific approach to handling paint with her contemporaries, the 'strong and powerful' experimentation evident in her distinct treatment of paint was something she had in common with the diverse techniques of British Symbolist and Aesthetic painters, including Watts, Burne-Jones and James Abbott McNeill Whistler. Unlike them, however, Swynnerton's experimentation with the application of paint was inspired by her passion for light. In the early 1880s she made her decisive move away from her early practice of traditional chiaroscuro techniques, which involved modelling figurative form through contrasting light and dark in controlled studio environments, to painting outdoors, in the 'glorious light of the sun'.[8] She would later explain that she sought to capture daylight effects that she believed enhanced the drawing and modelling of forms. In an interview with AB Cooper published in *Pearson's Magazine* in 1922, Swynnerton also declared the importance of depicting the tones and moods associated with particular seasons. As her biographers and obituarists recognised, painting outdoors was a priority for her.[9] This is borne out in her mature portraits – as in *Mrs A Scott-Elliot and Children* (Catalogue No. 45) – and nudes, as much as her subject paintings and imaginative works.

It seems significant, then, that during her periods in Italy and France, she was surrounded by artists who were experimenting with ways of applying paint to

---

8 *Jebsa (Roma Lady)* (Catalogue No. 2) and *Italian Mother and Child* (Catalogue No. 14), respectively.

9 AB Cooper, 'Our Greatest Woman Artist: the story of Mrs. Swynnerton who was recently elected to be an Associate of the Royal Academy', *Pearson's Magazine*, no. 327 (London, March 1922), 194–200 and Anon., 'Obituary: Mrs Annie L. Swynnerton', *Manchester Guardian*, 25 October, 1933.

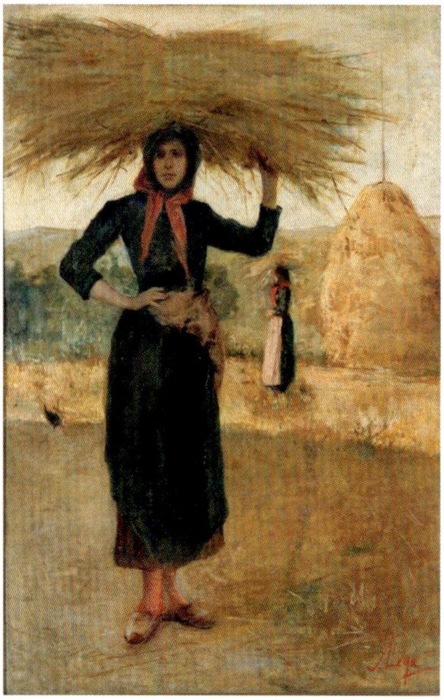

Silvestro Lega *La Fienaiola* (The Haymaker Woman) c.1890

canvas that were premised on painting outdoors. She first visited Rome in 1874 and, during her periods there over the following two decades, would likely have become aware of the contemporary 19th-century work of Tuscan artistic movement, the Macchiaioli, known for their realist subjects and representation of contemporary life. Their experimental paint application seen in Silvestro Lega's *La Fienaiola* (1890, Galleria d'Arte Moderna, Milan) for instance, was based on 'macchia' (light spots or flecks), which resulted in rough, sketchy surfaces that are thought to have pre-empted French Impressionism. Swynnerton's first forays into outdoor painting similarly display an earthy palette, which she makes her own through the incorporation of patches of rich colour created by sunlight falling on otherwise blandly coloured surfaces. Tellingly, too, the Impressionists mounted their fourth exhibition in 1879, the year that Swynnerton completed her studies in Paris. She was duly familiar with their focus on naturalistic scenes painted outdoors and use of very loose broad, layered and broken brushwork to convey light effects as well as their innovative representation of natural colours in shadows, which earlier artists had painted with black and brown. Such methods are exemplified in the work of Claude Monet, Pierre-Auguste Renoir and Mary Cassatt, to mention but a few.

Swynnerton's landscapes – including *The Town of Siena* (Catalogue No. 12) and *Italian Landscape* (Catalogue No. 19) – display broken brushwork and a concentration on light effects that cannot be ascribed to either the Macchiaioli or Impressionists entirely. What is more, she was more concerned with the human figure and approached the brushwork of her figures differently to her landscapes, making her landscapes important but secondary in many of her works.

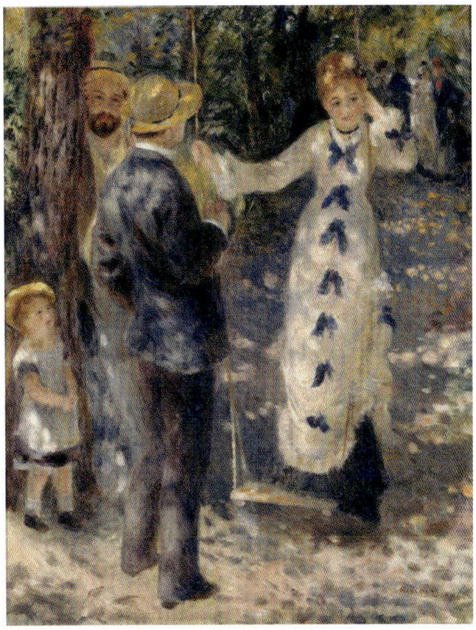

Pierre-Auguste Renoir *The Swing* 1876

In areas corresponding to her figures, her brushwork was less scumbled and more moulded than that of the Macchiaioli. Although she did employ light patches in a striking manner, they served to perfect the drawing and modelling form, often creating visible areas of impasto – thick application of paint leaving evident brushwork – and relief. In contrast, in *The Swing* (1876, Musée d'Orsay, Paris) for instance, Renoir employs patterns of layered brushstrokes representative of light in the depiction of his female subject's head, clothing and hands that cause her form to appear to dissolve into brushstrokes, or merge into the background.

There was no one Impressionist style, even in the years of the first exhibitions (1874–1886). So, although Impressionist artists shared ideas, paintings by Monet, Renoir and Sargent are very different in appearance, as is true of Aesthetic and Symbolist artists.[10] Like her now better-known contemporaries, Swynnerton can be understood as independently developing her own approach to painting, which resulted in her distinctive ways of handling paint. But she took this further than many artists, by resisting being tied exclusively to any particular movement or style. This was a brave strategy that provided her considerable creative freedom and enabled her to carve out her own niche within the international art world, which was so often obstructive to women artists.

Further distinctions between her style and that of even her closest peers can be observed. For instance, although, in her 20th-century portraits, Swynnerton shared an affinity with Sargent that was rooted in their focus on figures, they displayed different techniques. Like him, Swynnerton should be understood as

---

[10] Kenneth McConkey made this distinction clear in *British Impressionism* (London: Phaidon, 1989; rpt. 1998), particularly 76–77.

a significant contributor to the development of Impressionistic styles in British painting.[11] Sargent's portrait of Mary Hunter (née Smyth) (see 'Portraiture, Individuality and the Outdoors'), shows his delight in sweeping and lively brushstrokes, but also his rigorous draftsmanship, which produces solidly modelled three-dimensional bodily forms, with a clarity that contrasts with Renoir's earlier encountered work.[12] This is also the case for Swynnerton, although her figures are yet more solid than Sargent's, due to the way she layers paint and moulds form with her brushwork, which docs not become abstract. Indeed, the heaviness of Swynnerton's broken brushwork and her concentration on the realistic depiction of her models made stronger allusions to another artistic movement; namely, British Rural Naturalist painting.

British Rural Naturalism stemmed from French Rural Naturalist painting, championed by the Barbizon School and particularly Jules Bastien-Lepage. It was a form of modern realism practised by Swynnerton's friend George Clausen. His naturalism was spurred by an urge to portray the world of the rural poor in an accurate, unidealised and individual manner that had a social conscience, but was not without nostalgia and genuine sentiment, either.[13] Swynnerton's closeness to Rural Naturalism is borne out in the least diluted manner in her subject pictures of rural workers on the Isle of Man, *The Dreamer* (Catalogue No. 16) and *The Convalescent* (Catalogue No. 17). Her approach to landscape elsewhere in her oeuvre – in her stand-alone landscapes and those incorporated in her subject pictures, nudes and imaginative paintings, which combined allegorical modes and Symbolist ideas – was couched in direct study of nature outdoors, but enlivened by an imaginative sense that is often mystical. Meanwhile, her realistic treatment of her figures' flesh is not photographically replicative of nature, as Rural Naturalist painting aimed to be, but invigorated through expressive and moulded brushwork and colour. The subject of rural labour in her Manx paintings, nevertheless,

---

[11] McConkey, 1989; 1998 and McConkey, *Impressionism in Britain* (New Haven and London: Yale University Press and Barbican Art Gallery, 1995).

[12] Prettejohn, Elizabeth, *Interpreting Sargent* (New York: Stewart, Tabori & Chang, 1998), 9 and 14.

[13] This differed from French Realism, the 19th-century movement that depicted gritty social messages through generalised images of the lower classes.

provides further evidence that there was a political element to her subject paintings, in her case, one that was rooted in her belief in women's rights as well as broader social activism.

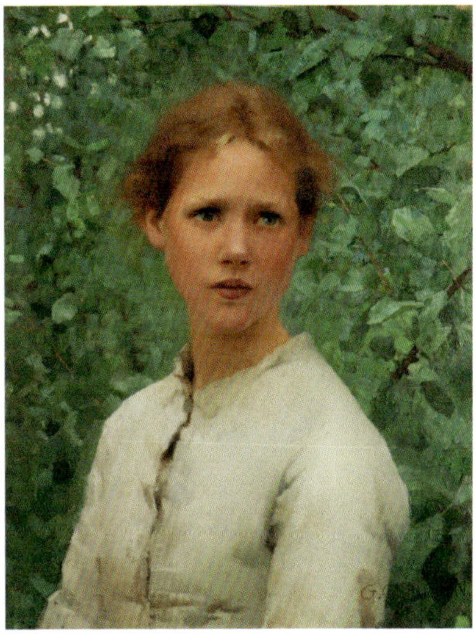

George Clausen *A Girl's Head* 1886

Swynnerton's self-positioning between traditional artistic conventions and styles associated with established and emerging art movements was an effective strategy. It gained notice for her work from the public, patrons, fellow artists and critics. The nature of the female personifications – often purposely indecipherable and enigmatic – are linked to this self-positioning and her women's movement commitments, expressing a desire to be independent of any one definition. Her work underlines the fact that, in the hands of some visionary artists, ideas and methods associated with specific artistic styles and movements co-exist within artworks. Such readings have only been suggested by art historians in the early 21st century, before which the study of artistic movements and styles tended to have rigid boundaries that often excluded women artists whose work resists categorisation. Thinking beyond categories enhances our reading of Swynnerton's work, enabling us to understand how she worked to create a niche for herself in the art world of her times while expressing her individual artistic passions.

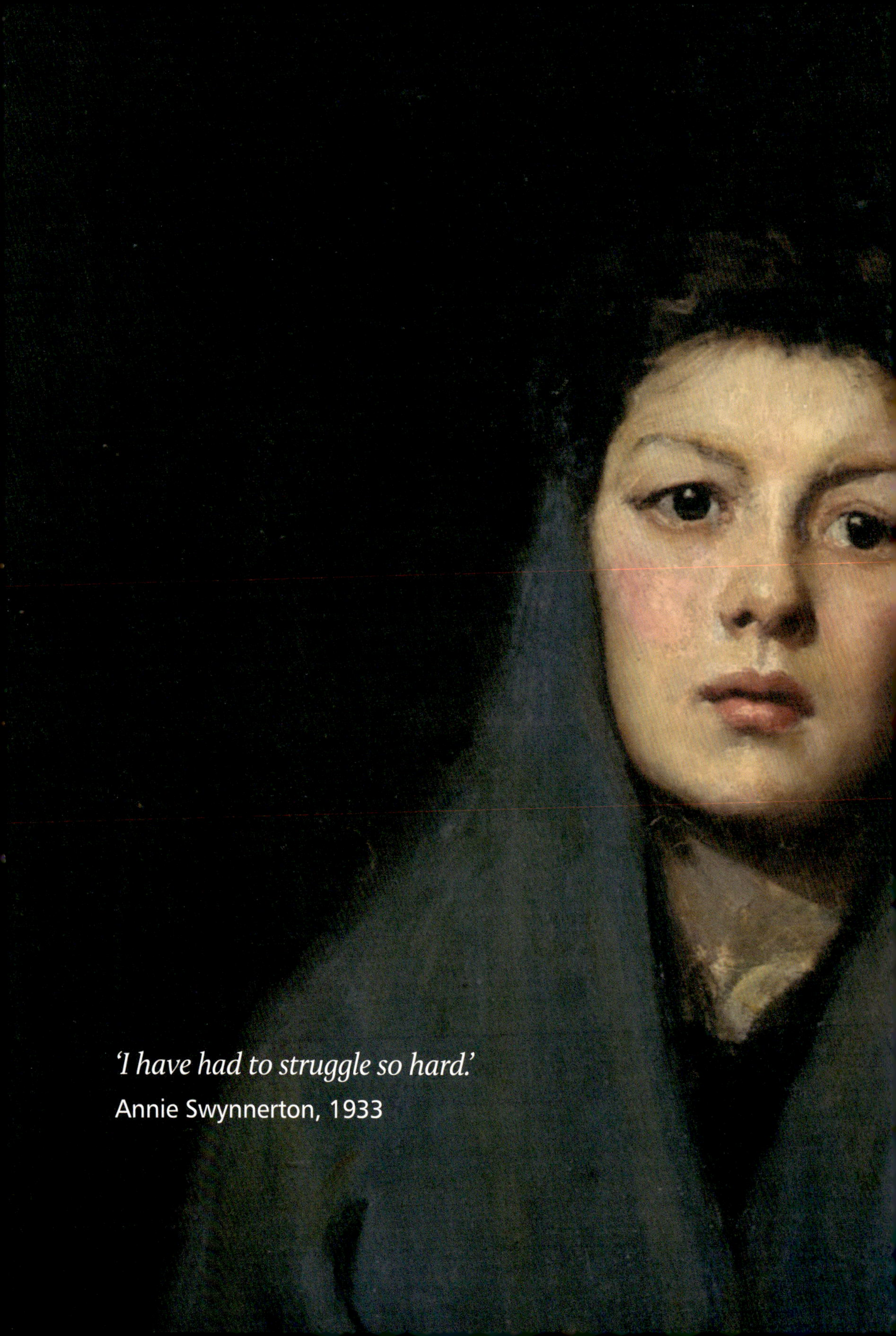

'I have had to struggle so hard.'

Annie Swynnerton, 1933

Becoming an Artist

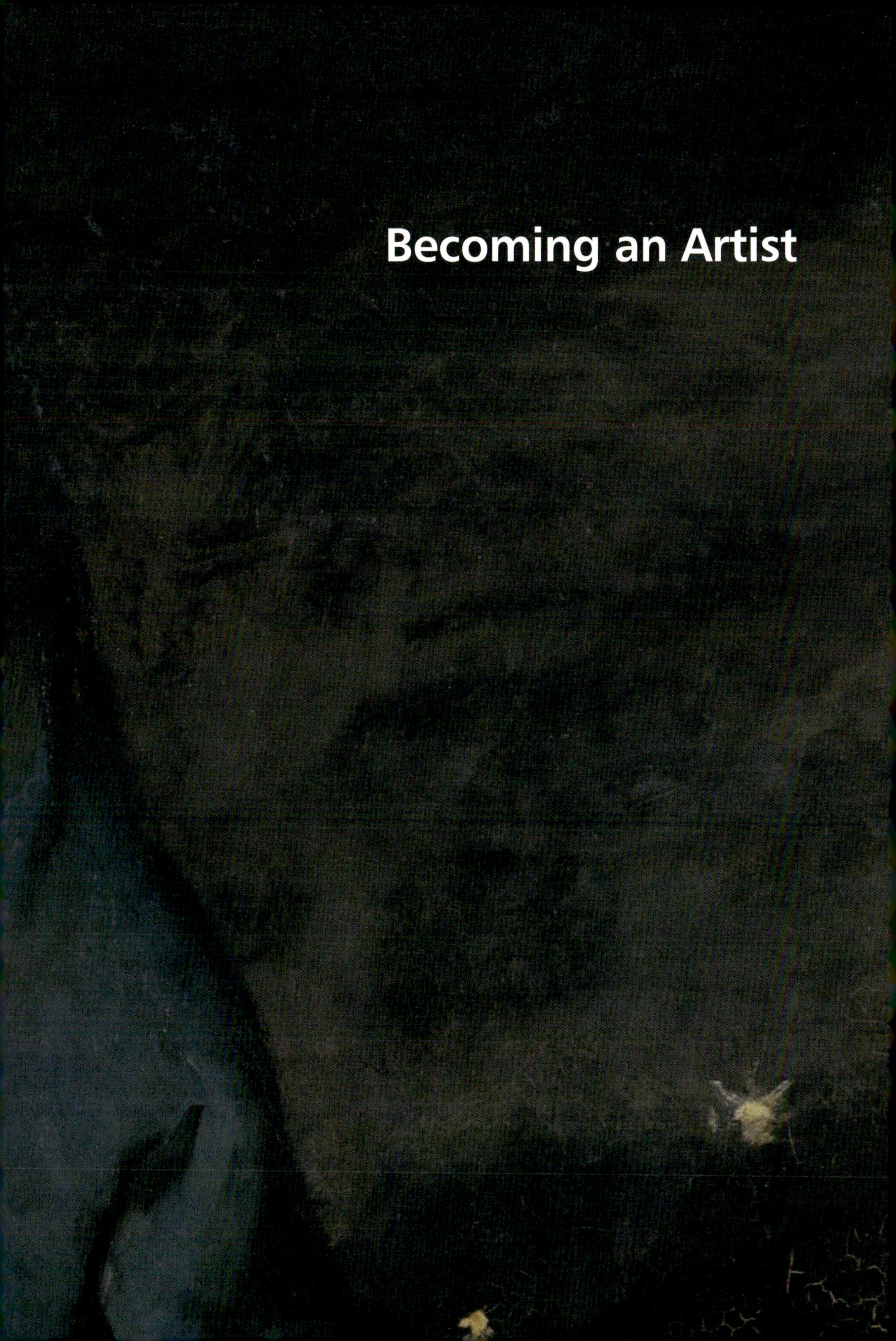

Becoming an Artist

Swynnerton was one of a generation of pioneering women who forged an independent artistic career in the 1870s to 1880s, at a time when the art world still presented obstacles to women becoming professionals. She later explained:

> *I have had to struggle so hard. You see when I was young, women could not paint – or so it was said. The world believed that and did not want the work of women, however sincere, however good. I refused to accept that. I fought and I suffered.*[1]

Mid-19th-century women artists had opened up opportunities for Swynnerton's generation, but women's access to artistic education was still not equal to men's.[2] At the Royal Academy of Arts (RA), London, for instance, women were initially barred from studying living figures and were not permitted to study draped nudes until 1893, denying them an essential component of a professional academic artist's skill set.

Swynnerton obtained academic fine art training through alternative routes, beginning with five years at the Manchester School of Art (MSA) from 1869 to 1873. MSA was a relatively liberal institution where women were trained in the fine as well as decorative arts, having access to study clothed figures and draped nudes. There Swynnerton began to contribute to exhibitions at the Royal Manchester Institution from 1871 and won a number of national prizes. This included a prestigious Princess of Wales Scholarship of £11, which enabled her first visit to Rome in 1874. Back in Manchester, she campaigned for women to exhibit at the Manchester Academy of Fine Arts and in 1875 she began to do so. At the Académie Julian, Paris, from 1878 to 1879, she benefitted from the continental art training system based on study of the, often undraped, nude and anatomy. Following her return from Paris to Manchester, in 1879 she sought to improve other women's artistic education by founding the Manchester Society of Women Painters. The same year she moved to launch her artistic career in London and began exhibiting at the RA.

---

1 Swynnerton, *The Evening News*, 15 February, 1933.

2 The Society of Female Artists, London, had been established in 1855, holding its first exhibition in 1857, and the first woman was admitted to the Royal Academy of Arts School in 1860.

Her portraits and subject pictures dating from the mid-1870s to 1880s reveal the extensive knowledge she had gained of British and European art of the past and how attuned she was to contemporary trends. They evidence her skilful engagement with a range of painting techniques and an expertise in representing light effects. Furthermore, these works show that she was concerned to represent women in ways that challenged conventions.

CAT 1 | *Mrs Annie L Swynnerton* 1928

Gwenny Griffiths 1867–1954
Coloured chalk on buff paper, 61.6 x 51.2 cm
Manchester Art Gallery. Gift of Gwenny Griffiths 1953.126

This is a rare portrait of Swynnerton who never sought to make her reputation through the cultivation of a fashionable persona. The precise circumstances that led to its production are unknown. Swynnerton and the artist of this work, Gwenny Griffiths, both studied at the Académie Julian in Paris and may have come to know one another there. They certainly knew one another at some point before 1914, when Swynnerton took up a studio at No.1A, The Avenue Studios, 76 Fulham Road, London, becoming a neighbour to Griffiths, who had previously occupied No.1A and then moved to No.5 in the same complex of studios. By the 1920s, Griffiths had become a close friend to Swynnerton and sometimes helped her with correspondence due to her failing eyesight. Both women utilised their spaces at Avenue Studios as their bases in London throughout their long careers, so it is highly likely that Swynnerton sat for this portrait there.

Produced six years after she became the first woman elected an Associate Member of the Royal Academy of Arts since its foundation in 1768, this portrait seems evocative of that pioneering accolade. A sense of Swynnerton's strength and determination, and also Griffiths's admiration for Swynnerton, is palpable in this portrait, while the simplicity of the unadorned image gives her a splendid and virtuous air. The medium chosen, and Griffith's reputation as a painter of official portraits, mean that this work may have been a study for an oil painting. It may, equally, have been a token of Swynnerton and Griffiths's friendship. Swynnerton's proximity to the picture plane and her attentive gaze suggests a congenial report between artist and sitter. More broadly, this painting evidences some of the ways in which 19th-century women artists supported each other, by modelling for and commissioning works by one another.

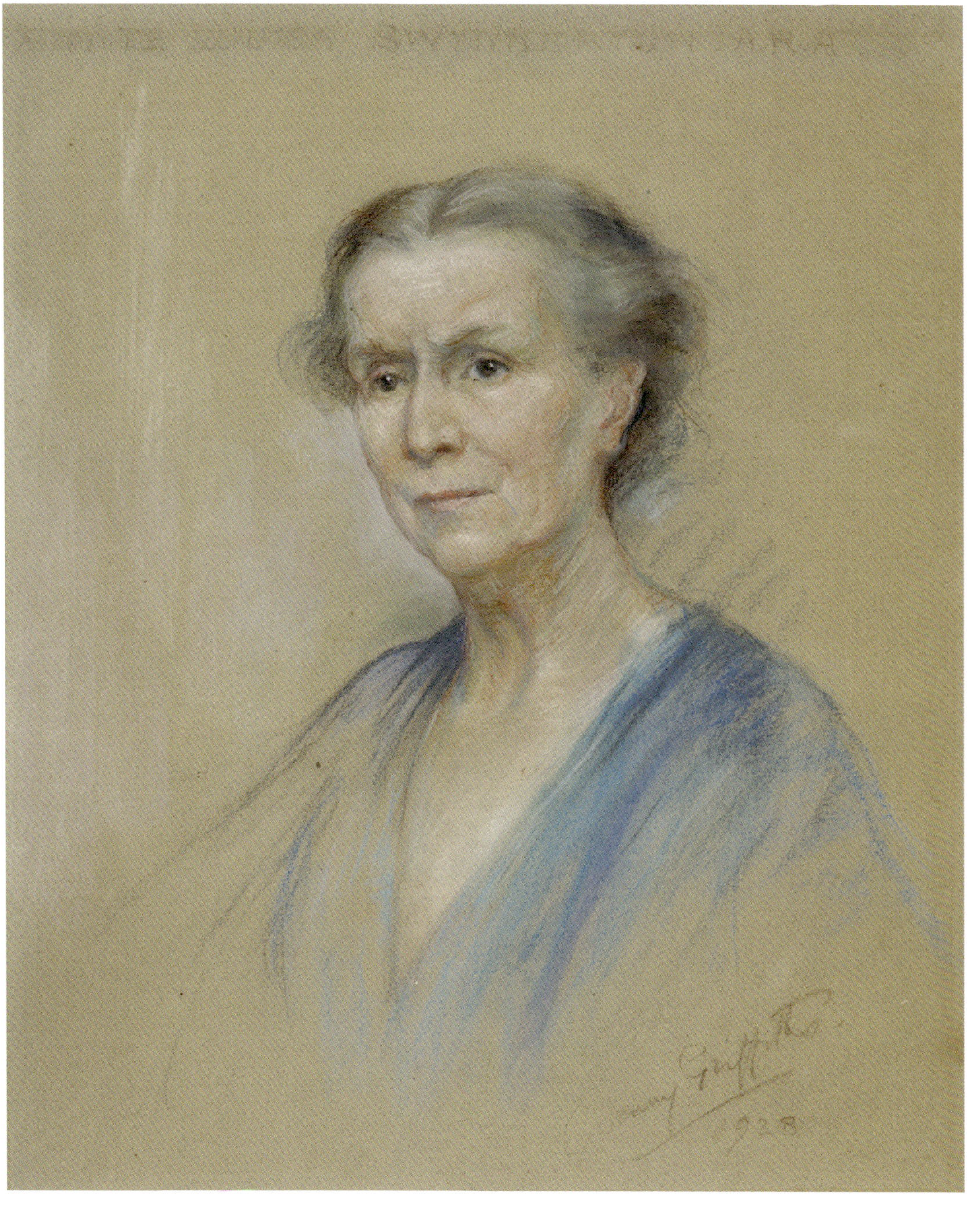
1928

CAT 2 | ***Jebsa (Roma Lady)*** 1874

Oil on canvas, 101 x 76 cm
Richard Taylor Fine Art
Presented to Priest Park Gallery by BL Bisgood Esq, 1937

This is Swynnerton's earliest known oil painting and one produced during her first visit to Rome. It reveals that during this visit she was pursuing an education in Italian art, as was common for many male artists. Her familiarity with the technique of modelling form through the stark contrast of light and dark (known as chiaroscuro) pioneered by High Renaissance Italian artists such as Leonardo da Vinci and Raphael, for example, is particularly apparent in this painting. Its earthy realism and drama is reminiscent, too, of the development of chiaroscuro by baroque artists Caravaggio, whose work was plentiful in Rome, and Artemisia Gentileschi-Lomi. Swynnerton's dramatic contrast of light and dark, most boldly represented through the application of thick white paint on top of the figure's headdress, lends striking plasticity to the modelling of her subject.[1] This approach informed her depiction of light and robust modelling of figures throughout her career.

The painting also tells us that her artistic training left her well versed in a combination of traditional painting techniques inspired by other 16th- and 17th-century Continental European painters. The presence of loose, broad brushwork, the thick application of paint leaving evident brush marks (known as impasto) and the inclusion of colourful fabrics in the figure's clothing, for instance, signal her awareness of portrait paintings by Titian, Rembrandt and Velazquez.[2]

That the middle-aged woman depicted wears the traditional costume of working-class Roman women of the second half of the 19th century indicates Swynnerton's early interest in the lives of contemporary women. The primary title, *Jebsa*, does not seem to be taken from a literary story, and suggests Swynnerton knew her sitter on first name terms. Even if this is a professional model posed in a studio, Swynnerton's depiction is realistic and unsentimental compared to picturesque figures in traditional costume produced around Europe by 19th-century British and French male artists, such as Frederic Leighton's *A Roman Peasant Girl* (unknown date, Manchester Art Gallery).

1 Swynnerton may have been inspired by study of Caravaggio's *Boy with a Fruit Basket* (1593, The Villa Borghese Collection, Rome) which, though different in subject, is lit from above in a similar manner.

2 The brushwork in this painting would have appeared thicker before its surface was visibly flattened by over-cleaning in the painting's recent history.

Frederic Leighton *Roman Peasant Girl*
date unknown

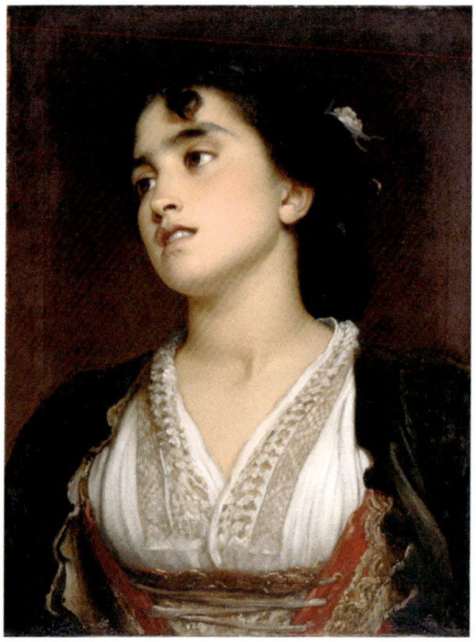

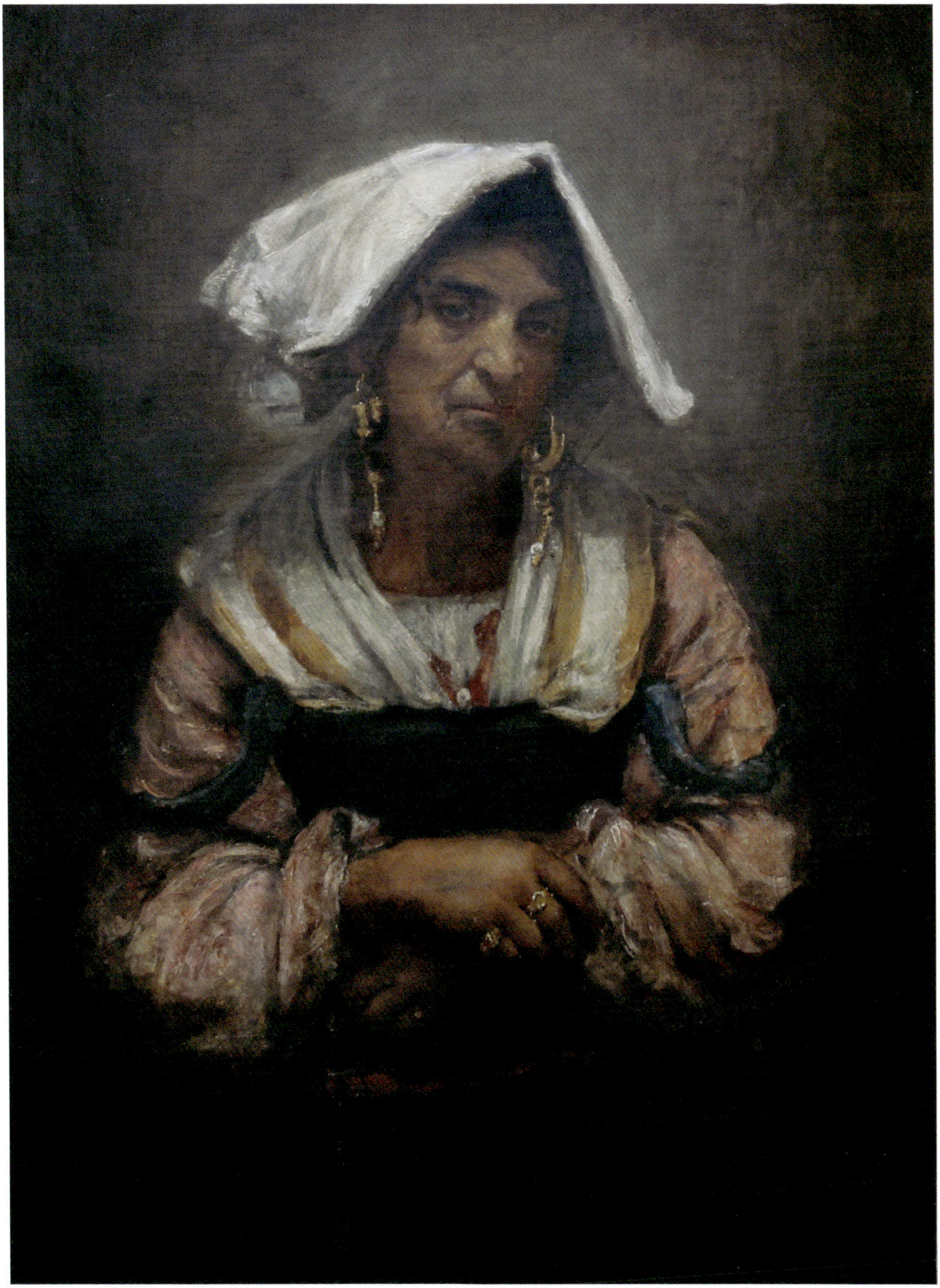

CAT 3 | ***The Reverend William Gaskell*** 1879

Oil on canvas, 86.6 x 71.1 cm
Manchester Art Gallery. Mrs ME Gaskell Bequest 1914.1

This portrait depicts Manchester charity worker and champion of education for the working classes, Unitarian minister The Reverend William Gaskell (1805–1884), widower of the novelist Elizabeth Gaskell (1810–1865). It was painted to commemorate his forty years of service as chairman of the Portico Library in Manchester and therefore depicts him in secular dress. Gaskell was asked whether he would prefer a portrait painted by 'Miss A. Robinson' or a bust sculpted by her future husband Joseph Swynnerton. He remarked 'a portrait by Robinson would be more desirable.' He added, 'My daughters tell me that she has painted a portrait which they like very much'.[1] Enough money was subscribed for the production of this portrait, which was given as a personal gift to Gaskell, and a bust by Joseph Swynnerton, which is displayed at the Portico Library.

The painting's three-quarter format, its depiction of a well-lit head against a dark background and the active brushstrokes employed to render Gaskell's wispy thinning hair, show Swynnerton's admiration of the works of Titian, Rembrandt and Velazquez – an admiration she shared with John Everett Millais, whose studio was close to the one she moved to London in 1879.

Swynnerton's Manchester social connections go some way towards explaining how she was able to establish her artistic career in London. She was introduced to Burne-Jones, Millais and, later, Sargent by her Manchester friends Julia and Meta Gaskell, the daughters of the sitter in this portrait.[2] Her intention, by this time, to become a professional artist is signalled by the prominence of her monogram – a motif made by overlapping the initials of her name ALR – in the upper left third of the canvas.

1 Barbara Brill, *William Gaskell, 1805-84: A Portrait* (Manchester Literary and Philosophical Publications), 110-11.

2 Anon., 'Mrs. Annie L. Swynnerton Dies: British Artist and Academician', *The Hull Times*. Ontario, Canada, 25 October, 1933.

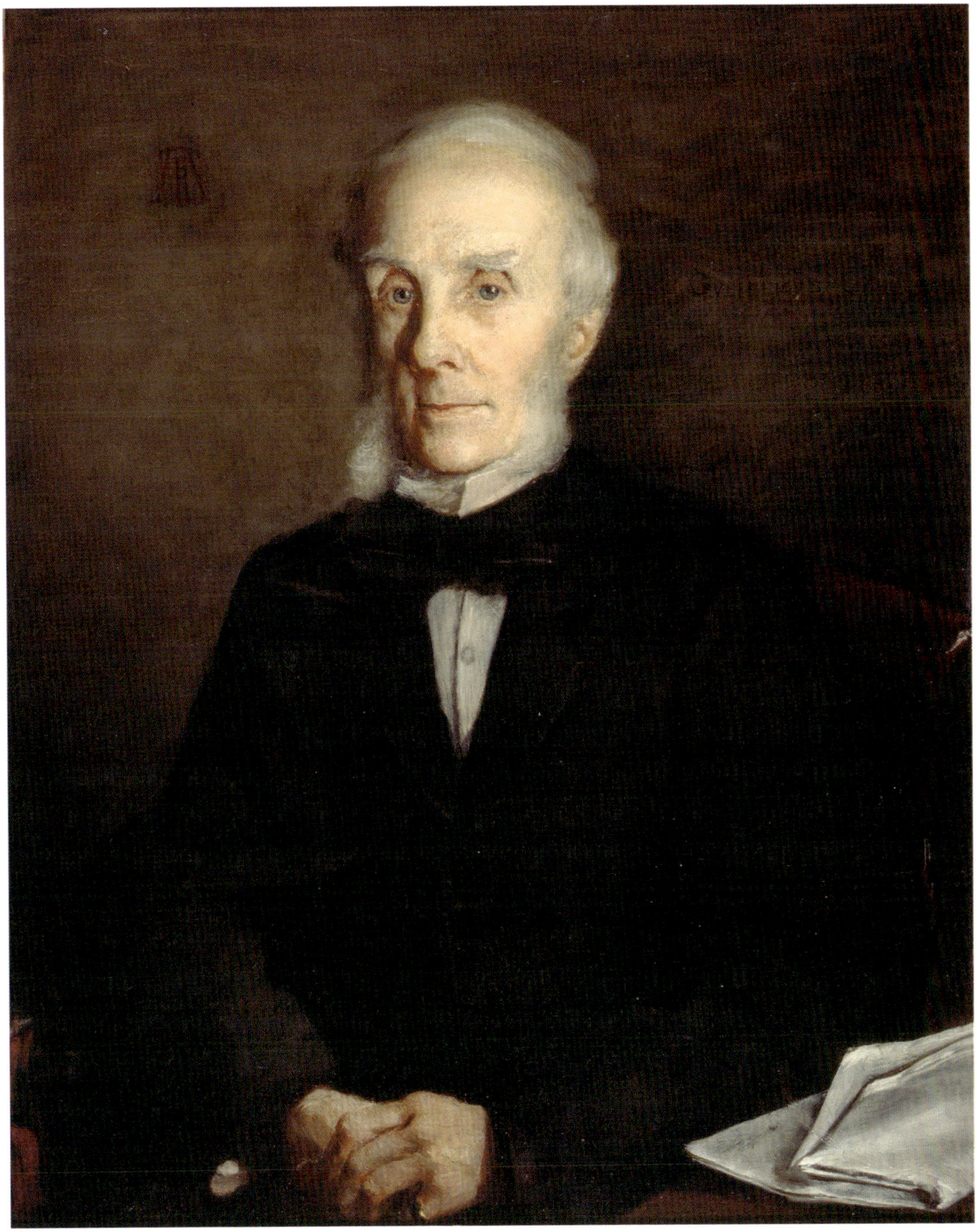

CAT 4 | *Susan Isabel Dacre (A Mon Amie)* 1880

Oil on canvas, 70.3 x 51.9 cm
Manchester Art Gallery. Gift of Susan Isabel Dacre 1932.15

In 1879, Swynnerton had made her debut at the Royal Academy with a now untraced painting *Portrait of a Lady,* which critics recognised as showing 'profitable studies of old Italian portraiture and Dutch *vraisemblance*' (appearance of truth).[1] Similar stylistic affinities can be seen in this portrait, exhibited at the Royal Academy in 1880. Dacre's head, similarly to Swynnerton's *The Reverend William Gaskell* (Catalogue No.3), is set strikingly against a dark buff ground and exhibits active brushstrokes, particularly in her fur-necked cloak, that show her admiration of 16th- and 17th-century Italian painters. Like many 19th-century British painters associated with the Aesthetic movement, such as Millais and James Abbott McNeill Whistler, she was experimenting with the application of paint; Whistler's *Arrangement in Brown and Black: The Fur Jacket* (1876, Worcester Art Museum) is reminiscent. Yet, Swynnerton certainly also looks back to 17th-century Dutch portraits, known for their realism, and 19th-century British Pre-Raphaelite notions of truth to nature.[2]

Swynnerton met fellow artist Susan Isabel Dacre (1844–1933) at the Manchester School of Art, where they formed a lifelong friendship, supporting each other's careers. This portrait is a visual sign of friendship between the pair, indicated by the alternative French title *A Mon Amie* (To My Friend). Swynnerton's faithful depiction of Dacre's face is also indicative of both women's feminist politics. Swynnerton champions 'real' women over idealised ones and rejects patriarchal images of femininity, including none of the colourful decorative flourishes seen in Millais's *Louise Jopling* (1879, National Portrait Gallery), for instance. This is not surprising, considering the studio Swynnerton and Dacre shared in London was close to a community of women artists and activists and that the pair contributed to various campaigns for women's rights and opportunities.

1 Anon., *Athenaeum*, 1879, 734.

2 Frans Hal's *Gypsy Girl* (1628–30, Musée du Louvre, Paris), for instance.

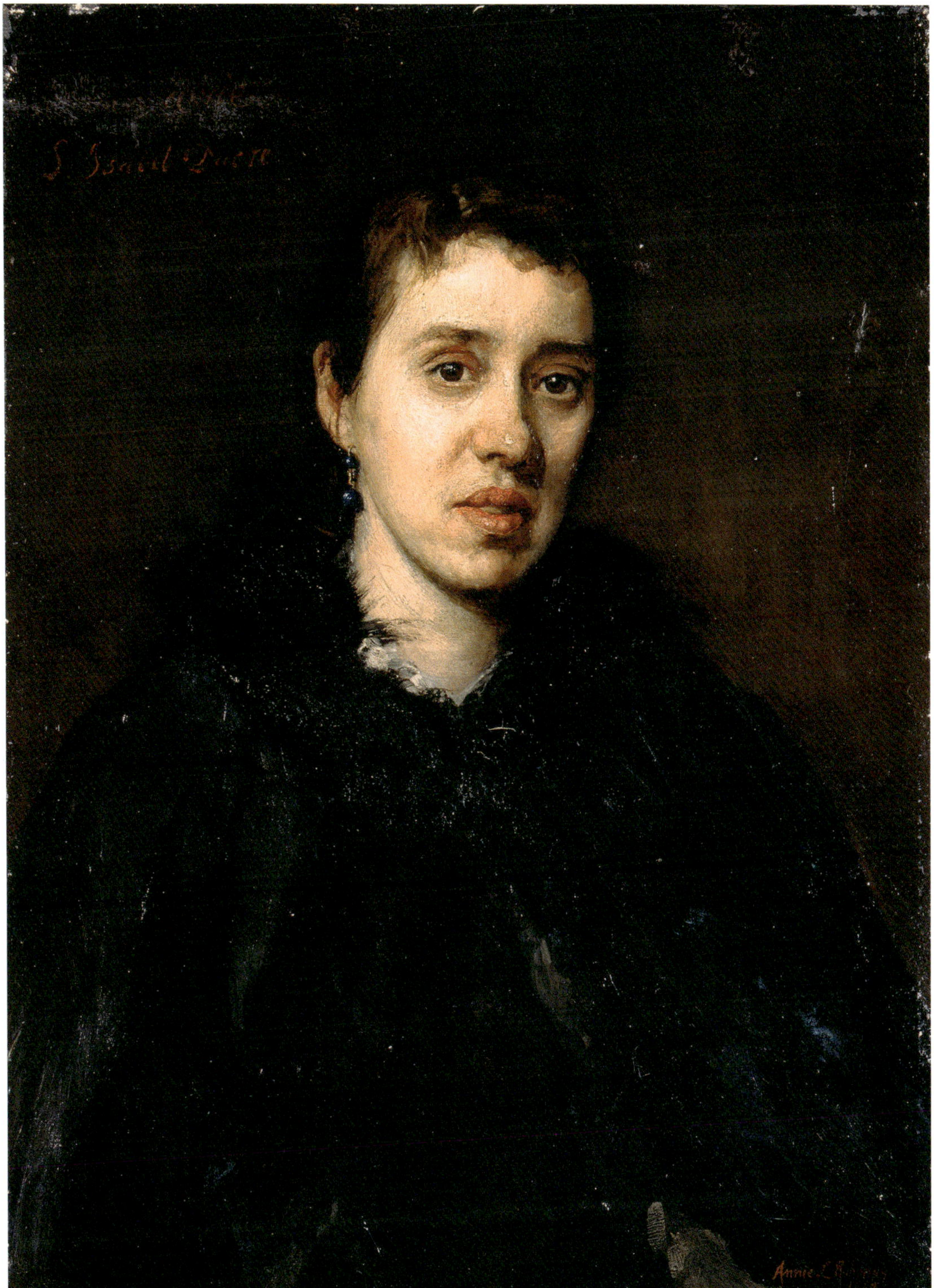

CAT 5 | *Florence H Musgrave* 1888

Oil on canvas, 49.5 x 40.6 cm
Nottingham City Museums & Galleries
Bequeathed by Mrs FH Musgrave, 1934

The sitter in this portrait, Florence Hawksley Musgrave (née Hawksley) (1851–1930), was the daughter of Nottingham civil engineer Thomas Hawksley FRS, but little is known about her or the circumstances of this portrait's production.[1] In 1881 she was the last child living with her father in Kensington, London, so this painting may plausibly have been a society portrait devised to secure a marriage for her. However, she remained unmarried until after her father's death in 1893 and the inscription of her first name in the picture is more fitting for a personal keepsake.

Genteel fashionable images of women in interiors were expected from a woman artist and played an important part in establishing Swynnerton's career in London. Yet, her work invites us not simply to admire the sitter's beauty and fashionability but also to consider the individual woman. The half-length format is intimate and Musgrave is caught in contemplation. Her unadorned head is allowed to command the top half of the canvas. Her face is particularly well modelled and the light upon it is sensitive.

Both the historical depth of Swynnerton's work and the modernity of her approach is identifiable here. The profile composition confirms Swynnerton's knowledge of 15th-century Italian portraiture and demonstrates her skill in tackling different formats. The profusion of shades of pink employed, meanwhile, is strikingly modern. The same year this portrait was produced, Swynnerton exhibited a painting titled *Harmony in Pink and Gold* (untraced) at the Society of Women Artists, London, that alluded to similarly titled Aesthetic paintings produced by Whistler around this time. A joy in the impressions and movement of fabrics celebrated through gestural brushstrokes demonstrates that Swynnerton was well aware of developments in Impressionist painting of the same period, recalling, for instance, Renoir's treatment of fabric, and Millais's incorporation of similar techniques.

1 With thanks to Lauren Turner's unpublished family history research.

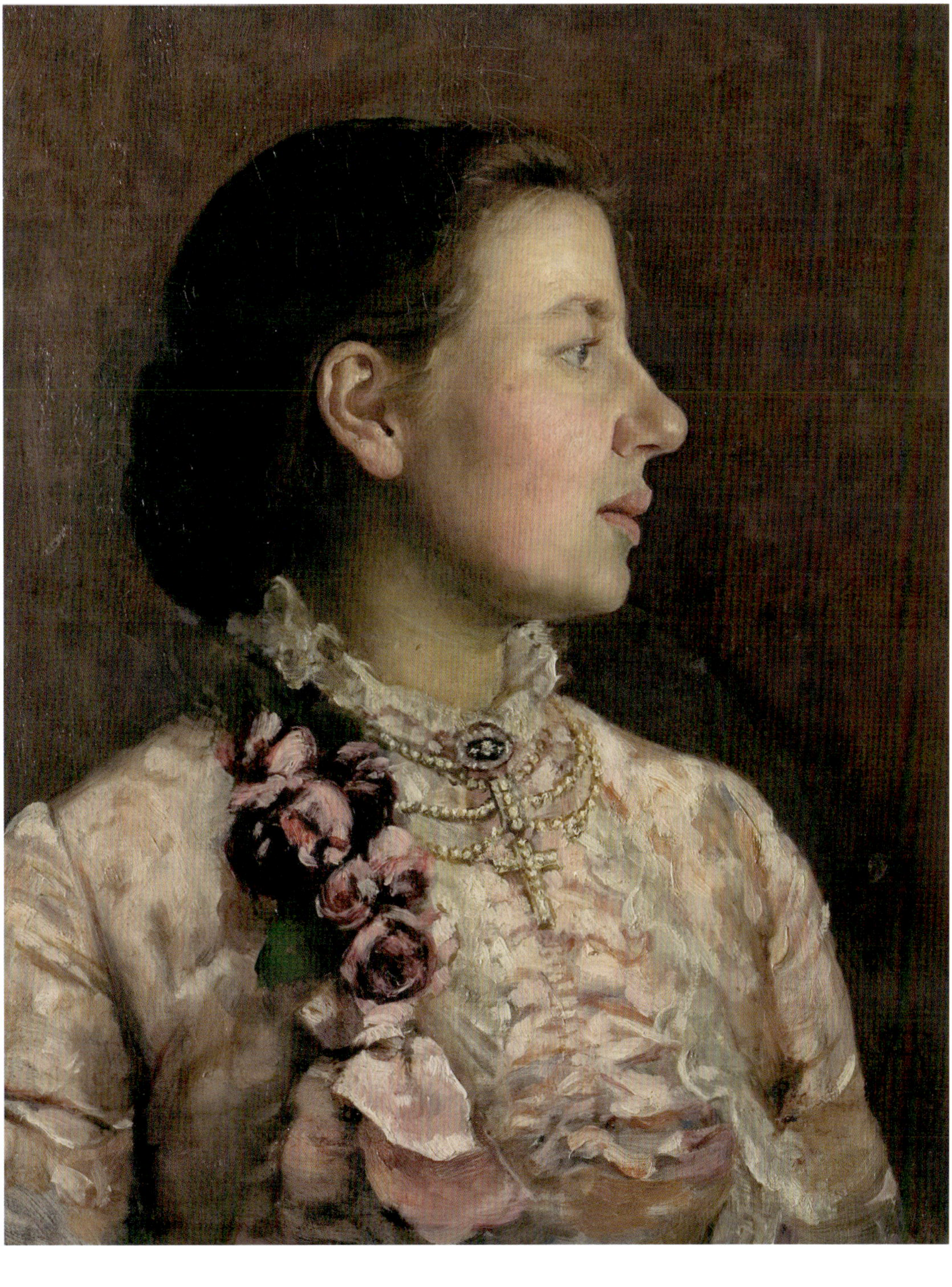

CAT 6 | *The Tryst (The Factory Girl's Tryst)* 1880

Oil on canvas, 114 x 78.5 cm
Salford Museum & Art Gallery
Gift from H Boddington, Jnr, 1880

In this early subject picture, exhibited at the Royal Academy in 1881, Swynnerton focused on the depiction of night-time light effects within a real landscape. The distant lights, reflected on water behind the figure, point to her awareness of Whistler's *Nocturne* series of Aesthetic paintings showing the River Thames at night, produced in the 1870s. However, although finished in London, Swynnerton's backdrop seems to be Peel Park, Salford. A windmill of the kind that stood on the bank of the River Irwell, surrounded by textile manufacturing factories, and was a prominent landmark of old Salford, can be seen in the background.

A tryst, a meeting – usually a secret one – between lovers, was a popular theme in 19th-century painting, frequently chosen by Pre-Raphaelite painters. Unusually for the subject, Swynnerton represents only a female figure. She shields her body from the cold with her shawl, looking searchingly into the darkness, on the brink of despair. This raises questions about the nature of the meeting, who the girl might be and her potential vulnerability.

Swynnerton's inspiration may have come from a local Manchester legend according to which a son of the Stanley family, who owned the land around the windmill, had fallen in love with the miller's daughter. Unfortunately, his family had sent him away to court, leaving the distraught miller's daughter to drown herself in the River Irwell, which prompted the son's own suicide. In remorse, his father ordered that the windmill that was the lover's trysting place should stand forever.[1] The female figure is also evocative of the portrayal of working-class women in popular 19th-century British novels, including Elizabeth Gaskell's *Mary Barton: A Tale of Manchester Life* (1848), whose plights were a social concern at the time.[2] This signals Swynnerton's interest in visualising working-class and peasant women, which continued throughout her career.

1 With thanks to Danny Morrell's unpublished research on the windmill and legend.

2 In the 1860s the Factory Acts of the 1840s and 50s – which had reduced the working hours for children and women to 10 hours and ensured ventilation, sanitation and guarding of machinery – had been extended to further industries but not all.

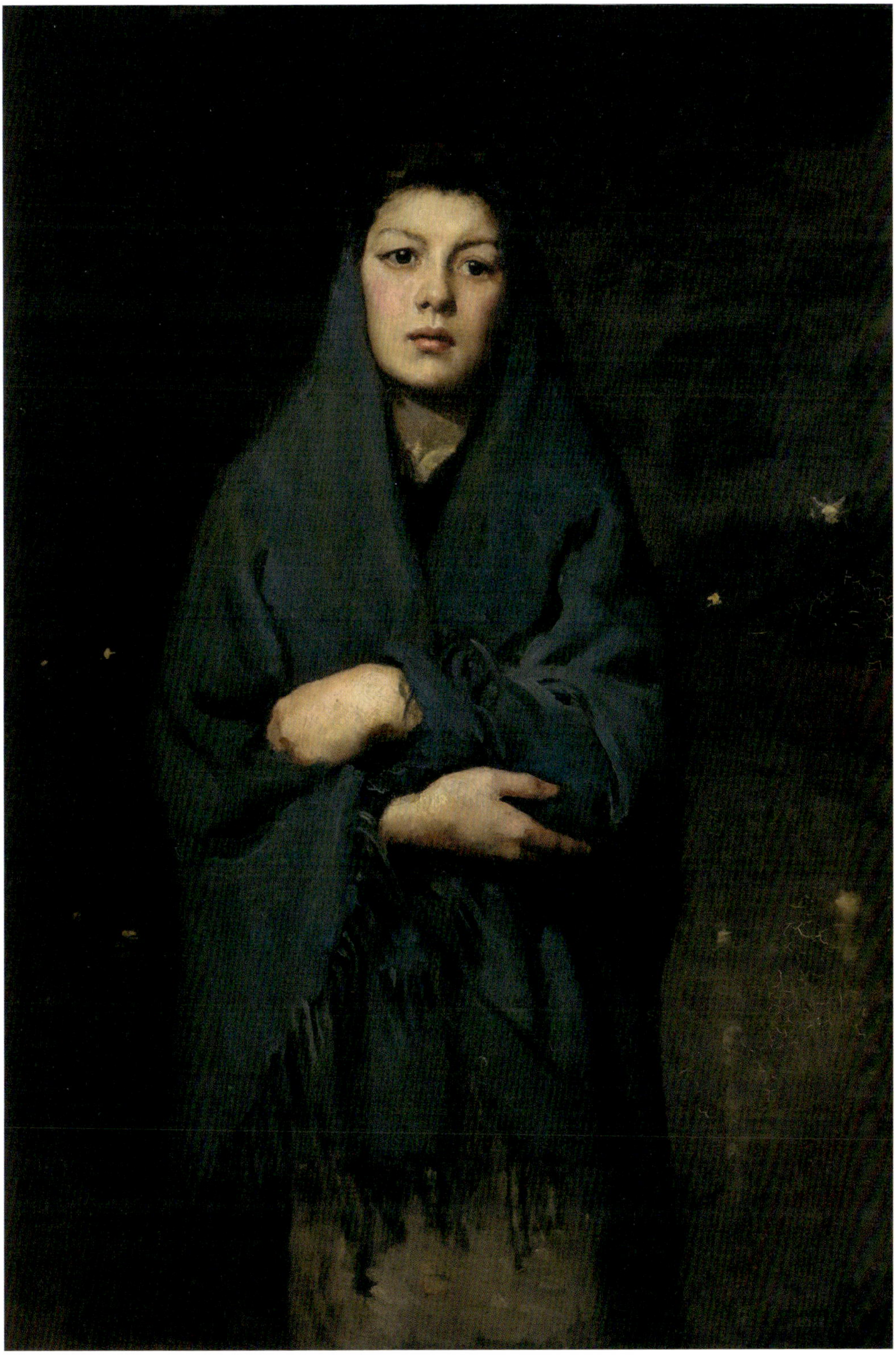

CAT 7 | ***The Letter*** date unknown

Oil on canvas, 101.6 x 48.2 cm
Royal Academy of Arts, London
Purchased by the Edward Stott ARA Fund, 1934

The subject of the receipt of a letter was popular in 19th- and early 20th-century British paintings where a female figure was often presented reading the letter in a well-lit room, with an open window symbolic of the outside world close by.[1] However, drawing on her knowledge of 16th- and 17th-century Northern Renaissance and Dutch Golden Age painting, Swynnerton experimented in this painting with the effect of natural light falling into a dark interior. The profile composition and yellow hues of the figure's dress recall Johannes Vermeer's *Girl Reading a Letter at an Open Window* (1657–59). However, the proximity of Swynnerton's figure to the window and the spectator, together with the manner in which the figure raises the letter to catch the natural light from a tiny open window, produces an intense feeling of claustrophobia that is particular to Swynnerton's portrayal.[2] This is emphasised by her employment of a stark contrast between the illuminated figure and dark background, a chiaroscuro technique. This approach, together with the use of incisive outlines, gives robustness to the young girl's form.

The significance of the letter remains a mystery. A sense of the girl's separation from the outside world is, nevertheless, made poignant, particularly through the decorative bullseye windows that punctuate the darkness and represent the light of the outdoors that is denied to the closeted girl.[3] The figure's concentration on the letter writer's words and the altar-like window ledge, which bears a vase filled with flowers perhaps symbolic of her relationship with the correspondent, gives an overarching sense that the painting is about devotion. Yet, there is little indication that it is of the romantic kind.

1 For instance, see *The Letter* by Leonard Campbell Taylor (Ferens Art Gallery) and the same subject by Ambrose McEvoy (The New Art Gallery Walsall).

2 The effect of claustrophobia is more extreme than that seen in John Everett Millais's *Mariana* (1851), which Swynnerton would no doubt have been familiar with.

3 Bullseye windows are a relatively rare feature that appears in a small number of British Pre-Raphaelite paintings. They are more common in the work of the Northern Renaissance painters that inspired the Pre-Raphaelites, such as Jan van Eyck's *The Arnolfini Portrait*, which entered the National Gallery, London's collection in 1842.

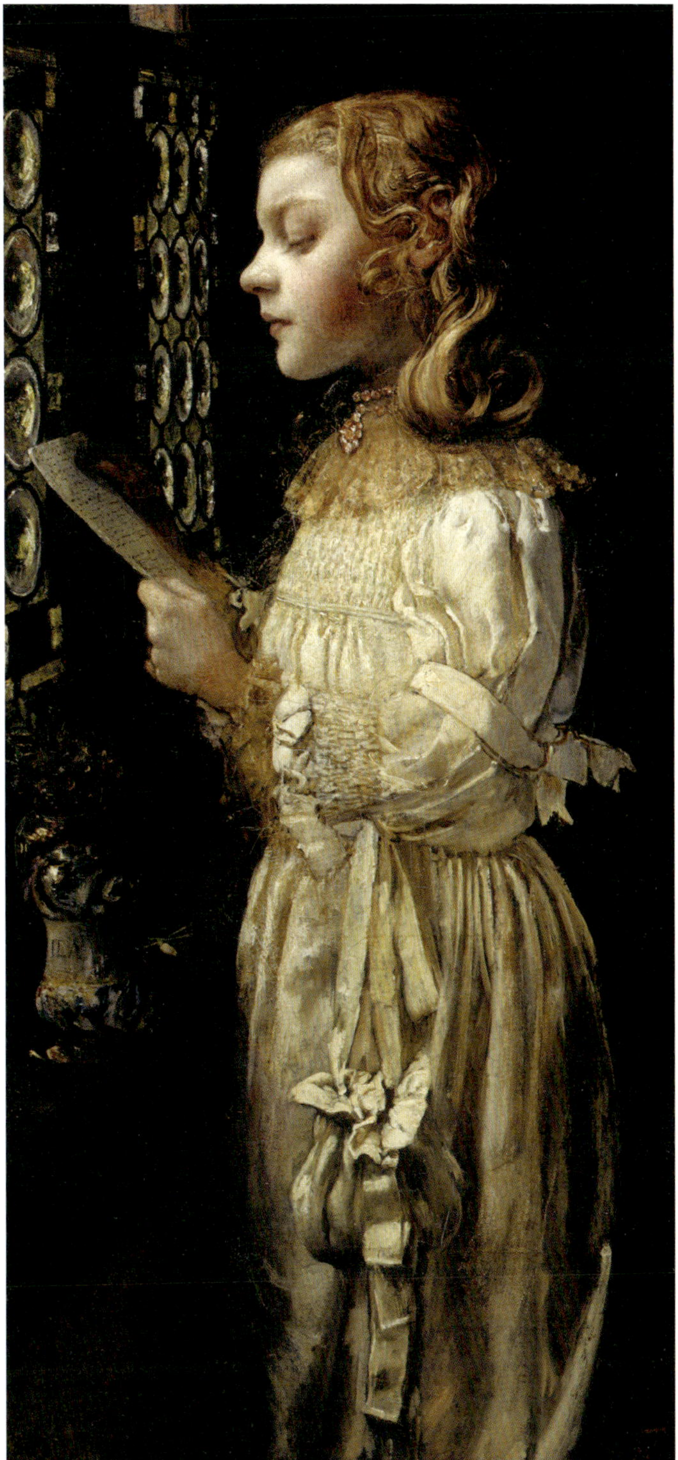

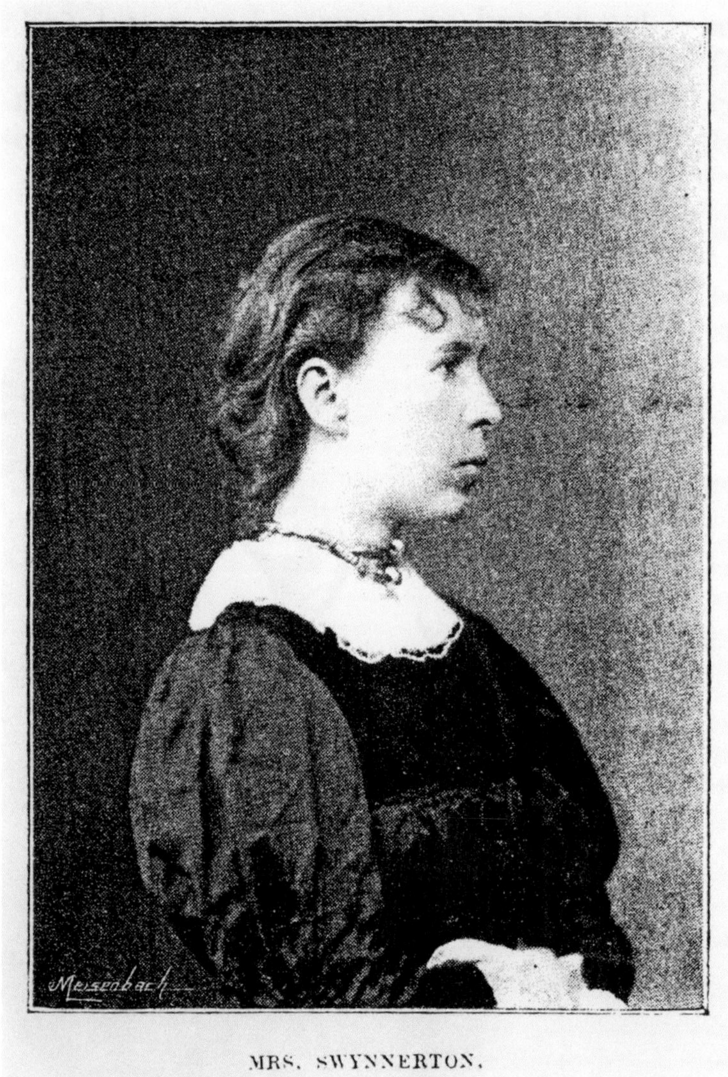

CAT 8 | **Annie L Swynnerton (née Robinson)**
c.1860s-70s

Georg Meisenbach & Co.
Facsimile of photograph published in *Sylvia's Journal*, June 1893
Manchester Art Gallery Archive

This photographic portrait of Swynnerton dates from her late twenties to early thirties, when she was becoming an artist. That it was used to illustrate an article about women artists in *Sylvia's Journal* in 1893 demonstrates that she, and other women artists, received some recognition in their lifetimes.

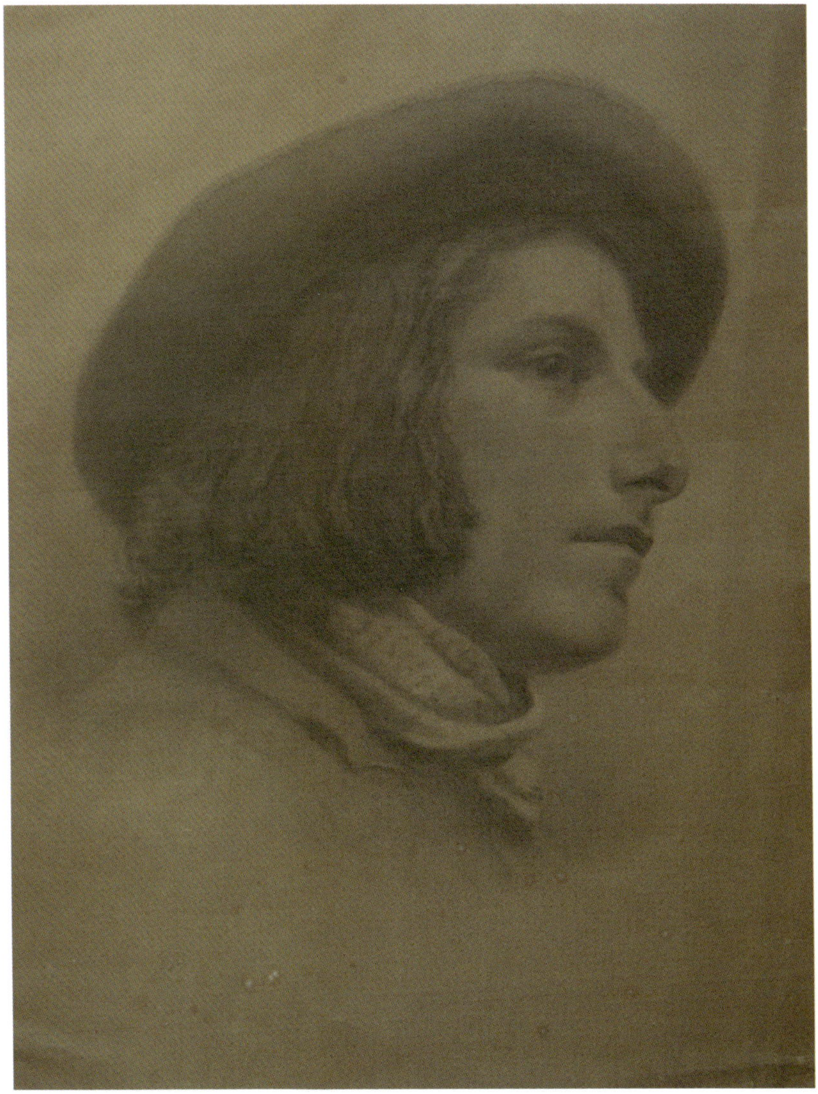

CAT 9 | ***The Head of a Young Man*** c.1870s

Pencil on paper, 43.6 x 32 cm
The Executors of Christine Brownlie Allen (1953-2014)

This rare surviving drawing produced by Swynnerton in the 1870s, while she was a student at the Manchester School of Art, illustrates her early skill in figure study. The figure may be a life model or someone Swynnerton knew; it could be her future husband, Joseph Swynnerton, which might explain the work's survival.

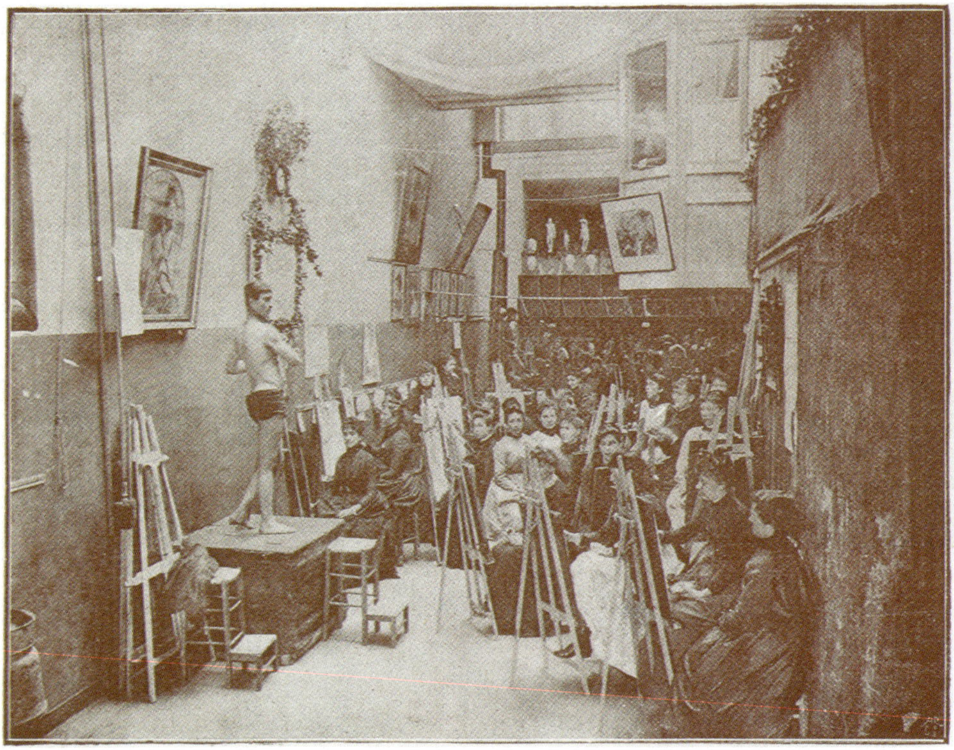

CAT 10 | **Women art students at work at the Académie Julian, Paris** 1893

Unknown photographer
Facsimile of photograph published in *The Sketch*, June 1893
British Library

This photograph shows female students studying a male life model at the Académie Julian, where Swynnerton studied in 1878-9. The progressive art education provided at this Parisian art school attracted women from across Europe and America, hence the crowded conditions. Fellow Académie Julian student, Russian artist Marie Bashkirtseff, kept diaries that reveal a rigorous training schedule, involving drawing from male and female undraped nudes, study of anatomy and observation of human dissections. In order to prepare for a professional career, female students also studied Parisian art collections and took part in competitions with their male peers.

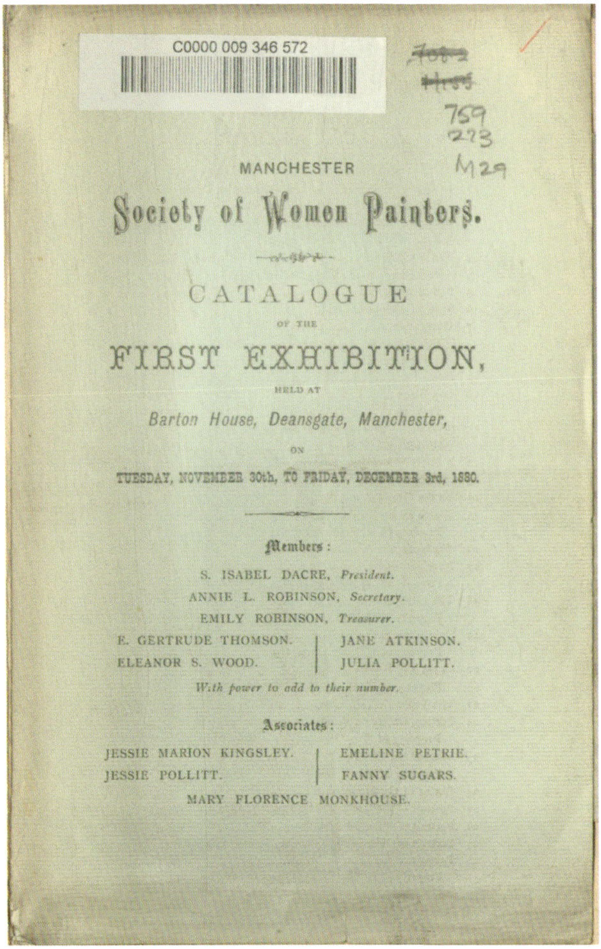

MANCHESTER

Society of Women Painters.

CATALOGUE

OF THE

FIRST EXHIBITION,

HELD AT

Barton House, Deansgate, Manchester,

ON

TUESDAY, NOVEMBER 30th, TO FRIDAY, DECEMBER 3rd, 1880.

Members:

S. ISABEL DACRE, *President.*

ANNIE L. ROBINSON, *Secretary.*

EMILY ROBINSON, *Treasurer.*

E. GERTRUDE THOMSON. | JANE ATKINSON.

ELEANOR S. WOOD. | JULIA POLLITT.

With power to add to their number.

Associates:

JESSIE MARION KINGSLEY. | EMELINE PETRIE.

JESSIE POLLITT. | FANNY SUGARS.

MARY FLORENCE MONKHOUSE.

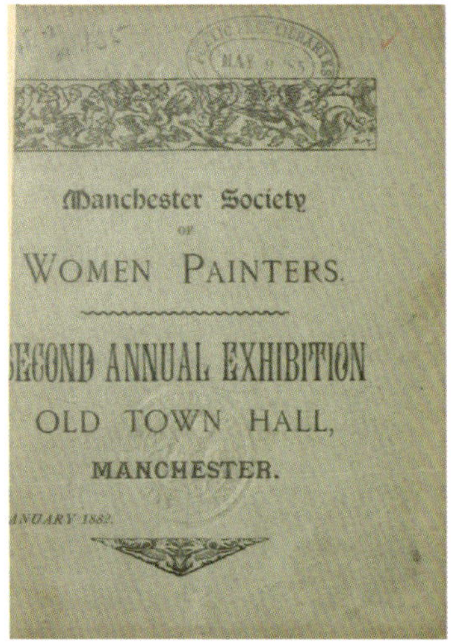

Manchester Society

OF

WOMEN PAINTERS.

SECOND ANNUAL EXHIBITION

OLD TOWN HALL,

MANCHESTER.

JANUARY 1882.

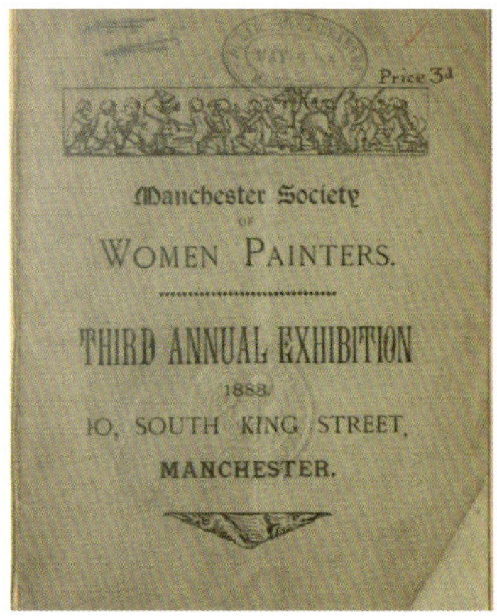

Price 3d

Manchester Society

OF

WOMEN PAINTERS.

THIRD ANNUAL EXHIBITION

1883.

10, SOUTH KING STREET,

MANCHESTER.

CAT 11 | **Manchester Society of Women Painters Exhibition Catalogues** 1880, 1882 and 1883

Susan Isabel Dacre, Annie L Robinson et al
Manchester Central Library Special Collections

Inspired by what she had learnt at the Académie Julian and unsatisfied with the opportunities available to women artists in Manchester, Swynnerton co-founded the Manchester Society of Women Painters in 1879. In addition to their exhibitions, the society's provision of 'facilities for members working together and studying from the life' evidences how central Swynnerton, and other women artists, thought real human bodies should be to women artists' practice.

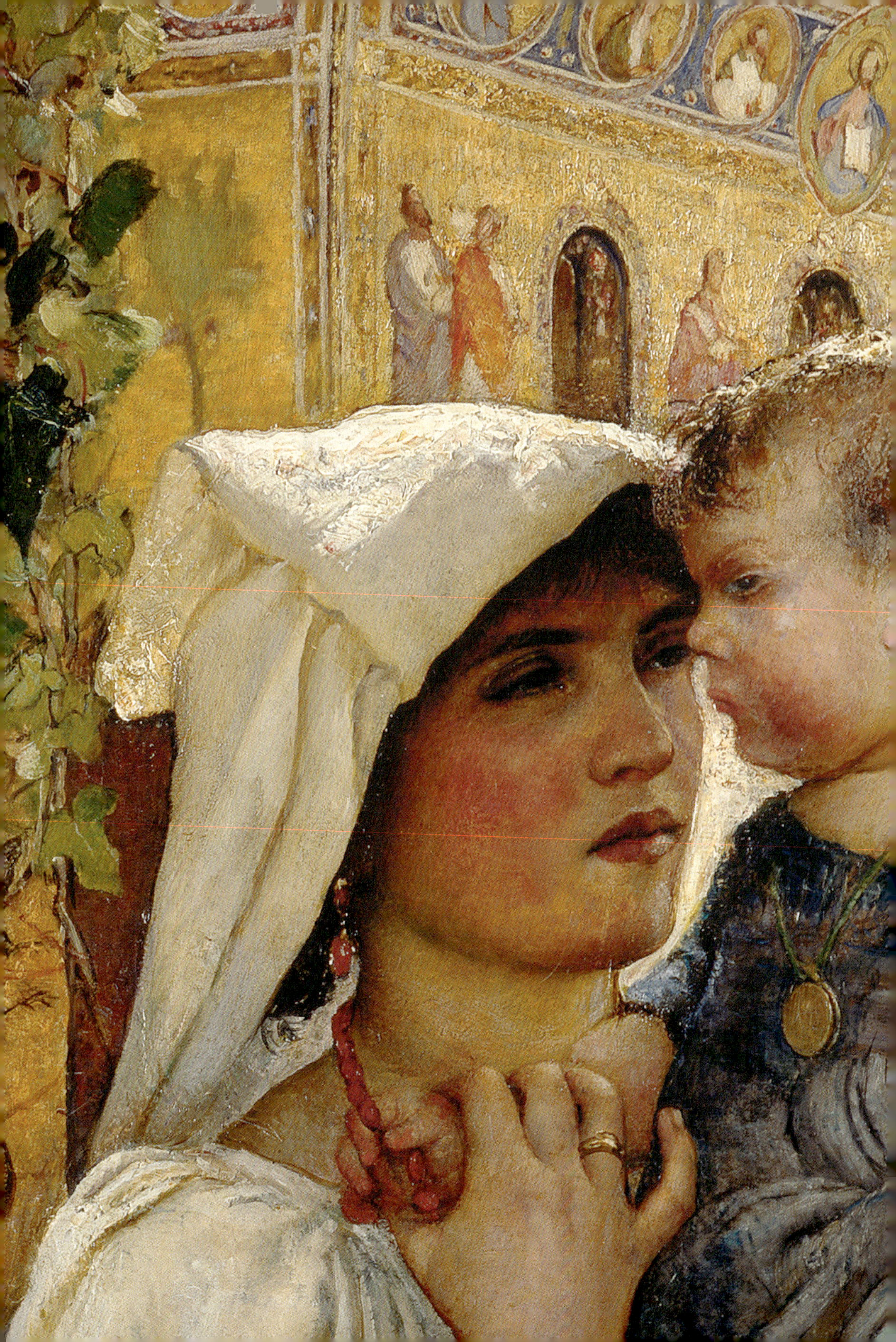

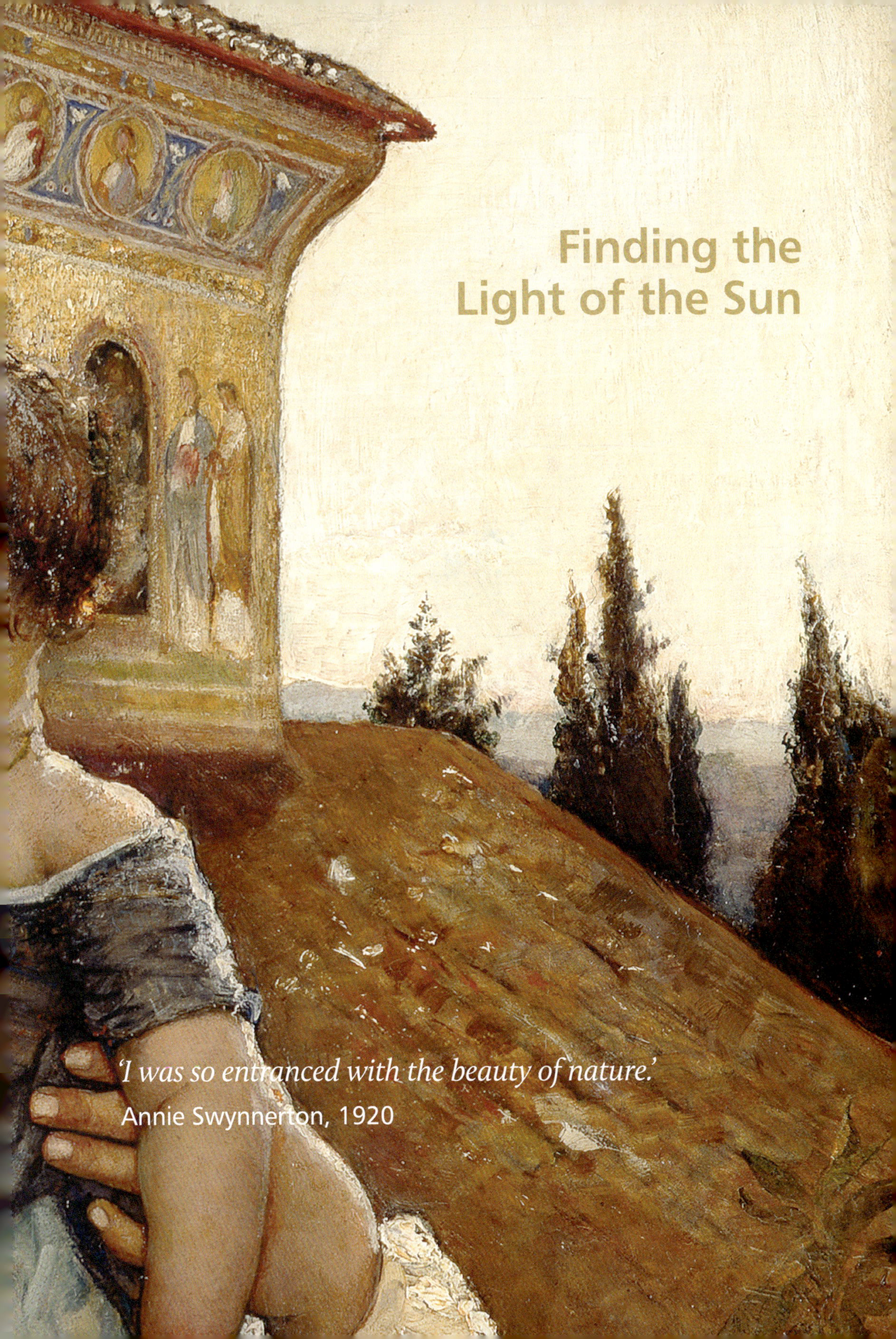

Finding the Light of the Sun

'I was so entranced with the beauty of nature.'

Annie Swynnerton, 1920

Finding the Light of the Sun

Swynnerton benefitted from a level of freedom to travel and develop as an artist that was unusual for British women in the 1870s and 1880s. This was enabled for over a decade by her friendship with fellow artist Susan Isabel Dacre. The pair acted as one another's travelling companion, visiting Rome in 1874 and attending the Académie Julian, Paris, in 1878–79. Paintings they produced in the 1880s, including landscapes, townscapes, paintings of architecture and depictions of contemporary Italian women outdoors, are evidence of their extensive travels throughout Italy.

This was a time of experimentation for Swynnerton, during which she began painting chiefly outdoors. She turned from the depiction of dark backdrops to light landscapes while continuing her exploration of light. She later explained:

> *I was early convinced that perfection of drawing and modelling was as possible in the glorious light of the sun as ever it was in the chill monotony of the studio. – nay much more. ... In this I was opposed to all the artists I ever spoke to ... However, I was so entranced with the beauty of nature and such a vista opened out to me of things never yet seen or recorded that I persevered, not intentionally, but because I could not help it.*[1]

Her preference for painting outdoors was influenced by 17th-century Dutch and Flemish landscape artists, early 19th-century British and Continental European Romanticists, Pre-Raphaelites and contemporary 19th-century painters.[2] The earthy colour palette she employed in the early 1880s is most reminiscent of the landscapes of the 19th-century Macchiaioli movement and Rural Naturalist paintings, but she developed her own independent style.

Swynnerton's earthy palette is punctuated by rich blue, emerald green and deep purple touches of her own innovation. Her figures, painted with a tight and smooth handling, are characterised by an incisive grasp of form, but enhanced by her distinctive way of depicting the action of strong sunlight on her subjects' bodies, through highlights consisting of

---

1 Swynnerton, Letter to Mr Brown, 6 June, 1920, National Gallery of Canada Archives.

2 The fourth Impressionist exhibition had taken place in Paris in 1879, the year Swynnerton completed her studies in the city. However, it is not until the 1890s to 1900s that her work reflects any admiration for their colour palette.

thick white paint. This inventive approach is paired with a loose, broken handling of paint in landscapes, architecture and costumes.

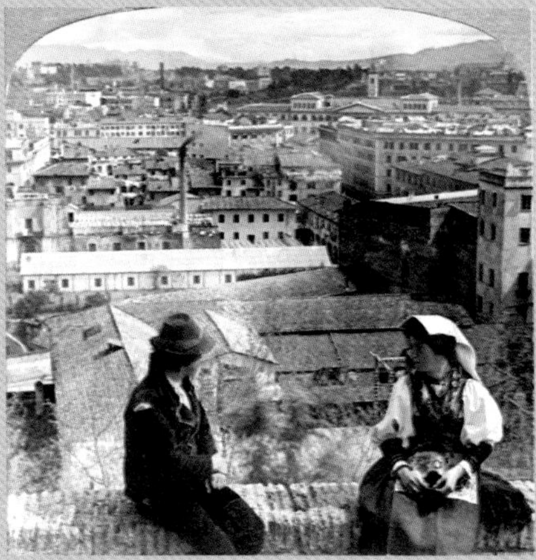

A rooftop view of Rome similar to that from Swynnerton's studio

Swynnerton continued to paint outdoors back in Britain in the later 1880s. Her paintings produced in this decade, abroad and at home, illustrate her early preference for depicting figures in landscapes.

She had begun living in Rome for sustained periods each year, from the time of her marriage to the sculptor Joseph Swynnerton in 1883, and would do so until his death in 1910. There she was in close proximity to the Italian countryside, and travelled yet more widely throughout Italy.[3] By the 1890s this embodiment within nature, and her passion for the light of the sun, had led her to develop a signature mature style. Swynnerton had, by the mid-1880s, adopted a white canvas primer, which had been innovatively used by the Pre-Raphaelites, and colour mixtures prescribed by her friend William Holman Hunt, with the intention of preserving the intensity of her colours, as the Pre-Raphaelites did.[4] Her colour palette had become light and bright, consisting of blues, pinks, purples and greens, and her brushwork both gestural and layered. Although her mature palette and technique shows her admiration for 19th-century British and French Impressionism, her unique approach to light and modelling form remains the dominant feature of her canvases.

[3] At the home the Swynnertons occupied from the early 20th century, 114 Via Montebello, Rome, Swynnerton had a rooftop studio overlooking the British Embassy Gardens from where she would have been able to see the nearby Alban Hills and Aventine Hill.

[4] Swynnerton, Letter to Mr Brown, 16 September, 1922, National Gallery of Canada Archives.

CAT 12 | ***The Town of Siena*** c.1880s

Oil on canvas, 37.8 x 51 cm
Manchester Art Gallery. Louisa Mary Garrett bequest 1936.210

Painted from the outskirts of the town of Siena, central Italy, Swynnerton's depiction of the topography of this hill town shows a high level of observation. This historic capital of Tuscany with its largely 12th- to 14th-century medieval architecture was popular with 19th-century artists. The low and distant view point Swynnerton has chosen gives the landmarks of the Cathedral of Siena and Torre del Mangia (Tower of the Eater) prominence. Comparison between this painting and Dacre's *The Walls of Siena* (date unknown, Manchester Art Gallery) illustrates the pair's practice of painting the same subject from different viewpoints. Their townscape paintings indicate both reciprocity in their practices and space for independent artistic development.

Swynnerton's loose, sketchy handling of paint in this work, with thin transparent and opaque layers that often allow the canvas to show through, is typical of her approach to landscape painting in the early 1880s. Her earthy palette is punctuated by rich purple passages that denote the effect of light on the terracotta rooftops and distant buildings. The foliage in the near distance is similarly made luminous green by the touch of light.

Artists often sold this type of painting to tourists in Italy. Yet, Swynnerton seems to have found homes for some of her early works back in Manchester. This example was owned by Louisa Mary Garrett, sister-in-law to suffrage leader Dame Millicent Garrett Fawcett's sister, suffragist Agnes Garrett.

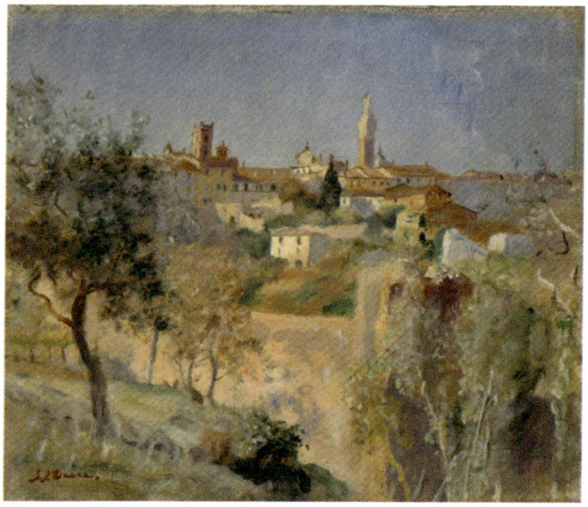

Isabel Dacre *The Walls of Siena* date unknown

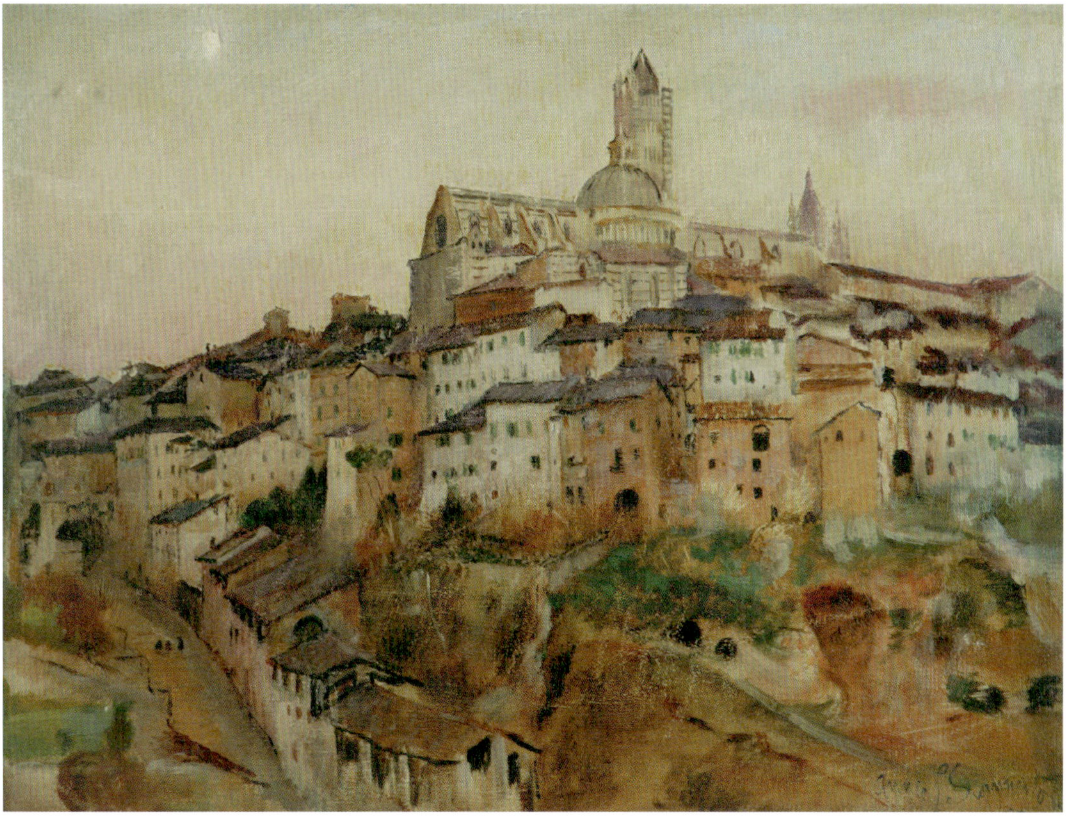

CAT 13 | *A View in Venice* 1880

Susan Isabel Dacre 1844–1933
Oil on canvas laid onto panel, 34.6 x 27 cm
Manchester Art Gallery. Gift of Thomas Gough 1928. 5

The paintings that Dacre and Swynnerton exhibited at the first Manchester Society of Women Painters exhibition held in 1880, including many now untraced works, tell us that they spent an extended period in Venice around that time. This included a variety of depictions of canals, waterfronts and landmarks, one of which was this painting by Dacre.[1]

The pair would have been familiar with depictions of panoramic scenes of Venice's major canals and lagoon by painters such as Canaletto in the 18th century, and later, Turner. However, Dacre's work depicts a picturesque, minor, anonymous canal. Such everyday views were a trend among many British painters, including James Holland, and Swynnerton and Dacre's contemporaries, including William Logsdail and Anglo-American John Singer Sargent. The quality of light, the reflective effects of moving water, the rich colours and decaying beauty of Venetian Gothic Architecture that enticed a plethora of painters to visit the city are apparent in Dacre's work.

1 Swynnerton's exhibits included the following untraced works: *Riva degli Schiavoni, Portico, St Mark's, Venice* and *West Door, St Mark's*. Her attention to St Mark's suggests she was attuned to 19th-century art critic John Ruskin's advice to young artists to study Venetian Gothic architecture.

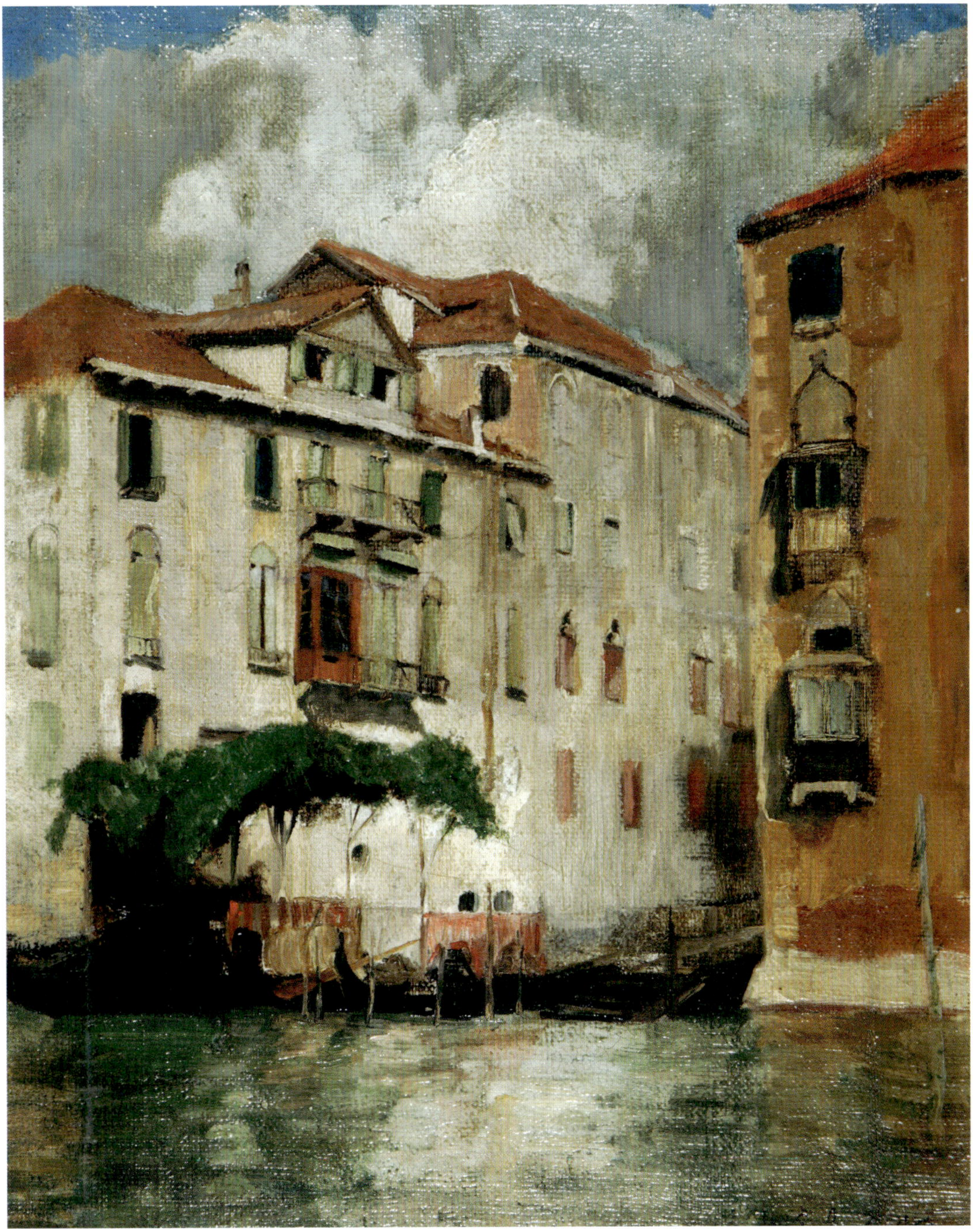

CAT 14 | ***An Italian Mother and Child*** 1886

Oil on canvas, 125.8 x 73.5 cm
Manchester Art Gallery. Louisa Mary Garrett bequest 1936.208

This painting is one of a series of contemporary Italian woman and child paintings that Swynnerton produced throughout the 1880s. Her composition references traditional Italianate depictions of the Madonna and Child by 15th-century Florentine artists whose work she would have had opportunity to study while visiting Florence in the 1880s.[1] Paintings by Sandro Botticelli, Fra Filippo Lippi, Lorenzo di Credi and Cosimo Rosselli, and relief sculptures by Lorenzo Ghiberti and Andrea Orcagna, all of whom sought to depict figures and landscapes naturalistically, were the most likely sources of inspiration.

Swynnerton's *An Italian Mother and Child* was not painted in Florence, but produced outdoors at a real location in Rome. The Basilica of Saint Lawrence Outside the Walls, Rome, dominates the landscape behind the figure. Its distinctive 13th-century façade adorned with gilt frescos and mosaic work, which was unfortunately destroyed in 1943 by bombing during World War II, is represented in detail by Swynnerton.[2] A 19th-century photograph of the surrounding area reveals that Swynnerton posed her figure in an arch of the walled Campo Verano cemetery that overlooks the basilica.

The principle that solidity of form is best achieved by light falling against it, which is the basis of traditional chiaroscuro painting techniques, is developed by Swynnerton in this painting through the use of the sun's natural light. Her characteristic application of thick white paint (using the technique known as impasto) recalls her earlier painting *Jebsa (Roma Lady)* (Catalogue No. 2). However, here, where the sun touches the mother's headdress, arms and knees for instance, the white patches express the intensity of the sun's light and heat.

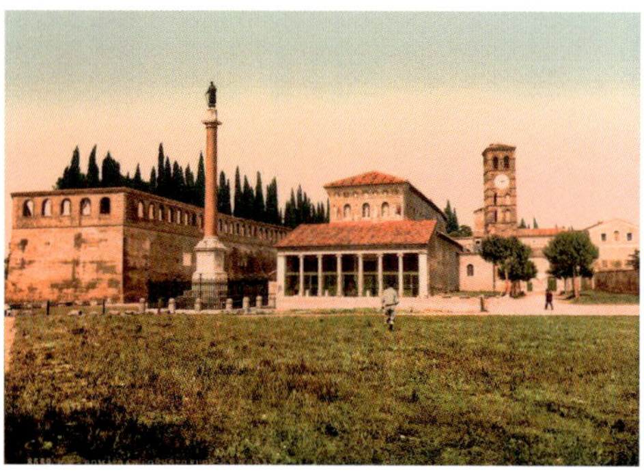

The Basilica of Saint Lawerence Outside the Walls, Rome, as seen in *An Italian Mother and Child*

1 Swynnerton and Dacre showed Florentine subject pictures at the 1882 MSWP exhibition that evidence that they spent a sustained period of time there prior to that show. Swynnerton's exhibits included *Florentine Mother and Child* (Private Collection) and *Interior of San Miniato, Florence* (1881, Manchester Art Gallery) among others.

2 The imagery related to the lives of the deacons St. Lawrence and St. Stephen, who is interred with St. Lawrence in the crypt.

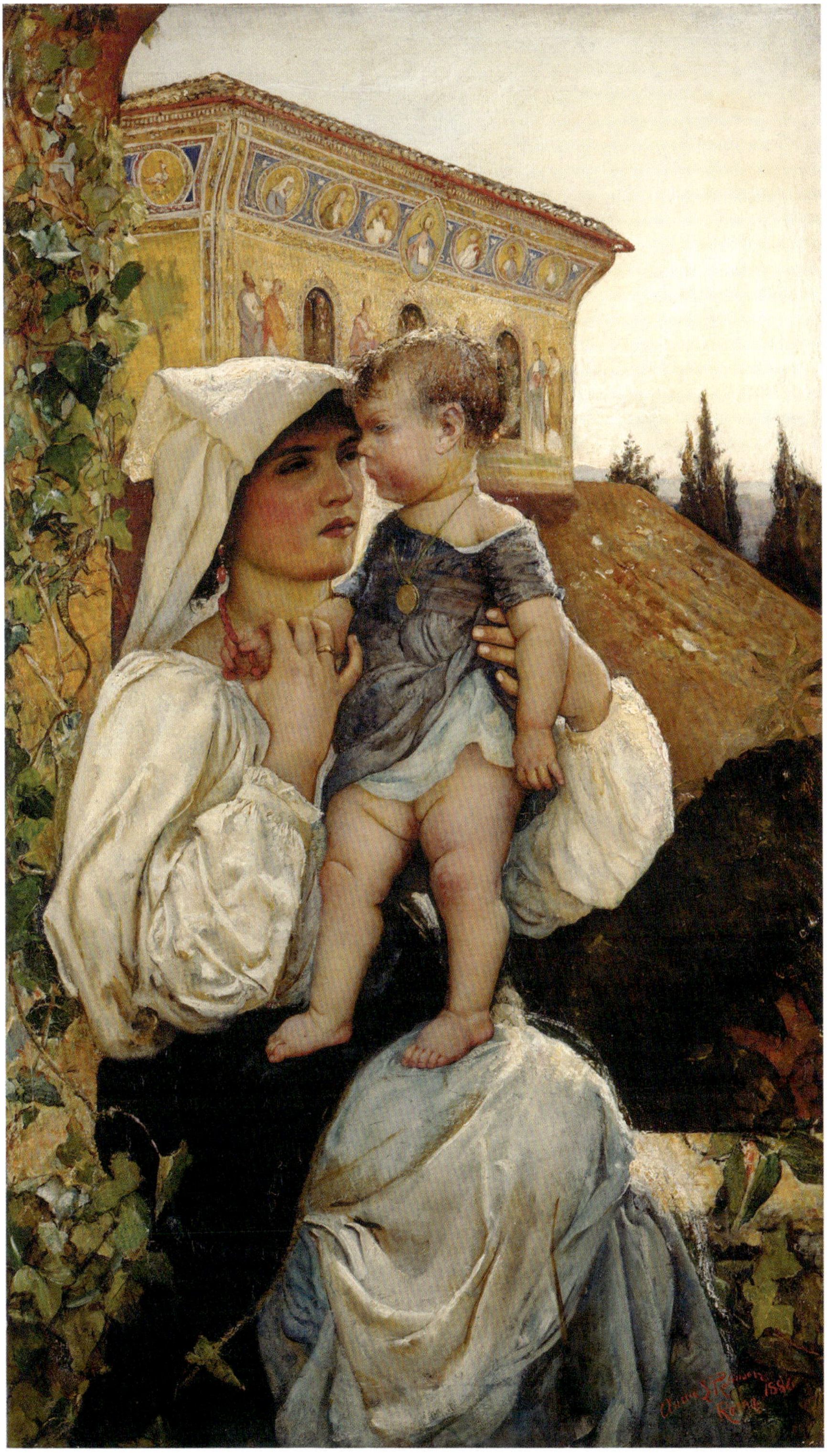

CAT 15 | ***The Young Mother*** c.1880s
Exhibited as ***Through the Orchard*** 1885

Oil on canvas, 134.5 x 86 cm
Dublin City Gallery, The Hugh Lane. Lane gift, 1912

Painted outdoors at Clovelly, Devon, this painting demonstrates the sustained influence of Swynnerton's experience of the Italian sun on her work during her periods in Britain. The intensity and skill she showed in the representation of the play of light on surfaces in the natural world is palpable here. The close attention to nature in the depiction of the apple tree evokes early Pre-Raphaelite notions of truth to nature. However, the use of the branches and fruits as a kind of decorative backdrop signals her desire to develop and stylise Pre-Raphaelitism, which she shared with its later exponents, including her friend Edward Burne-Jones.

There is a continued influence, too, from 15th-century Florentine artworks depicting the Madonna and Child, as well as a clear continuity between this work and Swynnerton's own series of Madonna and Child-style paintings depicting contemporary, low-status Italian women and children of the 1880s. The earthy palette and loose technique employed in this painting, meanwhile, together with the proximity of the figure to the viewer and her direct gaze, are attuned to depictions of working-class women in the work of 19th-century Rural Naturalist painters, including her friend George Clausen and French painter Jules Bastien-Lepage.

Swynnerton's depiction of a contemporary British working-class woman in this painting shows her attention to women's divergent roles; the female figure balances motherhood with the physical work of collecting water. She sent this painting to Dublin to replace a three-quarter length imaginative painting of a mature female nude, *St Martin's Summer* (now in the National Gallery of Canada); the former purchase having offended audiences at Dublin with its unabashed nudity. Swynnerton's modestly clothed Madonna-like figures, such as this one, certainly contrast with her bold nude women, for example *Oceanid* (Catalogue No. 25). The range she showed in the representation of female figures demonstrates her ability to cater to the tastes of different patrons, which was essential to making a career as a professional artist in the 19th and early 20th century.

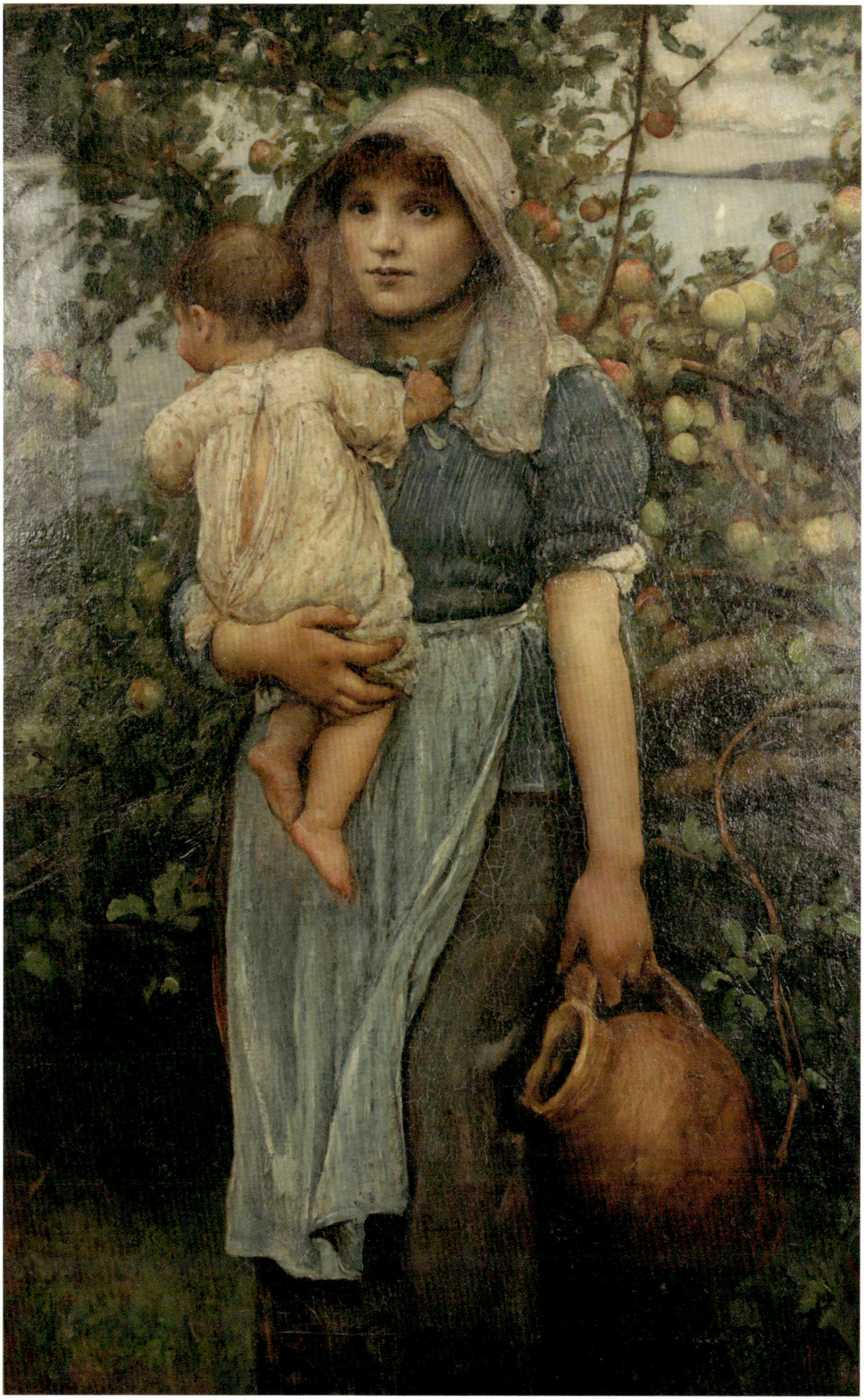

CAT 16 | *The Dreamer* 1887

Oil on canvas, 53.3 x 42.8 cm
Manchester Art Gallery. Gift of Fanny Rollo Wilkinson 1936.267

Depictions of female figures knitting outdoors are a common picturesque subject in 19th-century British, French and Italian paintings by William Dyce, Jean-François Millet and Giovanni Segantini, for instance. Working-class women, such as Swynnerton's knitting figure, are customarily depicted undertaking circular knitting, which created seamless tubes for socks and jumpers for their male relatives.[1] The activity is usually presented as a meditative pursuit, with the female subject looking down, concentrating on her work. This would correspond with *The Dreamer's* imaginative title, but the agency of Swynnerton's figure, her direct gaze and the way she holds her knitting and ball of wool apart, placing tension on the yarn, challenges such conventions. Her gaze and proximity to the picture plane more closely recall the confrontational figures of more socially conscious Rural Naturalist paintings, by George Clausen, for instance.

Swynnerton's enigmatic composition may allude to the character Queen Eurydice, in Sophocles's Ancient Greek mythological play *Antigone*. Eurydice is forced to 'knit until time comes for her to go to her room and die'. Her suicide, by her own needles, alludes to the Fates, three Greek goddesses who controlled the thread of every mortal life. That the painting evokes women's ability to realise the dream of determining their own fates, and those of others, seems appropriate given that it was produced on the Isle of Man – in 1881, the island's parliament, the High Court of Tynwald, became the first in the world to give women the right to vote in a general election.[2]

It is not surprising then that an artist with early feminist sensibilities was attracted to Manx subject matter. Swynnerton was also familiar with Manx culture through her marriage to Joseph Swynnerton, himself from the Isle of Man. In this painting, the three double-point needles form a triangular frame reminiscent of the Manx triskelion symbol, often seen as three legs linked at the thigh. The dark brown wool this woman is knitting with is typical of Manx Loaghtan sheep and the background is likely the fishing village of Laxey.

1 Women of higher social status were also depicted knitting as a form of genteel accomplishment or hobby.

2 Manchester women's movement leader Lydia Becker, who was a friend of Swynnerton and Dacre, led a group of women who travelled to campaign on the Isle of Man. They were instrumental in the realisation of the amendment that enabled unmarried women to vote there.

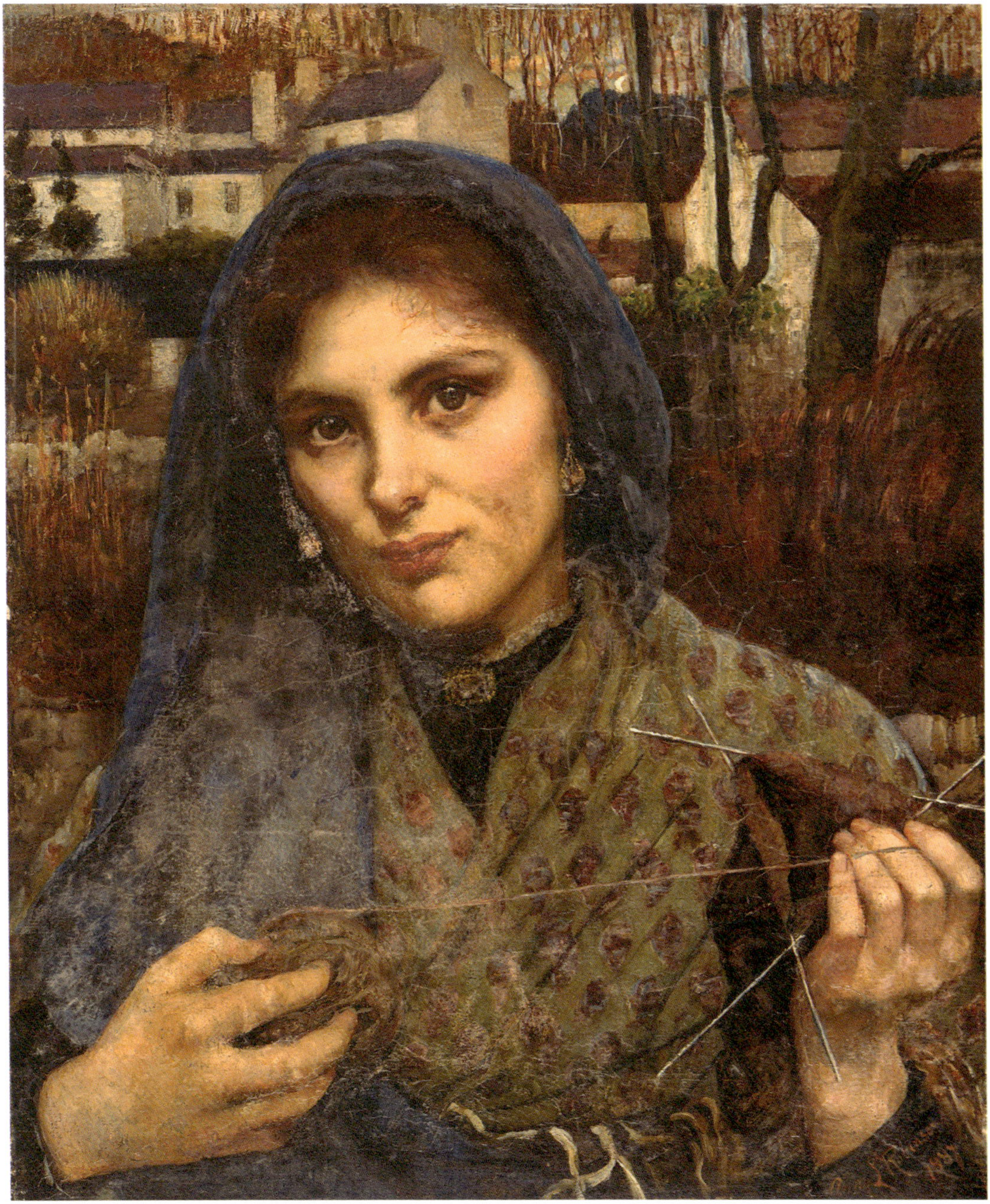

CAT 17 | ***The Convalescent*** c.1887

Oil on canvas, 57.1 x 63.5 cm
Tate. Presented by the Trustees of the Chantrey Bequest 1929

The Convalescent features the same model as seen in *The Dreamer,* wearing the same shawl. These paintings also share an earthy colour palette and loose handling of paint in their backdrops. They are part of a series, produced around 1887, depicting contemporary working-class Manx women, painted outdoors.[1] Swynnerton includes symbols of the island here: a sheep alluding to the Manx Loaghtan breed and the clusters of the yellow wild flower *cushag* (ragwort), the Manx national flower.

The theme of a person recovering from illness was frequently employed in 19th-century British and French painting to depict the fragility of people of all ages, sexes and social classes. The depiction of a lone female convalescent of this kind also enabled artists to explore the subject's emotional and psychological states. Swynnerton chose to embrace the representation of *reverie,* a state of being lost in one's pleasant thoughts.[2] With a world of sensation around her, the female figure closes her eyes, looking inward, absorbed. Her slight smile signifies her contentment in the world of her imagination, yet her closed eyes and relaxed posture also tell us she is comfortable in her natural surroundings. Her lower body is encompassed by the tall moorland scrub, giving a sense of her oneness with the landscape, and her flushed cheeks imply she is benefitting from the restorative power of the outdoors.

Swynnerton's direct study of a real landscape demonstrates a level of devotion to painting outdoors comparable to that of hardy early Pre-Raphaelite landscape painters. The vantage point from which she observed this panoramic view was likely the rugged slopes of South Barrule hill, above the village of Foxdale, close to the Manx capital, Douglas. In front of the Eary Dam, the body of water seen in the upper right background, are two lead-mining sites, and beyond it a mining tower, symbolic of the working-class community of which the depicted figure was part.

1 Another work by Swynnerton titled *Manx Maid* was exhibited at the Liverpool Autumn Exhibition and Grosvenor Gallery in 1887 and illustrated in the catalogue of the latter show.

2 The cracking of thickly layered paint (known as pentimento) in the areas relating to the figure's eyelids tells us that they have been painted over and indicates the figure's eyes were originally painted open.

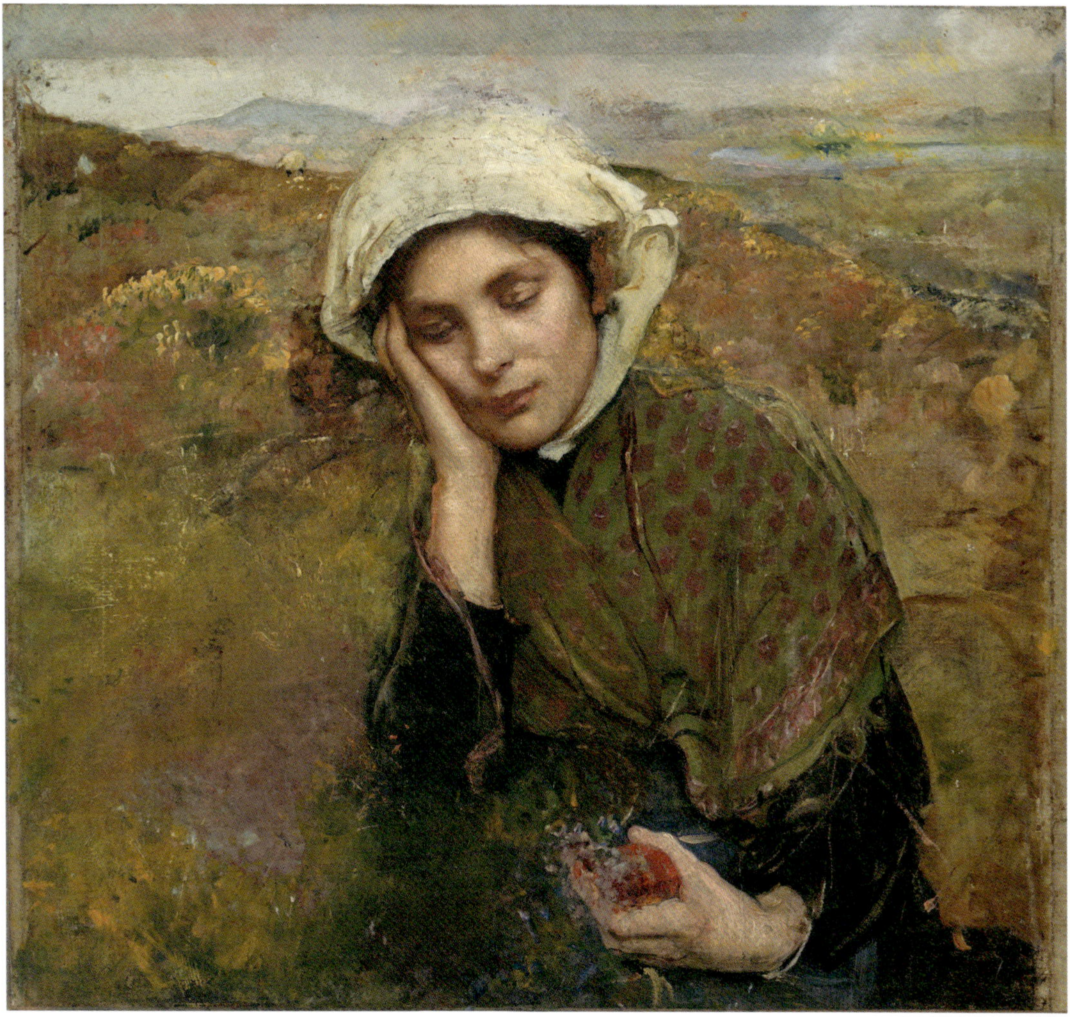

CAT 18 | ***The Olive Gatherers*** (also known as ***The Plain of Lombardy***) 1889

Oil on canvas, 38.5 x 71 cm
Manchester Art Gallery. Gift of Fanny Rollo Wilkinson 1936.268

Painted in 1889 and exhibited at the Society of Women Artists, London, in 1891, *The Olive Gatherers* was one of the earliest paintings in which Swynnerton applied her mature signature palette. Her liking for afternoon light, particularly the colours and light effects created as the day moves towards sunset, is also established here; the moon visible above the mountain range signals the coming of night.

In common with 18th- to 19th-century European Romantic paintings of pastoral landscapes Swynnerton represented nature as a comforting source of beauty and both physical and spiritual sustenance. Her unspoilt, uplifting panoramas and sunsets behind majestic mountains also contain a generous dose of the picturesque. This concept was developed in the late 1700s by clergyman and artist William Gilpin, and referred to the notion of the charm in discovering the landscape in its natural state. Her work develops what art historian Lindsay Smith has called a 'preoccupation with natural perception' – i.e. as perceived by the viewer without idealisation or stylisation – seen in Pre-Raphaelite landscape paintings, too.[1] This panoramic view is a real landscape in the plains of Lombardy, northern Italy, close to Milan. Here Swynnerton has created substantial depth, utilising the device of a zigzagging row of trees to guide the viewer's eyes far into the landscape. The haze hanging in front of the mountain range makes it seem yet more distant and separates it from the valleys and inhabited hill towns, giving the mountains an otherworldly, perhaps mystical status. This became a recurring theme in Swynnerton's work; see, for example, *Montagna Mia* (Catalogue No. 46).

Swynnerton's interest in working-class subjects is expressed in the title of this work and by the inclusion of two figures, a man and a woman, at work harvesting the olive trees together in the foreground. In common with her contemporaries, John Singer Sargent and Italian landscape painter of naturalistic scenes and revolutionary Giovanni Costa, for instance, she was interested in depicting the activities associated with rural life in Italy against its natural backdrops, with a social conscience as well as an eye for aesthetics.

[1] Lindsay Smith in Marcia Pointon (ed.), *Pre-Raphaelites Re-Viewed* (Manchester University Press, 1989), 86 and 87.

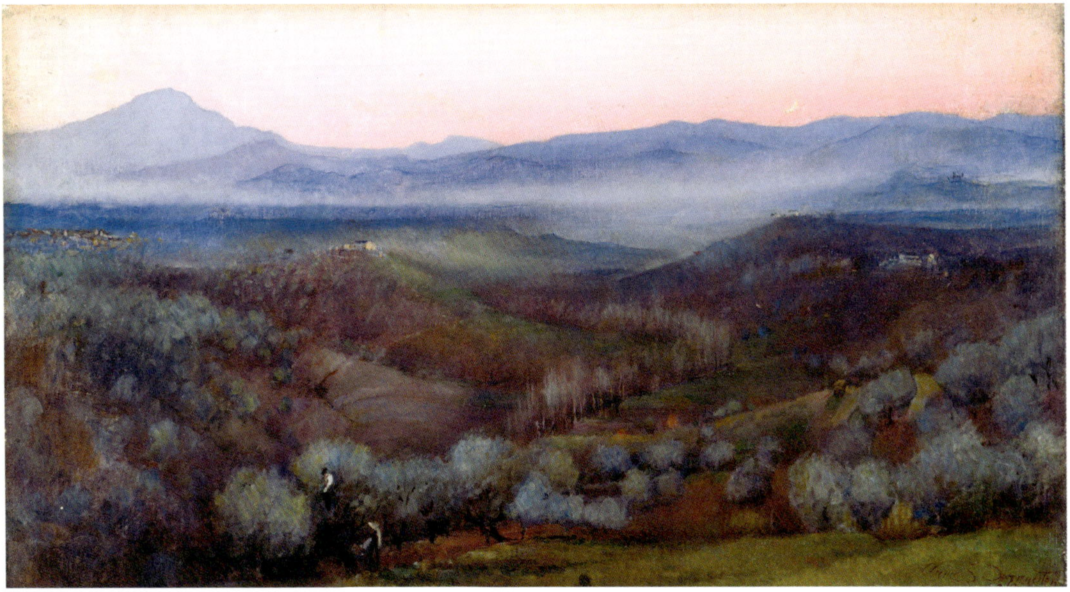

CAT 19 | *Italian Landscape* c.1900s

Oil on canvas, 84.3 x 119.1 cm
Manchester Art Gallery. Dr Jane CH Walker, LLD bequest 1939.20

Swynnerton's broad brushwork and thickly applied paint (known as impasto) in this work is reminiscent of 19th-century French Impressionism, a movement in which each individual artist approached the application of paint in their own distinctive way. It is telling that Swynnerton's friend John Singer Sargent displayed his 'much admired Annie Swynnertons' alongside French Impressionist works by Claude Monet, acknowledging the affinity between their practices. In Swynnerton's work, sunlight, represented by white paint, illuminates the distant mountains, rugged hills and hill town around the depicted crater-lake, which reflects the vibrant blue sky.

Although there is no record that confirms where Swynnerton painted this landscape, the small size of the volcanic crater-lake, the rugged appearance of the mountains and hills that surround it and the form of the town above its banks recalls Lake Nemi in the Alban Hills close to Rome – a place commonly painted by a variety of 18th- and 19th-century male European artists who undertook Grand Tours of Italy. Swynnerton painted other works there, including *Oceanid* (Catalogue No. 25) and *The Southing of the Sun* (Catalogue No. 22) in the early decades of the 20th century. The fig trees in the foreground of this painting link it to another contemporaneous landscape by the artist, too: *The Barren Fig* (Catalogue No. 21), painted at Lake Albano.

The landscapes, such as this one, that Swynnerton enjoyed exploring with her husband, their family and their friends are made vivid by Frederick Swynnerton's reminiscences of time spent with his brother Joseph in Italy:

> *We went riding among the Alban Woods and vineyards ... on foot, generally with congenial friends, we have climbed Mount Soracte, the Alban Hill, and Monte Gennaro, the highest peak of the Sabines, crossed Lake Bracciano in a ramshackle canoe ... and have trampled through the innermost recesses of the Sabine and Volscian mountains, visiting their classical sites ...*[1]

1 Frederick Swynnerton, 'A Manx Sculptor and his work', *Mannin*, vol. 2, no 3, 1914.

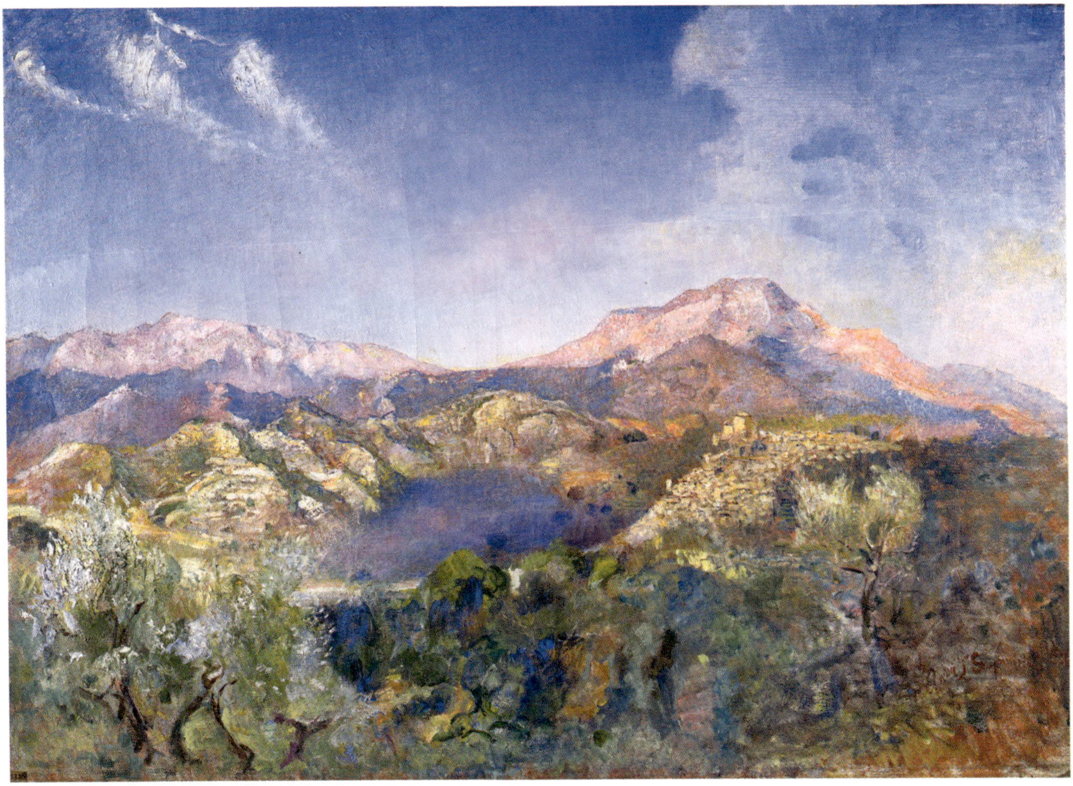

CAT 20 | *Capri* c.1900s

Oil on canvas, 61.3 x 29.2 cm
Private Collection

Capri is a coastal townscape painting depicting the largest harbour, Marina Grande, on the island of Capri. This painting indicates the extent of Swynnerton's travels across Italy, with Capri being the southern-most location she is known to have represented. Swynnerton took an accurate approach in documenting the harbour, town buildings and mountainous landscape beyond. She recalled in 1923, 'Once, at Capri, I sat on a rock in mid-stream every day for three weeks to get the motion of water in the sunlight.'[1] Her painting with its bright, harmonious colours, bold white highlights and gestural paint, which gives movement to the water and boat sails, successfully evokes the atmosphere of the place.

By the early 20th century a succession of artists from around the world had visited Capri and painted its coastline. Like the royal families, aristocrats, politicians and industrialists who holidayed there, artists and poets were attracted by its famed unassailable beauty and the quality of the light. A range of artists interested in working in an impressionistic style favoured the island, including John Singer Sargent and a number of Italian painters, most notably Antonio Leto, who lived on the island from 1882 onwards. The majority of Swynnerton's known townscapes depict inland locations, which makes this painting unusual among her landscape works, although she frequently painted the lakes of the hilly countryside around Rome. The portrait orientation of the canvas is also a rare choice. These aspects show her versatility and inventive approach to landscape.

1 Swynnerton in AB Cooper, 'Our Greatest Woman Artist: The Story of Mrs Swynnerton who was recently elected to be an Associate of the Royal Academy', *Pearson's Magazine*, March 1923, no. 321, 197–8.

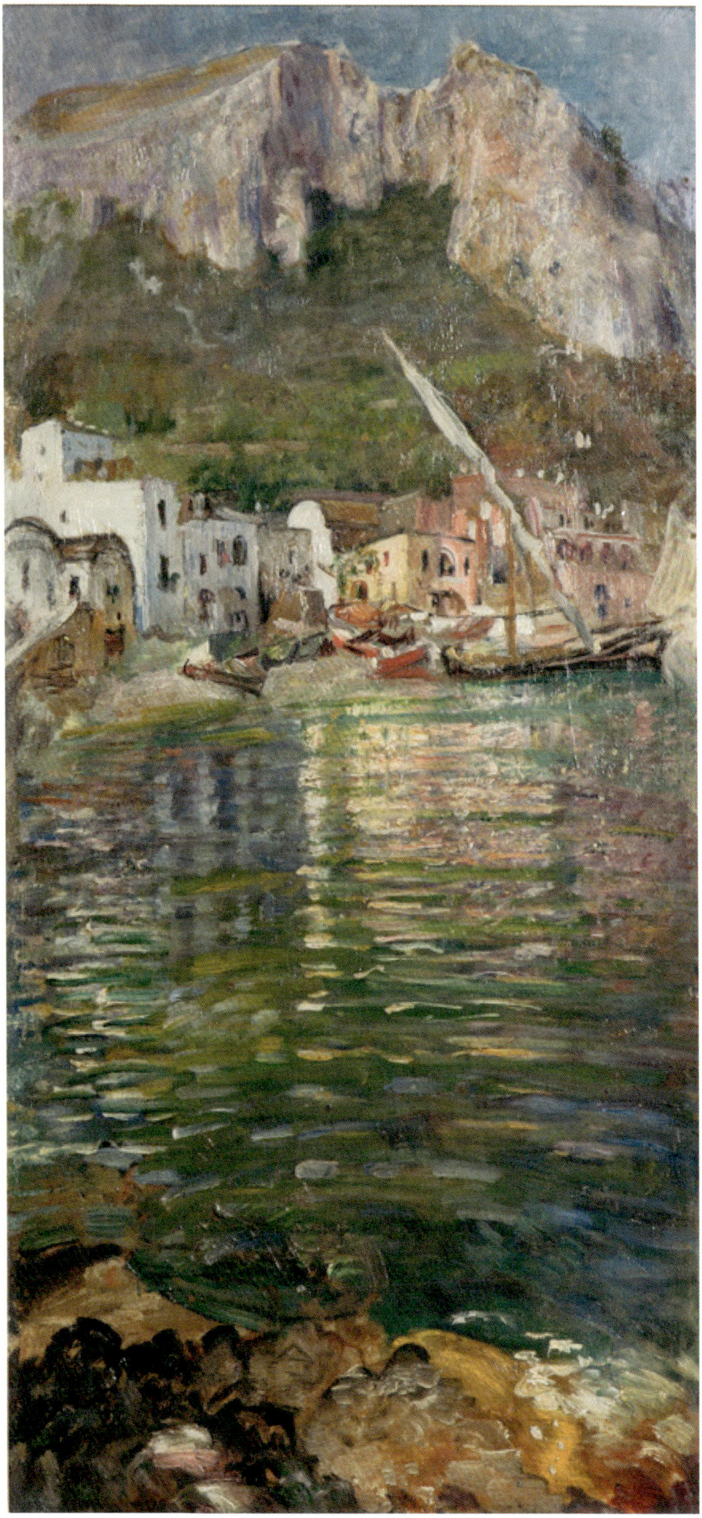

CAT 21 | *The Barren Fig* c.1900s

Oil on canvas, 29.5 x 50 cm
The Executors of Christine Brownlie Allen (1953-2014)

Produced at Lake Albano in the Alban Hills, approximately 13 miles southeast of Rome, this painting illustrates that Swynnerton took advantage of her close proximity to the Italian countryside during her long periods of residence in the capital. The tree that is positioned in the centre of the canvas, close to the picture plane, conceals and reveals a view of the small volcanic crater-lake at the foot of Monte Cavo. This unusual and visually engaging composition makes Swynnerton's physical presence within the landscape tangible. The majority of her known landscape paintings take the middle and far distance – the sky, mountains and undulating landscape, and features such as distant vegetation, buildings and people – as their focus, paying less attention to the foreground. The foregrounded fig tree in this painting is therefore rare.

This painting shows the high level of skill Swynnerton possessed when it came to the close study of nature, which is evident in other works such as *Landscape with Trees* (undated, Aberdeen Art Gallery & Museums). Such works also demonstrate how she combined Pre-Raphaelite principles of direct study from nature outdoors with an independent gestural approach to the application of paint.

Annie Swynnerton
Landscape with Trees date unknown

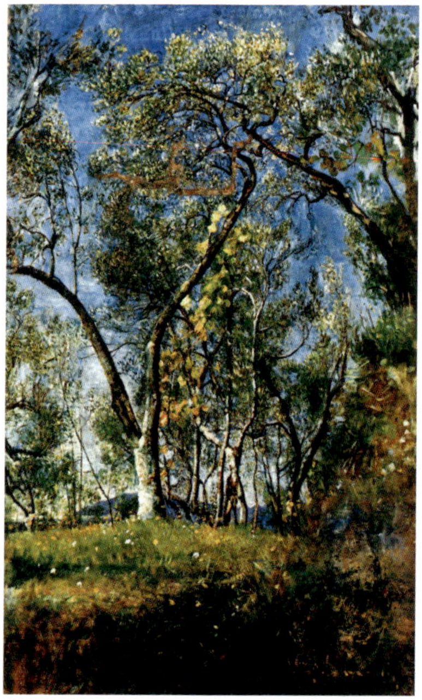

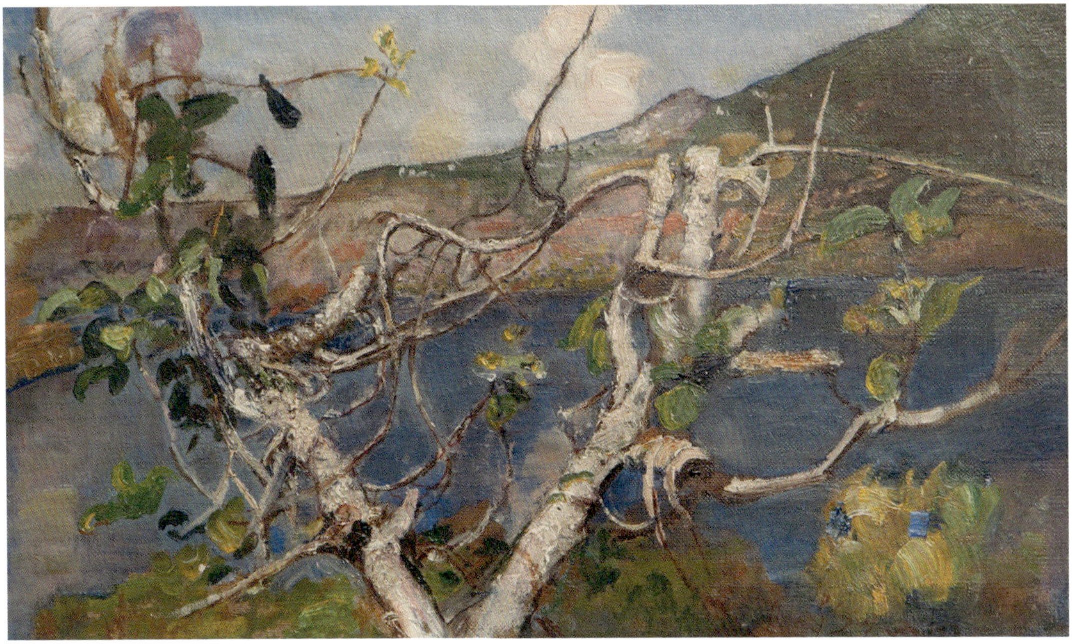

CAT 22 | ***The Southing of the Sun*** 1911

Oil on canvas, 111.90 x 88.9 cm
Manchester Art Gallery. Purchased from Annie L Swynnerton ARA 1923.47

Painted at Nemi, a town in the Alban hills, south of Rome, this painting epitomises the joy Swynnerton found in the light of the sun in Italy. The sun's warmth on the peasant woman's body is made tangible through the bold application of thick white paint. The woman's green dress emphasises her oneness with the landscape – which had become a recurring theme in Swynnerton's work by this time – while her open-armed gesture celebrates the sun's life-enriching properties.

The painting's title is taken from a line in verse 7 of 'May-Day',[1] a poem by American poet Ralph Waldo Emerson, the leading exponent of transcendentalism, a philosophical and social movement developed in the United States in the 1820s and 30s in reaction to rationalism. Swynnerton's imagery is in keeping with the awakening effects of spring described in Emerson's first verse. The poem's words seem to comment on Swynnerton's artistic preferences, too. In Emerson's poem, flora and fauna, unlike the artist who longed to paint outdoors, are content and busy living through the winter and do not chide 'the tardy Spring'. Neither do they pay attention to the setting sun that Swynnerton so prized for the light effects and colours it created.

Emerson's transcendentalist teachings that divinity exists in all of nature and humanity are apparent in Swynnerton's depiction of the female figure. The light that shines from behind her might be reflected from the crater-lake that the town of Nemi overlooks but it simultaneously gives her an ethereal, saintly, or even mystical, glow. The natural beauty of old age is embraced here, too – as it is in *The Vagrant* (c.1900s–10s, Manchester Art Gallery) – through the faithful replication of the lines and creases that give the sitter's face its individual character.

The eighth verse of Emerson's poem wisely advises patience and trust in the cyclical nature of the passing seasons. It seems appropriate, given that Swynnerton produced this painting the year after her husband's death, an event that likely felt like the close of a season in her life, which she much wanted to imagine coming round again. After 1910, she would spend less time in Italy each year.

1

The sparrow meek, prophetic-eyed.
Her nest beneath the snowdrift weaves,
Secure the osier yet shall hide
Her callow brood with mantling leaves, –
But though by science all undone,
Why only shall thy reason fail
To see the Southing of the Sun?

Ralph Waldo Emerson, from 'May-Day', 1867

Annie Swynnerton *The Vagrant*
c. early 1900s–10s

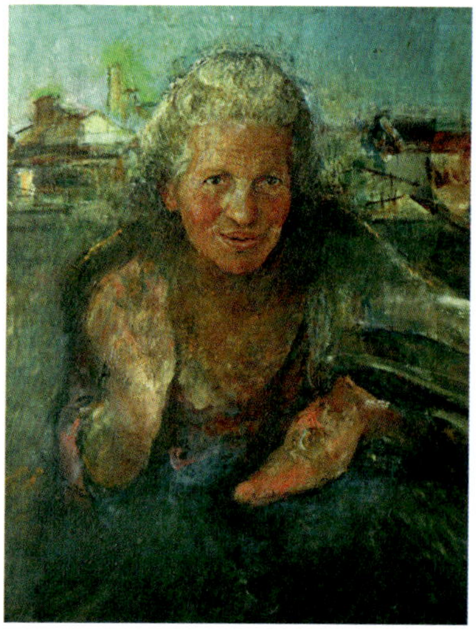

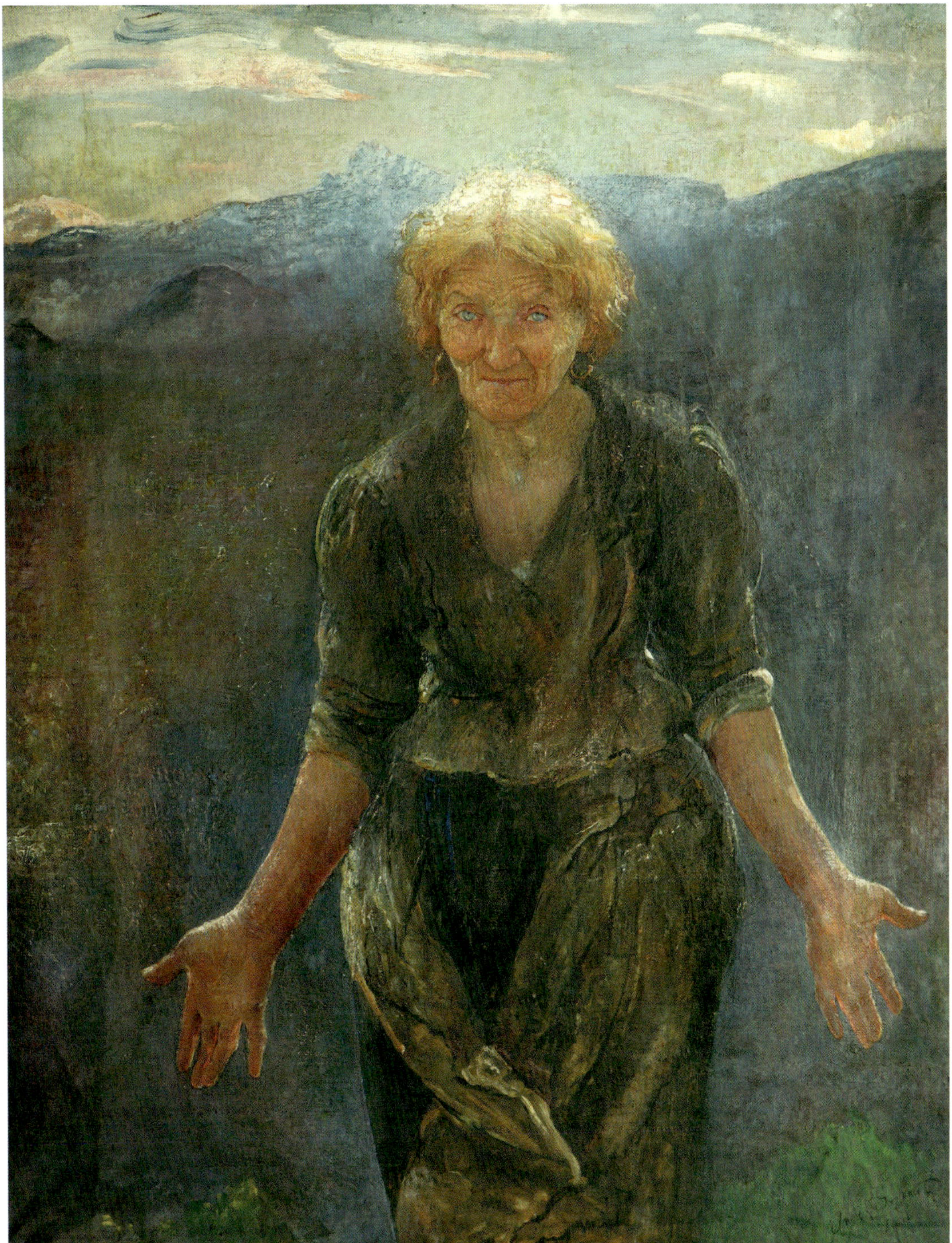

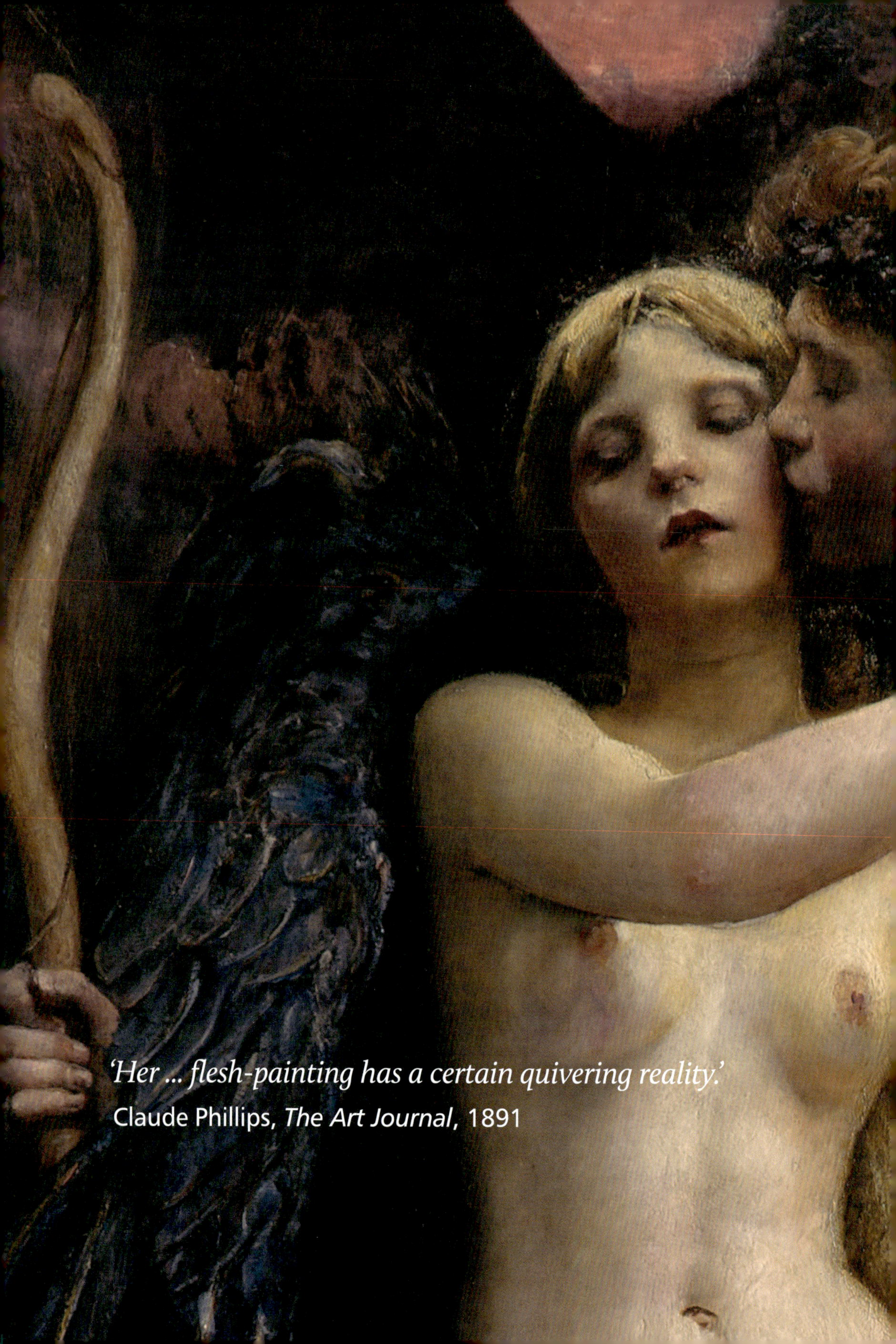

'Her ... flesh-painting has a certain quivering reality.'

Claude Phillips, *The Art Journal*, 1891

Embodied Nudes

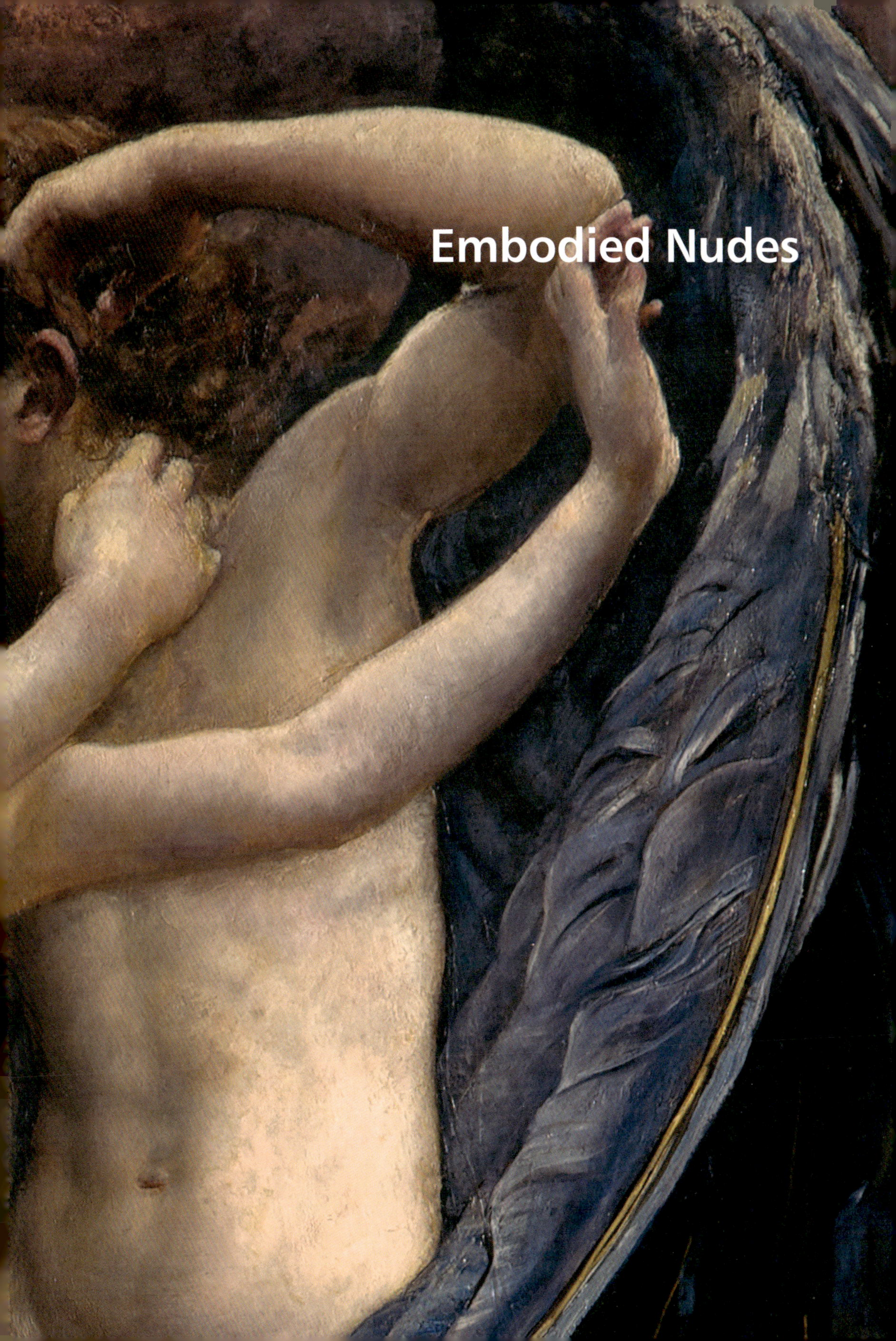

Embodied Nudes

The nude was a staple genre in Academic painting of the 18th, 19th and early 20th centuries that regularly featured in subject pictures inspired by mythology, biblical narratives, literature or history. It allowed artists to demonstrate their knowledge of the human body. Swynnerton was among a small number of late 19th-century women painters who depicted nude figures. Women who did so were unusual because, until the 1870s, professional training in this area had been denied to women.

The rigorous training, rooted in study from draped and nude models and classes in anatomy, that Swynnerton obtained for herself, through various routes, prepared her well for working in this genre. However, perhaps due to presiding opinions that the nude was an unsuitable subject for women artists, it was not until 1891 – after fellow women artists Anna Lea Merritt, Henrietta Rae and Evelyn Pickering DeMorgan had begun exhibiting paintings of nude figures – that she showed enough confidence to exhibit a foray into this genre, *Cupid and Psyche* (Catalogue No. 23). Just two years later her *Mater Triumphalis* (1892, Musée d'Orsay, Paris) won a medal for oil painting at the World's Columbian Exposition in Chicago of 1893. There, alongside the most highly acclaimed male artists of the time, she was among nine British women to be rewarded.[1]

Like other contemporary artists of both sexes, Swynnerton adopted allegorical subject matter inspired by classical Greek and Roman mythology in her paintings of nude figures in order to make them socially acceptable for public display. Her residence in Rome from the 1890s to 1910s no doubt provided ample inspiration. The broader influence of Italy can be seen in the light effects, landscape backdrops and vivid colour palette of her nudes, too.

The originality of Swynnerton's nudes lies in her emphasis on realistic, unidealised, female forms, which are robustly modelled, and her use of layered and textured paint in a variety of colours in the depiction of flesh.

---

1 This included John Everett Millais, Lawrence Alma-Tadema, George Clausen, Frederic Leighton, John William Waterhouse and Albert Moore and Laura Alma-Tadema, Anna Lea Merritt and Lady Elizabeth Southerden Butler. Anon., 'British Art Awards at Chicago', *The Times*, 19 August, 1893, 5.

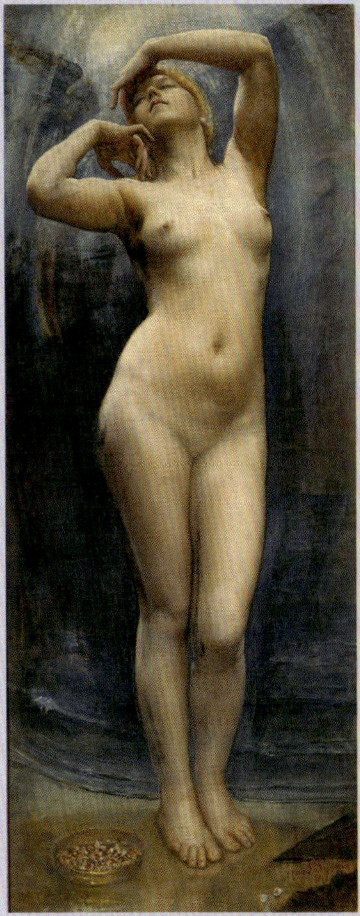

Annie Swynnerton *Mater Triumphalis* 1892

This challenged conventional idealised and stylised representations of female beauty in nudes by 19th-century male Academic artists, which depicted women as coy and their skin as smooth and consistent in colour. Swynnerton also communicated a tangible sense of what it feels like to inhabit the female human form that is influenced by her own lived experience. In her paintings, we see women's hands touching their own bodies, alluding to their self-knowledge. The contact of pleasurable, and occasionally uncomfortable, natural elements against their skin is sensitively evoked. She brings to the genre an innate knowledge of the female form that contradicted the fragile bodies and simple minds imagined by patriarchal ideology. Furthermore, the gestures of her nudes make them active and engaging, and their, often authoritative, connections with nature give visibility to women's creative powers. In combination, these aspects of her work encapsulate hope and potential at a time when the role of women was changing and opportunities were opening up. We might conclude that Swynnerton represented the female nude according to her own agenda, powerfully influenced by her beliefs in women's rights and agency.

Her embodied nudes prompted mixed responses from reviewers but admiration from contemporary artists, including John Singer Sargent and French sculptor Auguste Rodin, who were instrumental in ensuring important examples of her work were acquired by British and French national art collections.

CAT 23 | *Cupid and Psyche* 1890

Oil on canvas, 147 x 91 cm
Gallery Oldham. Gift of Charles Edward Lees, 1892

Depictions of Cupid and Psyche in art throughout the ages commonly feature a nude, or partially draped, male and female figure together. The subject comes from Roman writer Apuleius's 2nd-century novel *The Golden Ass*. Apuleius recounts how the goddess Venus, jealous of human woman Psyche's beauty, sends her son Cupid to wound Psyche with his arrow so that she might fall in love with a lowly man. However, Cupid falls in love with Psyche and makes her his wife, ensuring their marriage remains secret by forbidding Psyche to look upon his face. In Swynnerton's composition, Psyche's barely closed eyes and out-reached hands imply that she desires knowledge of Cupid's identity. Women's beauty, vision and knowledge are therefore key themes represented in this painting.

The classical narrative here made the figures' nudity and intimacy acceptable for public display.[1] Yet, while 19th-century Academic nudes focused on idealised bodies and were characterised by a consistently smooth paint surface – seen in the work of Frederic Leighton and Lawrence Alma-Tadema, for instance – Swynnerton challenged those conventions. Here, the range of colours she used in the depiction of flesh, including the suggestion of blue veins, is realistic and emphasises the life force of the two protagonists. This is underlined by the strong modelling of the figures, through the contrast of the moonlight that illuminates their bodies and the low light of breaking dawn behind them.

Swynnerton's realism was not unusual in itself, but when combined with her heavy working of paint and broad brushwork modelled into relief in places, it was startling to some. Art critic Frederic George Stephens found Psyche's 'features are coarse and blubbered' and 'her flesh is without the sweetness, evenness, or purity of youth'.[2] By the 1890s, broken and gestural approaches to painting had become acceptable in clothed figures, but remained shocking in the depiction of nudes. Swynnerton's original approach was noted by Claude Phillips in the *Art Journal*: 'The artist, in love with the unidealised truth, has not departed from her vigorous and over-British young models' but he did find a redeeming quality in her work: 'her flesh-painting has a certain quivering reality not to be found in many renderings of the nude by contemporary English artists'.[3]

1 In 1890 this work had been purchased by a private collector, industrialist Charles Edward Lees.

2 'The New Gallery', *The Athenæum*, 9 May, 1891, 610.

3 'The Summer Exhibitions at Home and Abroad II – The Academy and the New Gallery', *The Art Journal*. vol.53, July, 1891, 189.

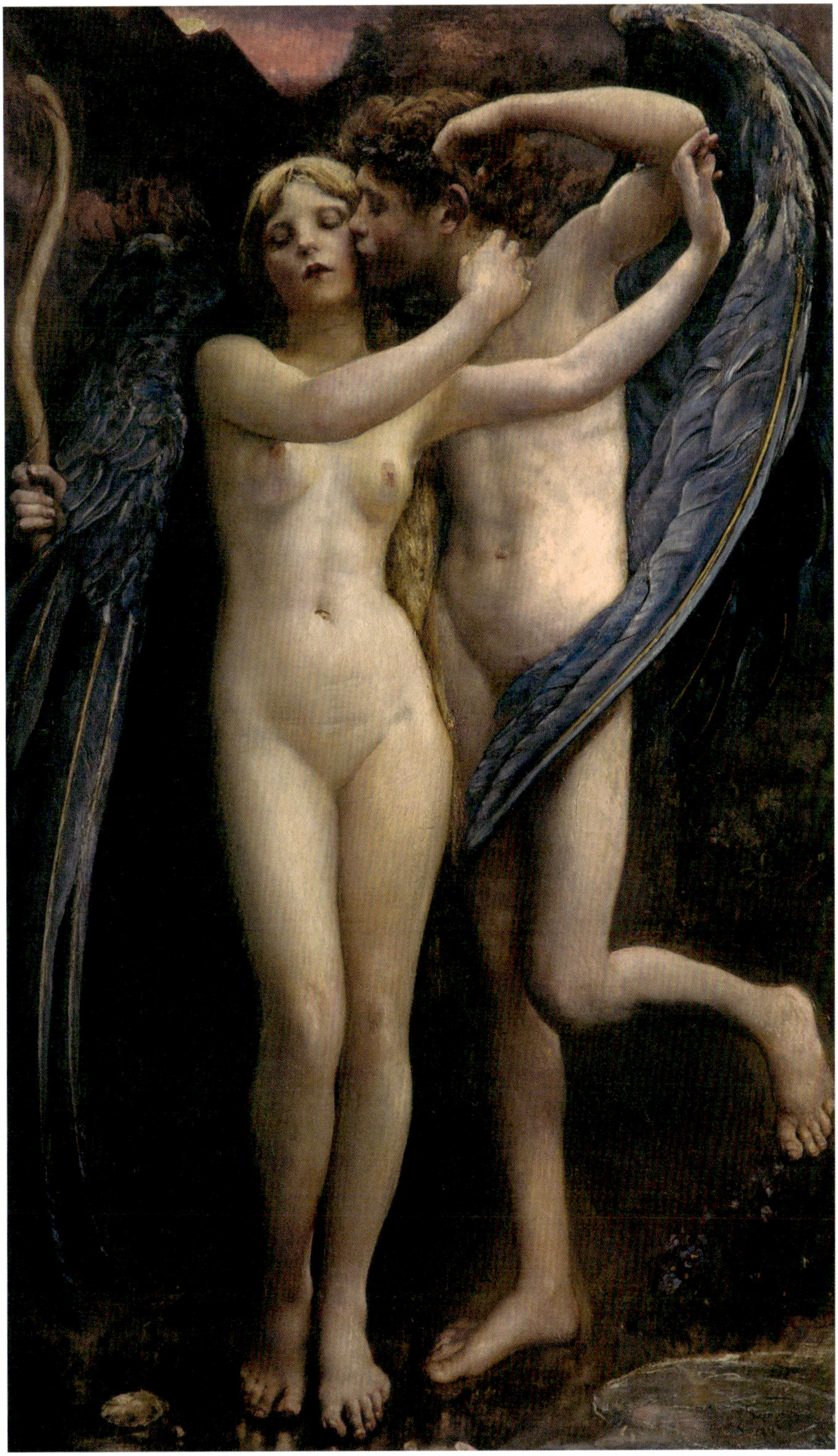

CAT 24 | ***Oreads*** exhibited 1907

Oil on canvas, 177.8 x 177.8 cm
Tate. Presented by John Singer Sargent 1922

This painting depicts a group of Oreads, which are tree and mountain-ravine nymphs in classical mythology. The epic poem *Dionysiaca*, a 5th-century tale about a flood, by Greek writer Nonnus, tells us that 'The sea rose until Nereides became Oreiades on the hills over the woodland.'[1] The figures stand and sit precariously atop tree branches over which breaking waves splash. They cling together, variously mourning the loss of others of their kind – a mood that is reflected in the dark tones of the painting – and singing to guide survivors to safety. The flesh-coloured projection among the waves, which resembles a human knee, in the right foreground, might represent a Naiad lost to the sea, or provide opportunity for the viewer to imagine one's self embodied in the scene. The rainbow in the background to the right of the figures symbolises a glimmer of hope that counters the foreboding stormy sky behind them at their left. The figures' entwined hands, the contact of their bare feet against the tree branches and the effect of the water and wind against their skin makes tangible their outdoor location and embodied experience of their environment.

Swynnerton has characteristically modelled the figures with white highlights and thick contour lines so that they appear robust and muscular. Here, though, she combines that mode with more roughly textured and layered paint. The number of figures shown together, and their contorted positions, meanwhile, demonstrate her ambition and skill in figure study. This is a work that was admired and purchased by John Singer Sargent in 1907, who came to think of her as 'one of the greatest modern painters'.[2]

Painted at Rome, the composition, together with the depiction of foaming water, also recalls sculptural fountains in the round that adorn numerous piazzas in the city. The semi-circular arrangement of the figure group, within a circular canvas, adds to this by creating a dynamic sense of three-dimensionality. It is surely not coincidental either that Swynnerton's husband was a sculptor who designed a handful of monumental fountains involving multiple figures, such as his *Immortal Youth* (untraced, before 1894).

1 With thanks to unpublished research on the subject of this painting by Tate Senior Curator, Carol Jacobi.

2 Anon., 'Annie Swynnerton Dies; British Artist and Academician', *Herald Tribune*, 25 October, 1933, 19.

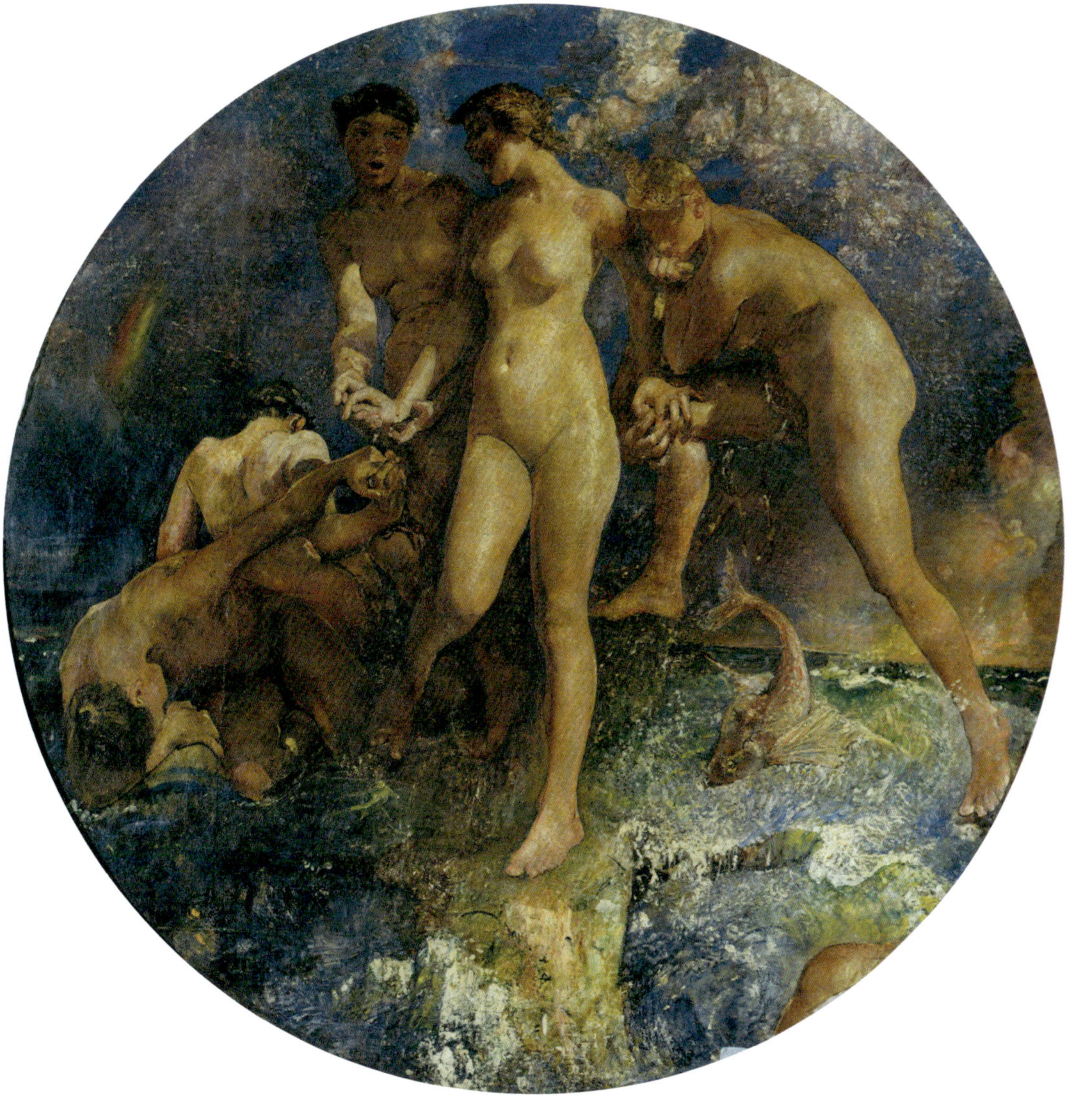

CAT 25 | ***Oceanid*** before 1908

Oil on canvas, 99.8 x 109.8 cm
Museums and Galleries, City of Bradford MDC
Purchased from Christiana Jane Herringham, 1908

According to *Theogony* written around the 8th century BCE by Greek poet Hesiod, Oceanids were sea nymphs who were each the patron of a particular spring, river, sea, lake, pond, pasture, flower, breeze or cloud. The three serpents in the water in the bottom right foreground seem purposely subtle and enigmatic. The Oceanid is unperturbed by them, so we might read them as creatures she coexists with or wields power over.

Details such as the figure's face and hands may have been finished in Swynnerton's rooftop studio in central Rome. However, the landscape backdrop, water and body of the figure were likely studied at one of the crater-lakes close to Rome. The virtuoso depiction of light and translucency and movement in the water around her is too realistic to have come from the artist's imagination alone and suggests a sustained study of water in situ. Indeed, Swynnerton's depiction of intense sunlight here, which is emphasised by strong shadows, demonstrates her devotion to painting outdoors in nature, despite fatiguing conditions.

The way that Swynnerton captures the dappled light on the figure's wet skin, through the the skilful application of flecks of opaque white paint over the thick layers representing her flesh, evokes the sensual feel of water on skin. The figure also seems to take pleasure in the touch of her hair and experience of the sun's warmth on her body. Together, these aspects communicate a sense of her embodiment in the environment, with the reflection of flesh colours on the water's surface giving a further sense of the figure's oneness with the vivid water around her. The robust modelling of the figure through natural light effects also draws attention to, and celebrates, her unidealised nude body, which is in keeping with Swynnerton's feminist politics and truth to the individual appearance of her models and sitters.

Swynnerton's independent approach to the female nude appealed to fellow women artists and suffragists. This painting belonged to one such woman, tempera painter, art patron and director of a number of women's publications, Christiana Herringham, who was involved with administrating the women's movement in the early 20th century.

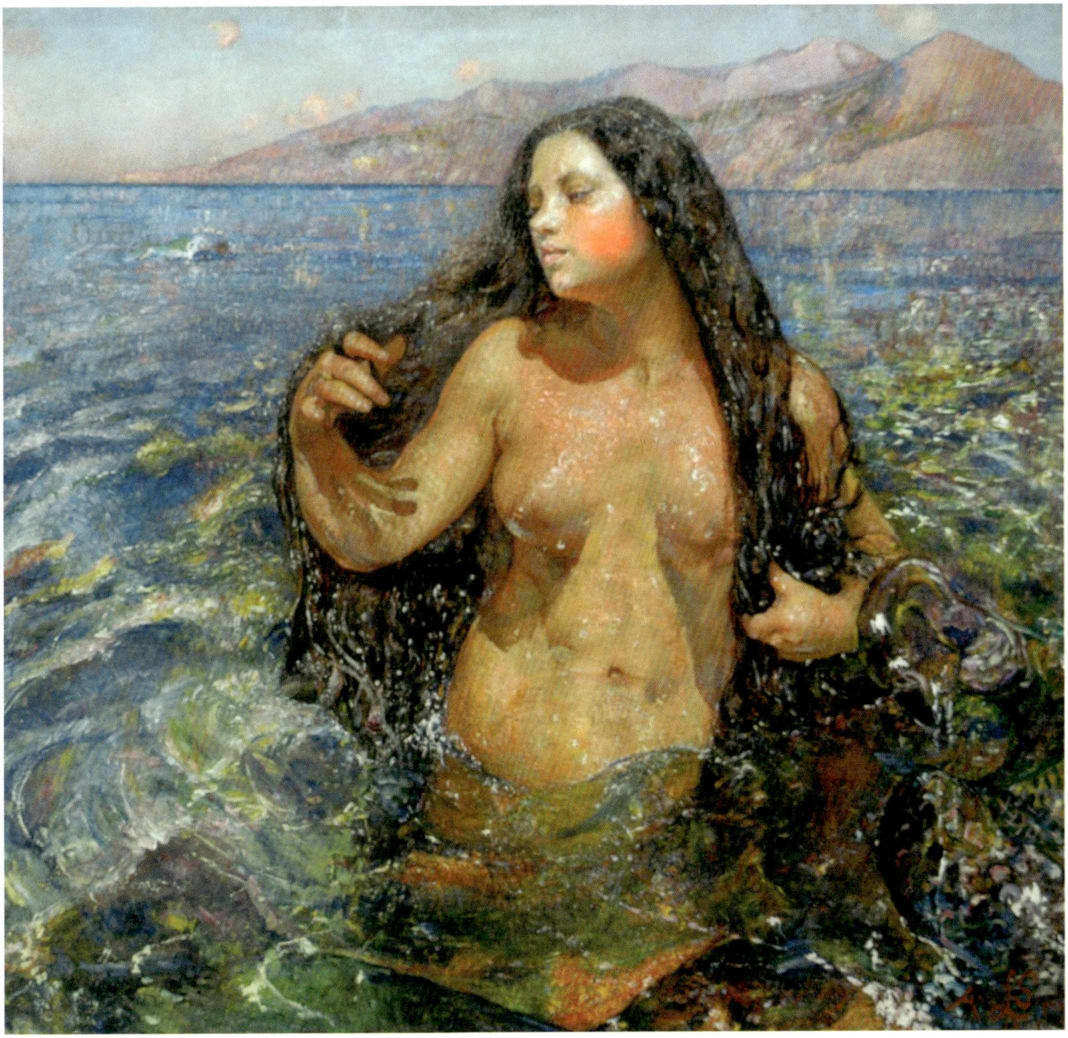

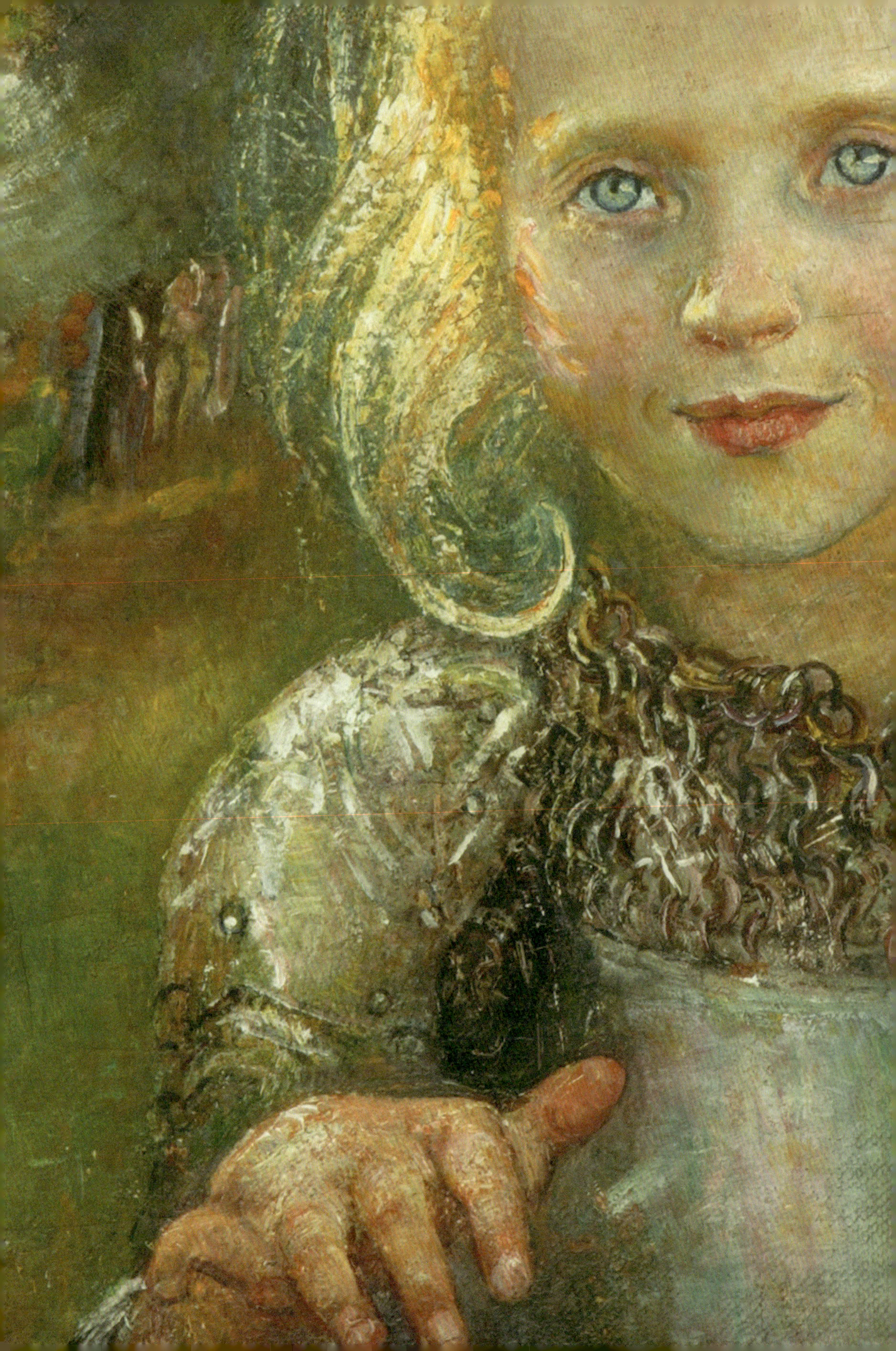

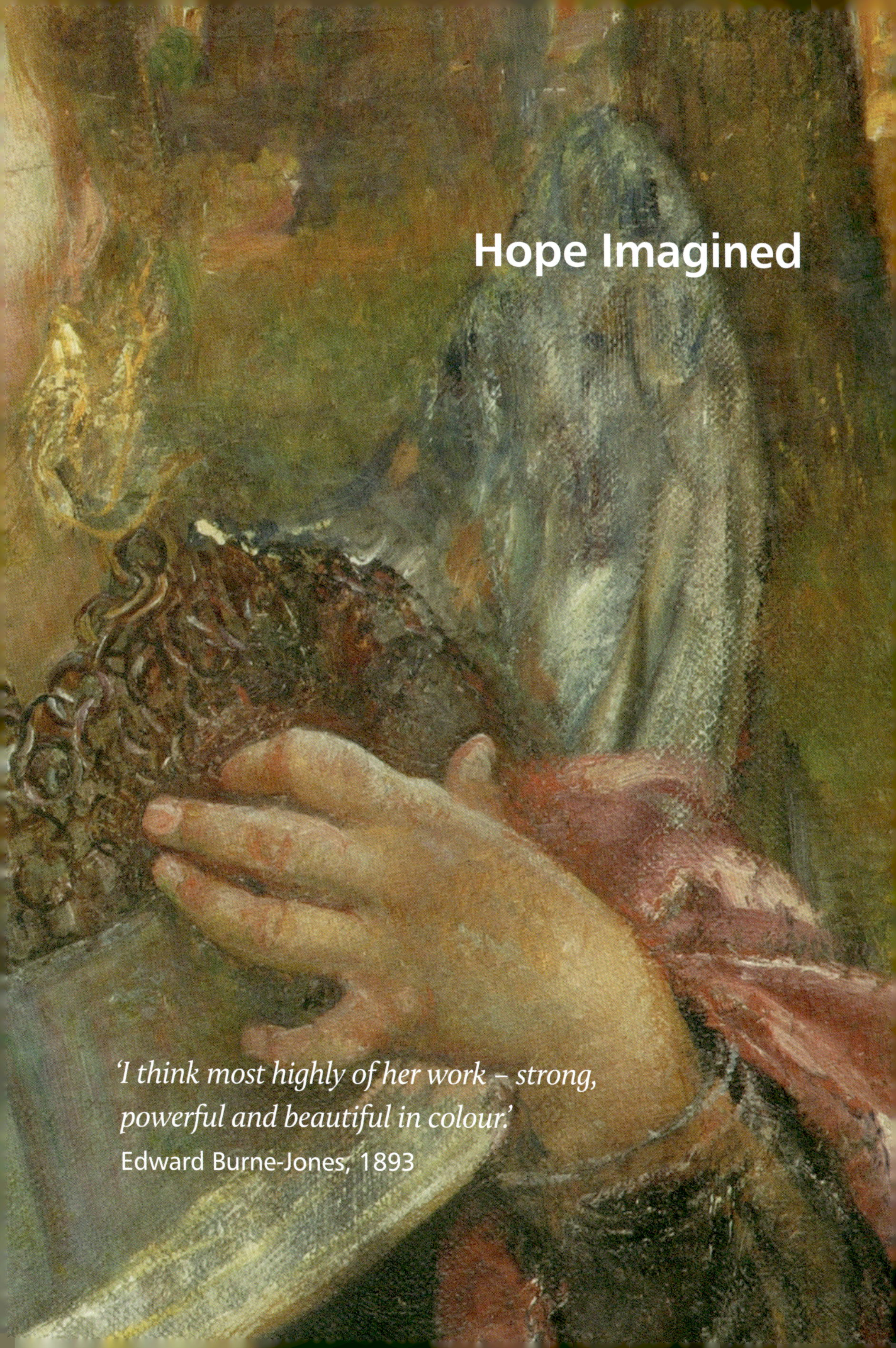

Hope Imagined

'I think most highly of her work – strong, powerful and beautiful in colour.'
Edward Burne-Jones, 1893

Hope Imagined

By the 1890s, the women's movement had been campaigning for women's rights in all spheres of life for over half a century. It had gathered momentum, winning some ground: in 1884, for example, women ratepayers in England and Wales were granted the right to vote in borough and county elections and women became more involved in party political campaigns from this time onwards.

The art world, too, saw changes, with moves towards women's achievement of equal access to artistic training being made. In 1871, while Swynnerton was studying at the Manchester School of Art, the Slade School of Art opened in London, admitting women and men to study the same curriculum from the outset. Then, in 1893, the Royal Academy Schools permitted women to study the draped model. More needed to be achieved, but small victories gave suffragists and women artists hope of obtaining equal rights.

Swynnerton's imaginative paintings of the 1890s and early 20th century are characterised by an ambiguity in meaning, but they nevertheless communicate a sense of spirituality, commitment to social justice and visionary imagination. These are aspects her work had in common with now better-known artists of the British Symbolist movement, including her close friends George Frederic Watts and Edward Burne-Jones. In their figurative paintings, such as Watts's *Hope* series, British Symbolists aimed to express subjective universal themes through an emphasis on form and colour. However, Swynnerton's vibrant use of light and bright colour and her gestural, sculptural approach to applying paint is distinctly of her own imagination and unlike her Symbolist friends' subdued palettes. Her representation of the theme of hope also differs strikingly from the melancholy found in the paintings of her male predecessors and peers. The hunched and blinded figure clinging to hope, but on the brink of despair, in Watts's *Hope* series, for instance, contrasts with Swynnerton's upright, wide-eyed figures moving forward with cautious but optimistic agency, in pursuit of a hopeful vision that has awakened their senses.

Politics and art are closely allied in Swynnerton's imaginative paintings of this period. In these works of her mature career she represented hope for women's

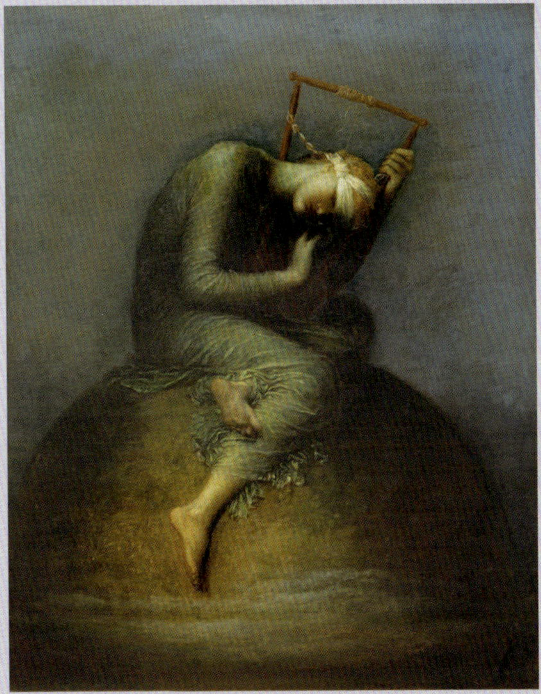

George Frederic Watts *Hope* 1886

future freedoms, employing symbolic imagery of powerful winged and armour-clad female figures. Works such as these by Swynnerton, and others by fellow women artists such as Evelyn Pickering DeMorgan (1855–1919), prefigured, and were likely a source of inspiration for, emblems adopted by the women's movement. Indeed, logos used by the militant Women's Social and Political Union (WSPU) include the *Angel of Freedom* and *Joan of Arc* figures (see 'Hope Realised', Catalogue Nos. 31 and 35).

CAT 26 | *Illusions* c.1902

Oil on canvas, 68 x 51 cm
Manchester Art Gallery. Louisa Mary Garrett bequest 1936.207

Around the time that Swynnerton painted her now untraced work *Joan of Arc* (c. early 1900s) she depicted other anonymous symbolic female figures of various ages wearing amour.[1]

Swynnerton was doubtless aware of John Everett Millais's painting *Joan of Arc* (1865, Private Collection) and Frank Dicksee's painting of the same name (1902, location unknown). Her male predecessors depicted young girls whose innocence and fragility is signalled by the weight of oversized armour, or lack of it. Yet, the armour and chain mail worn by the young girl in Swynnerton's *Illusions* is well fitting. Furthermore, despite her innocent and playful appearance, which is appropriate to her age, she wears her amour with confidence and exhibits powerful potential. The ethereal dappled sunlight falling on the right side of her body gives her form a robust three-dimensionality. Her wings provide a sense of freedom from her environment. She issues forth like a powerful vision from the woodland background, evoking Swynnerton's interest in myths and legends. One of the girl's raised hands touches her chest in a gesture of identification, while the other reaches out towards the viewer, perhaps offering an invitation to join her cause.

The illusions referred to in the painting's title remain ambiguous, but for any girl imagining a future in the first decade of the 20th century that included independent rights for women, such a reality was still an illusion. In 1903, the year after Swynnerton exhibited this painting, the Women's Social and Political Union was founded in Manchester by Emmeline and Christabel Pankhurst and members of this faction, known as suffragettes, began militant action.

1 Swynnerton was aligned with the moderate women's movement represented by the National Union of Women's Suffrage Societies. However, she undoubtedly came to know about the militant activites of the suffragettes, who adopted Joan of Arc as their patron saint.

Annie Swynnerton *Joan of Arc*
c. early 1900s

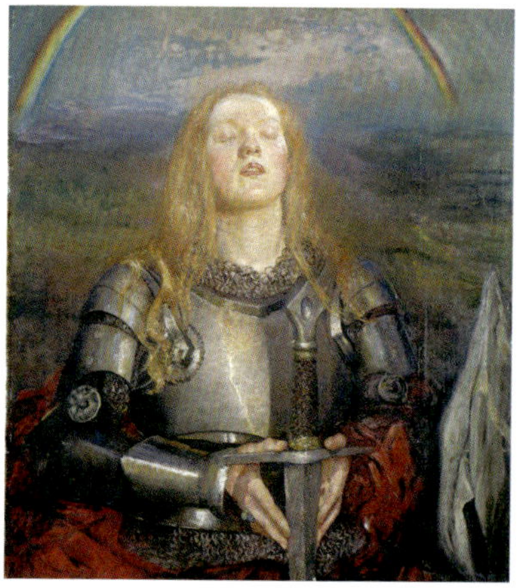

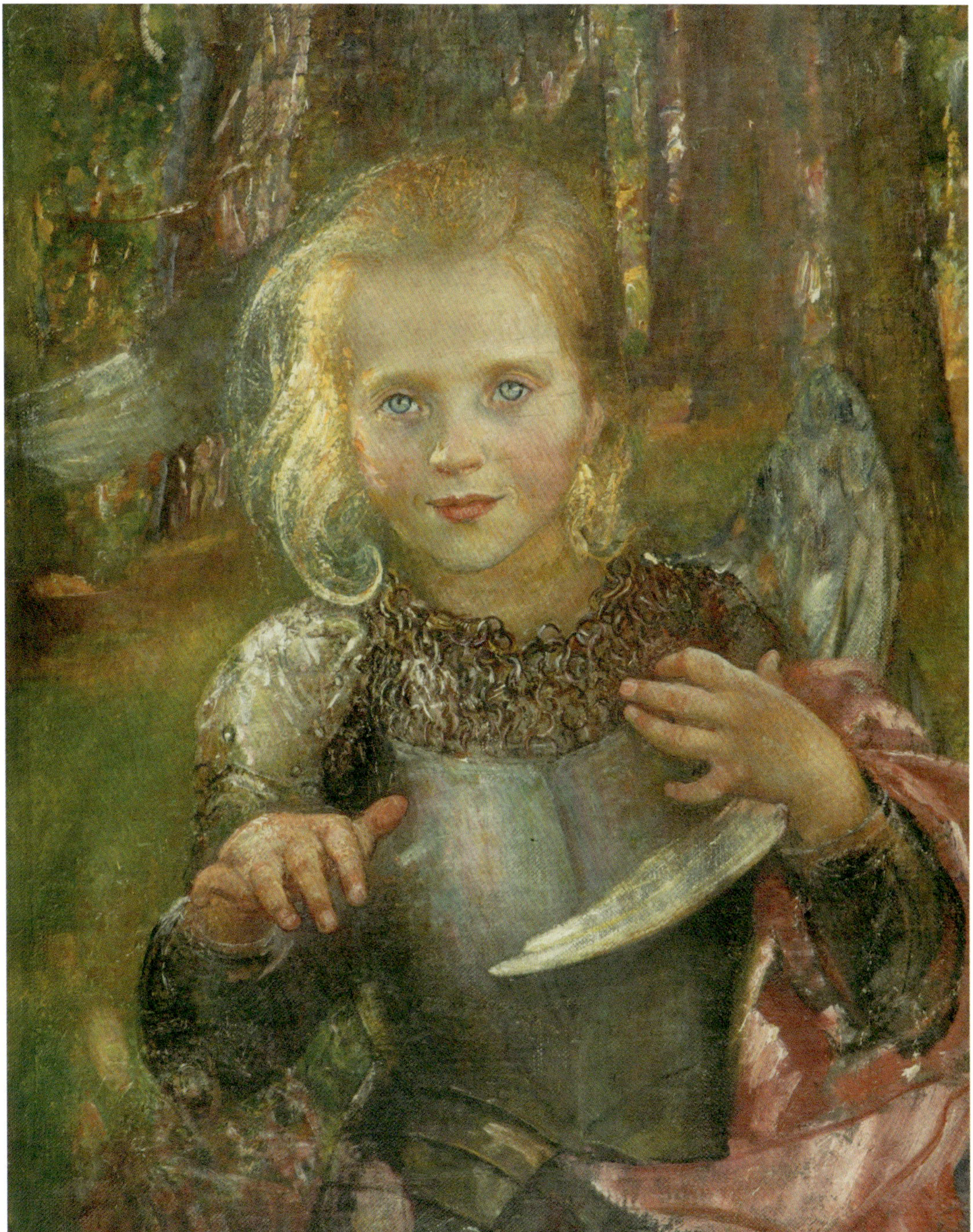

CAT 27 | ***The Sense of Sight*** 1895

Oil on canvas, 87.3 x 101 cm
National Museums Liverpool/Walker Art Gallery
Presented to the Walker Art Gallery by Charles J Proctor, 1896

When this painting was exhibited at the New Gallery, London, in 1895, an unnamed art critic writing in *The Athenaeum* acknowledged the proximity of Swynnerton's work to that of the British Symbolist movement, recognising the ambiguity of her 'winged woman, angel or spirit incorporate'.[1] In light of the momentum of the women's movement at the time, the figure's wings may represent a human woman's ambitions in various walks of life. Wings are an attribute of supernatural beings – angels in religious narratives – and are depicted in art throughout the ages. Swynnerton also alludes here to Spiritualist beliefs in the ability of spirits of the dead to communicate with the living, which was on the rise in late 19th-century Britain. Her figure combines these identifications, without being any of them alone.[2] Neither can we know what daunting sight or vision she gazes at with intense rapture and which catches her off guard, causing her to look slightly off balance.

Despite the ambiguity of the figure, there is nevertheless an overarching theme of vision. In fact, the patron who purchased *The Sense of Sight* from the 1895 Liverpool Autumn Exhibition took its title literally as representing the loss of eyesight that he was experiencing.[3] With knowledge of Swynnerton's feminist politics, however, we can read her sculptural handling of paint as alluding to women's visionary capability to imagine the world hopefully and to affect it positively. Swynnerton's emphasis on strong outline and contours and realistic treatment of the symbolic figure creates a tangible strength of form that is muscular and almost sculptural; indeed, some of her critics recognised the influence of Michelangelo in her bold outlines, which are particularly reminiscent of the sibyls of the Sistine Chapel.[4] The figure is also evocative of 15th-century Florentine high-relief sculptures, including examples by Lorenzo Ghiberti and Andrea Orcagna, which Swynnerton would have known from visits to Florence. Her technique creates a sense of agency in the figure, making her hands and head appear as though they could project beyond the canvas. Her wings, which are heavily modelled into low-relief, too, are meanwhile prevented from making a bid for freedom by the confines of the picture frame. Overall, there is a tension between the figure's tentative forward movement and impression of restriction that reflects the limitation of women's rights at this time.

1 'The New Gallery (Third and Concluding Notice)', 27 July, 1895, 135–36.

2 Swynnerton produced a second version of this painting *The Angel of Annunciation*, dated 1898. It displays subtle differences in the composition of drapery and its colouring. The more descriptive title may have been prompted by media criticism of the allusive nature of *The Sense of Sight*.

3 Letter from Swynnerton to the incumbent curator, Walker Art Gallery Liverpool, 18 July, 1927, Walker Art Gallery Archive.

4 PH Rathbone in *The Sphinx*, vol. 3, 1895, 34.

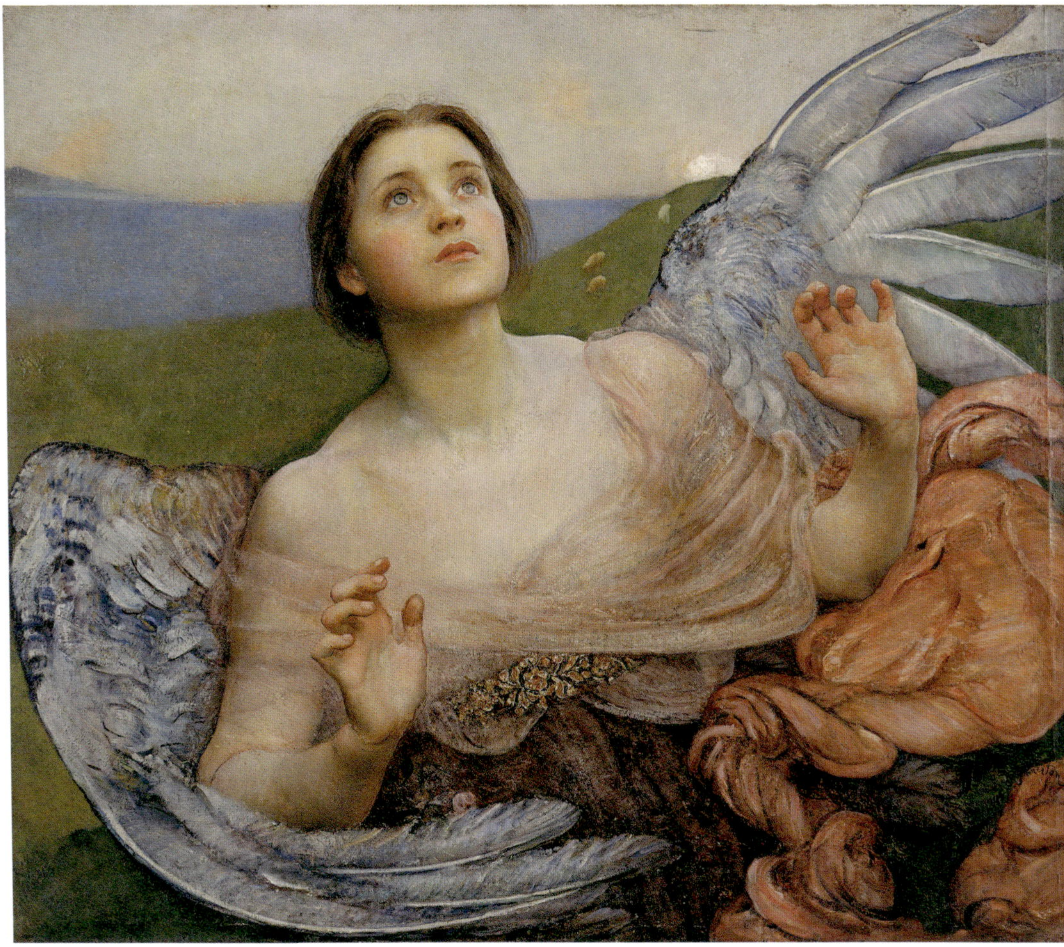

CAT 28 | ***New Risen Hope*** 1904

Oil on canvas, 57 x 51.9 cm
Tate. Presented by the Trustees of the Chantrey Bequest, 1924

New Risen Hope is a study for a completed painting of the same name that was bought on the recommendation of Swynnerton's friend George Clausen for the National Gallery of Victoria in Melbourne in 1906. In keeping with her passion for painting figures outdoors, which Clausen also favoured, Swynnerton painted this figure study in a Sussex field. However, the background comprising a faint hilly outcrop, in the upper sixth of the canvas, and the expanse of blue below it, recalls more closely the mountains and lakes she frequented close to Rome.

Technical examinations have revealed that Swynnerton experimented with giving the figure wings, which implies an initial affinity with her other paintings of winged figures, such as *The Sense of Sight* (Catalogue No. 27) and *Illusions* (Catalogue No. 26), which represent hope for women's future freedoms. Art historian Alison Smith has previously suggested that *New Risen Hope* is 'a statement of female emancipation, an affirmative alternative to Watts's forlorn Hope'.[1] Such a reading is reinforced by the title and inclusion of a rainbow, traditionally symbolic of promise and hope, in the complete 1906 work.[2]

There is a sense of the joy of embodiment in the human form here that is characteristic of Swynnerton's full-length female nudes. However, the half-length composition chosen here allows the gender of the young child to remain indefinite. Swynnerton remarked ambiguously that this work 'depicts a lovely English child rising out of a grey and mysterious mist'.[3] The intense sunlight, falling most strongly on the child's face and chest, together with the ambiguous white brushstrokes surrounding the subject's lower body, suggest oneness with the natural environment while also hinting at the mystically dramatised drapery and otherworldly atmosphere incorporated in the completed work. What is apparent in this study, though, is the child's wide-eyed innocence and uncertain forward movement.[4] Swynnerton's treatment of the child with realism and individuality also aligns her imaginative work with her sympathetic depiction of children in her portraiture.

1 Alison Smith, *The Victorian Nude* (London: Tate, 2001), 228.

2 Watts, similarly, included a rainbow in some of his *Hope* series paintings, but not others.

3 Anon., *The Evening News*, [6 February], 1922.

4 Swynnerton was apparently inspired to paint this work by a line from the poetry of Ralph Waldo Emerson. He held progressive views on feminism and championed individualism, which likely appealed to her. The poem and line remain unidentified.

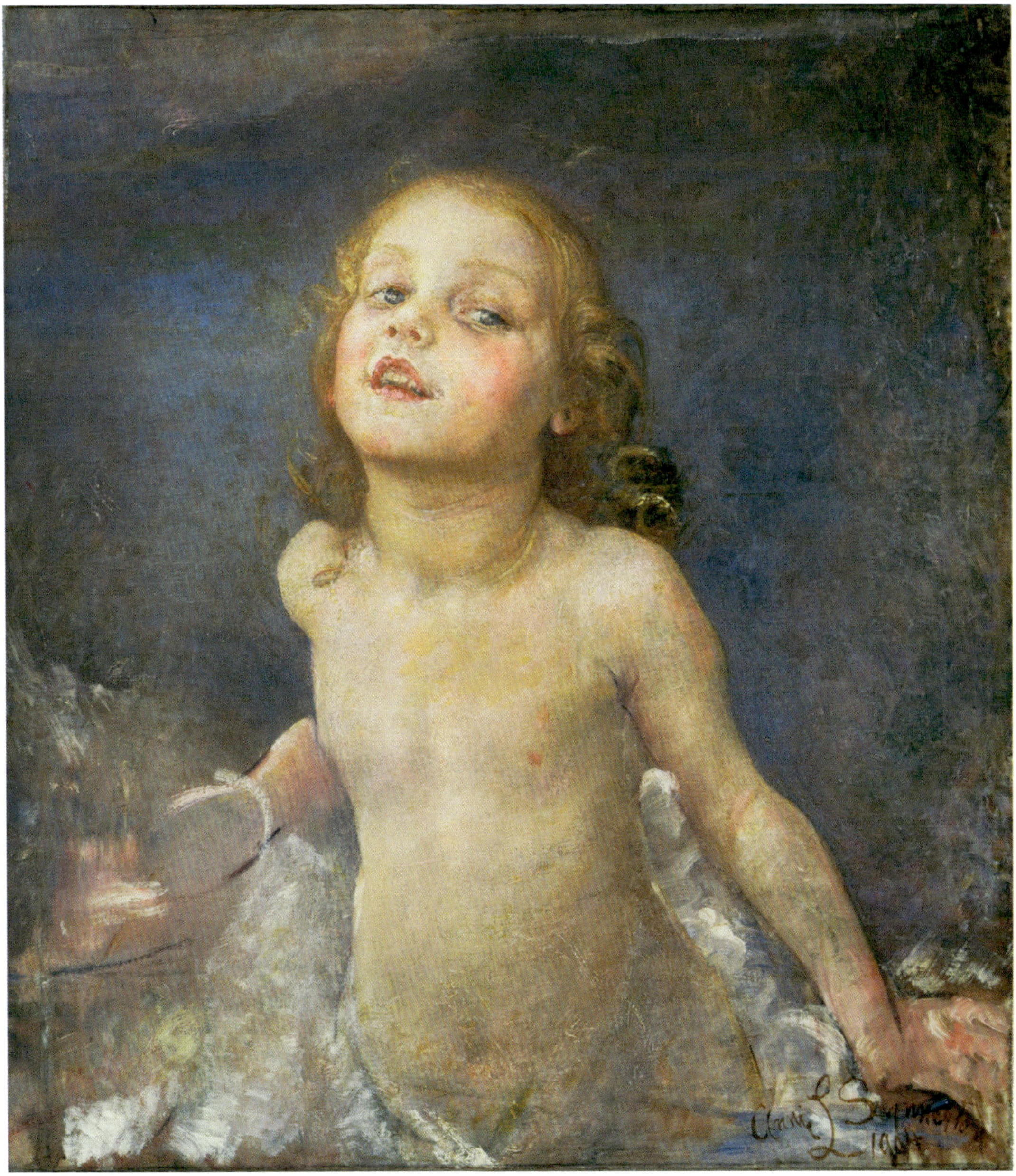

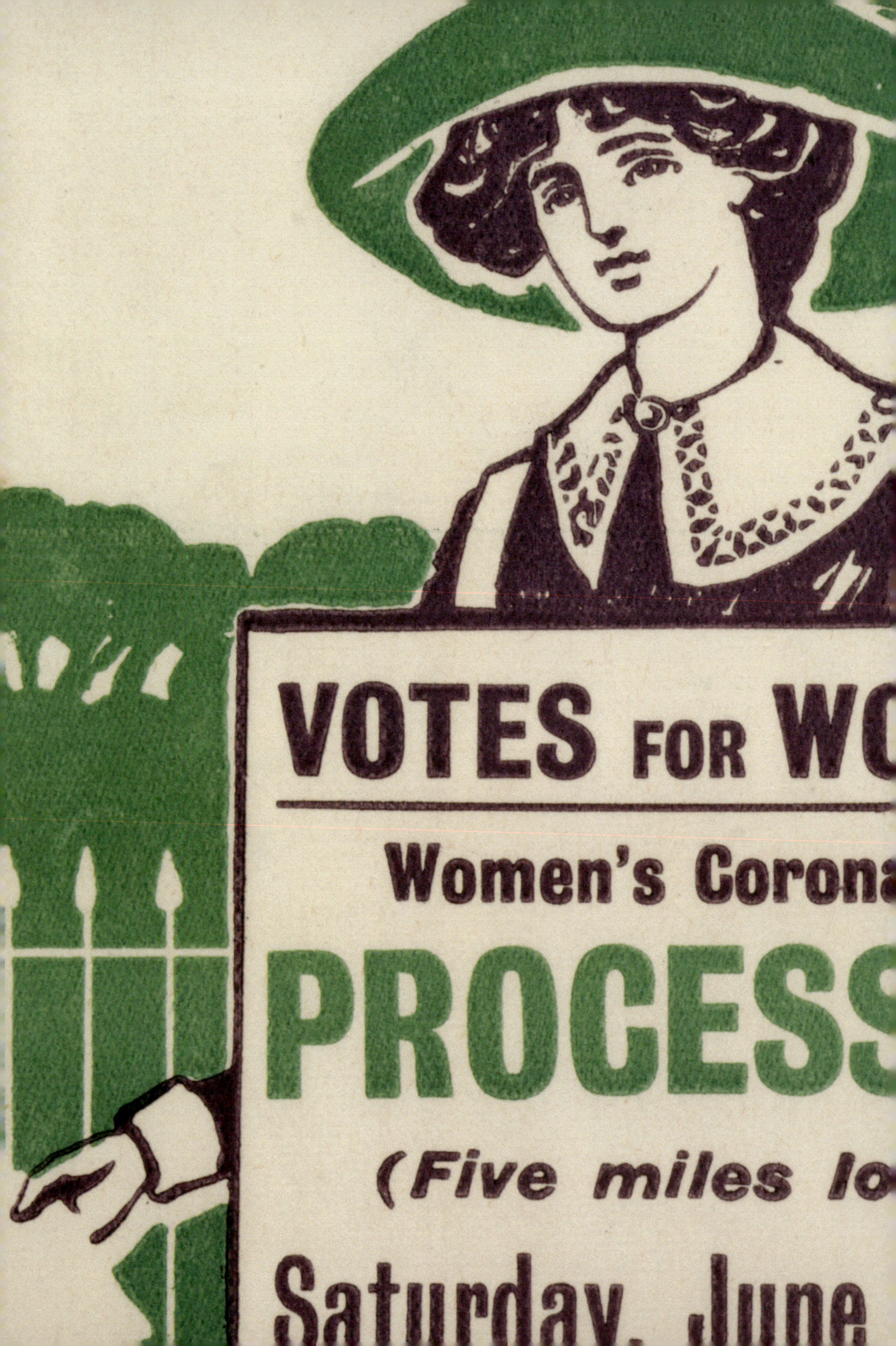
VOTES FOR WO
Women's Corona
PROCESS
(Five miles lo
Saturday, June

Hope Realised

'Deeds, not words.'

Women's Social and Political Union slogan

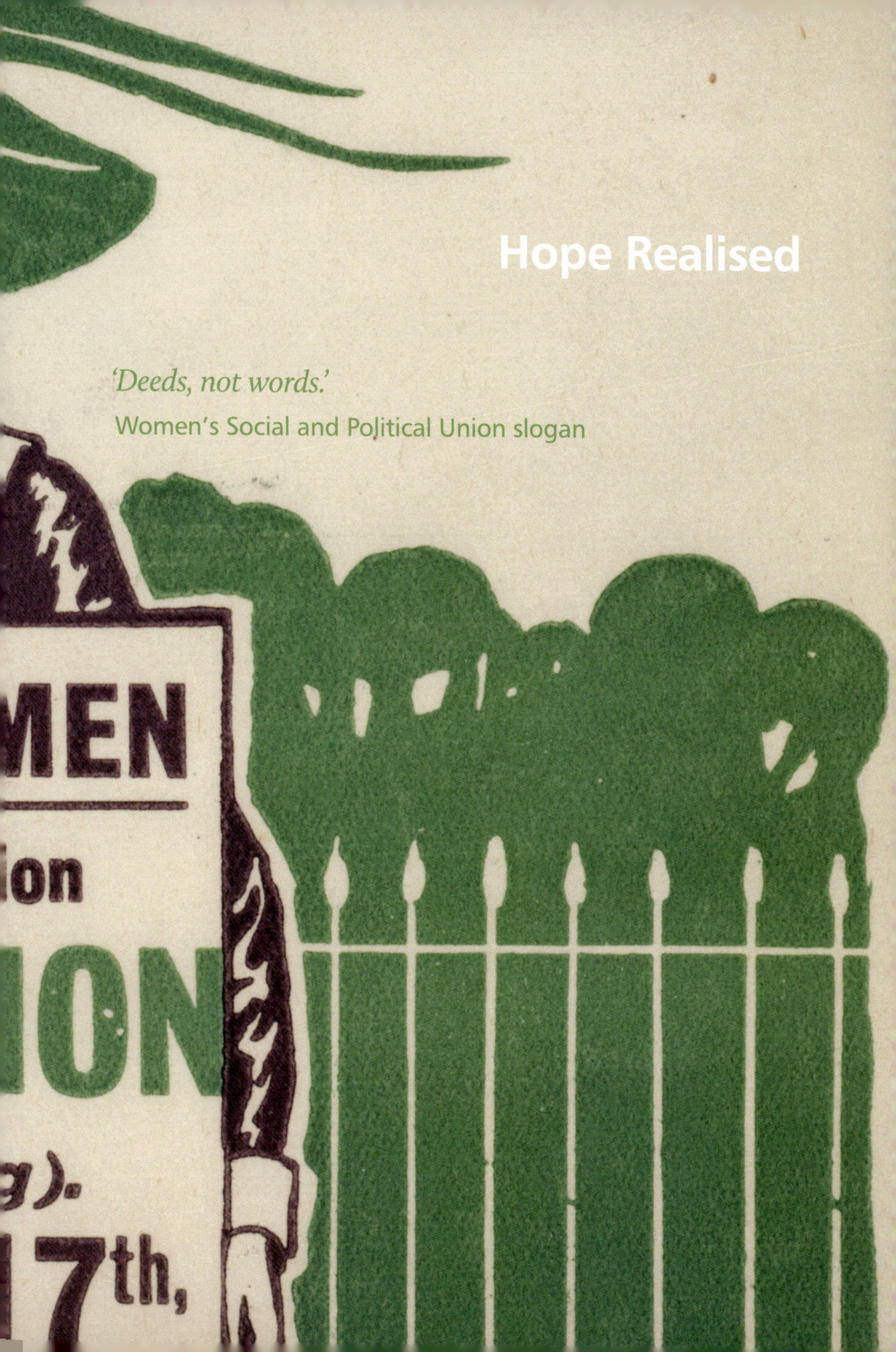

Hope Realised

In 1918 the Representation of the People Act granted the vote to British women over 30 years of age. This was a landmark step towards realising the hopes of women's rights campaigners. By that time, Swynnerton had been a passionate supporter of women's right to vote for over three decades. She had signed the Declaration in Favour of Women's Suffrage in July 1889, a campaign led by the committee of the National Society for Women's Suffrage. Then, in 1897, she put her signature to the claim for women's suffrage led by the committee of the National Union of Women's Suffrage Societies (NUWSS).[1] Her commitment to the cause had been publicly demonstrated when she headed the Artists' Suffrage League section of the Women's Coronation Procession in 1911. There, in a rallying speech, suffragette Emmeline Pankhurst had declared:

> *What does this demonstration of ours mean? It means victory! ... We have proved that we can combine; we have proved that women have great powers of organisation; we have proved that women have great artistic capacity... we know that providing all these things we have shown that women, alongside with men, are worthy to build up a humanity that men can never make without our help.*[2]

The fight for gender equality in all spheres of life that was waged in the late 19th and early 20th centuries certainly extended beyond social and political spheres and into the art world. The impact of artistic work in the political sphere is palpable, with a striking correlation between Swynnerton's use of powerful winged and armour-clad female figures and the motifs later employed by the militant women's movement.

Early in her career, Swynnerton had developed and would continue to maintain tight links with an extensive network of women involved in the moderate women's movement, including the liberal Garrett family women.[3]

---

1 In 1897 the National Society for Women's Suffrage merged with the National Central Society of Women's Suffrage to become the NUWSS.

2 June Purvis, *Emmeline: A Biography* (London: Routledge, 2003), 165.

3 Swynnerton painted Millicent Garrett Fawcett, her younger sister Agnes Garrett, who was a suffragist and interior decorator, and Agnes's sister-in-law Louisa Mary Garrett in 1885.

Connections born out of their political beliefs led Swynnerton and Dacre to paint esteemed portraits of a number of leading figures of the movement. These are portraits that, in inspiration and execution, foreground real women and their achievements. Swynnerton's shared beliefs with individuals within the women's movement facilitated her sensitive depiction of them and they, in turn, became important patrons of her work. Louisa Mary Garrett, for instance, ultimately made a bequest of four Swynnerton paintings, including *Illusions* (Catalogue No. 26), to Manchester Art Gallery.[4] Thus Swynnerton's politically founded connections played a significant role in the formation of the largest public collection of her work.

[4] *The Town of Siena* (c.1880s), *An Italian Mother and Child* (1886), *Rain-clouds Monte Gennaro* (1904) and *Illusions* (c.1902).

CAT 29 | ***Lydia Becker*** c.1885–1888

Susan Isabel Dacre 1844–1933
Oil on canvas, 66.5 x 52.3 cm
Manchester Art Gallery. Gift from the National Union of Women's Suffrage 1920.1

Swynnerton's friend Dacre was actively involved in the administration of the suffrage movement. For a decade, beginning in 1885, she was a committee member of the moderate organisation the Manchester National Society for Women's Suffrage. It was through her involvement that she befriended Manchester-born early women's movement leader, Lydia Ernestine Becker. Dacre likely met Becker after joining the MNSWS in 1885 and produced this portrait before Becker's mental breakdown in 1888.

A generation before the Garretts and Pankhursts, Lydia Becker convened the first meeting of the Manchester Society for Women's Suffrage – known as the Manchester National Society of Women's Suffrage (MNSWS) from 1867 to 1897 – the first organisation of its kind in England. By 1887 she had become President of the National Union of Women's Suffrage Societies (NUWSS). Unlike other early feminists, Becker argued there was no natural difference between the intellect of men and women and consequently championed a non-gendered education system in Britain.

In Dacre's portrait of Becker, her head is relatively unadorned. Her hair is plaited with ribbons and wound into a top bun, providing no distraction from her face, which is, in turn, undecorated. This, together with the neutral background,[1] allows her identity and strong, unfaltering gaze to be the focus of the painting, which seems appropriate in light of the unequivocal voice she gave to women's rights.[2] Becker's outfit, meanwhile, comprises a plain and darkly coloured silk dress and minimal decorative elements, which reflects her famed down-to-earth character. Dacre displayed her considerable skill in the unidealised likeness, complete with wire-framed reading glasses, and depiction of exquisite sheer lace, intricate jewellery and corsage. The latter alludes to Becker's other intellectual work as a published botanist, who corresponded with and contributed to Charles Darwin's work.

1 Retouching can be seen either side of the sitter's head. This was carried out in the painting's relatively recent history to repair damage caused by the canvas becoming stuck to the picture glass.

2 Becker's face did not always dominate the painting to the same extent, however. The artist cut the canvas down by fifty percent, forming the current half-length portrait, in 1920. The change was a stipulation of Manchester Art Gallery's acquisition committee, who viewed the composition to be stronger without the sitter's hands.

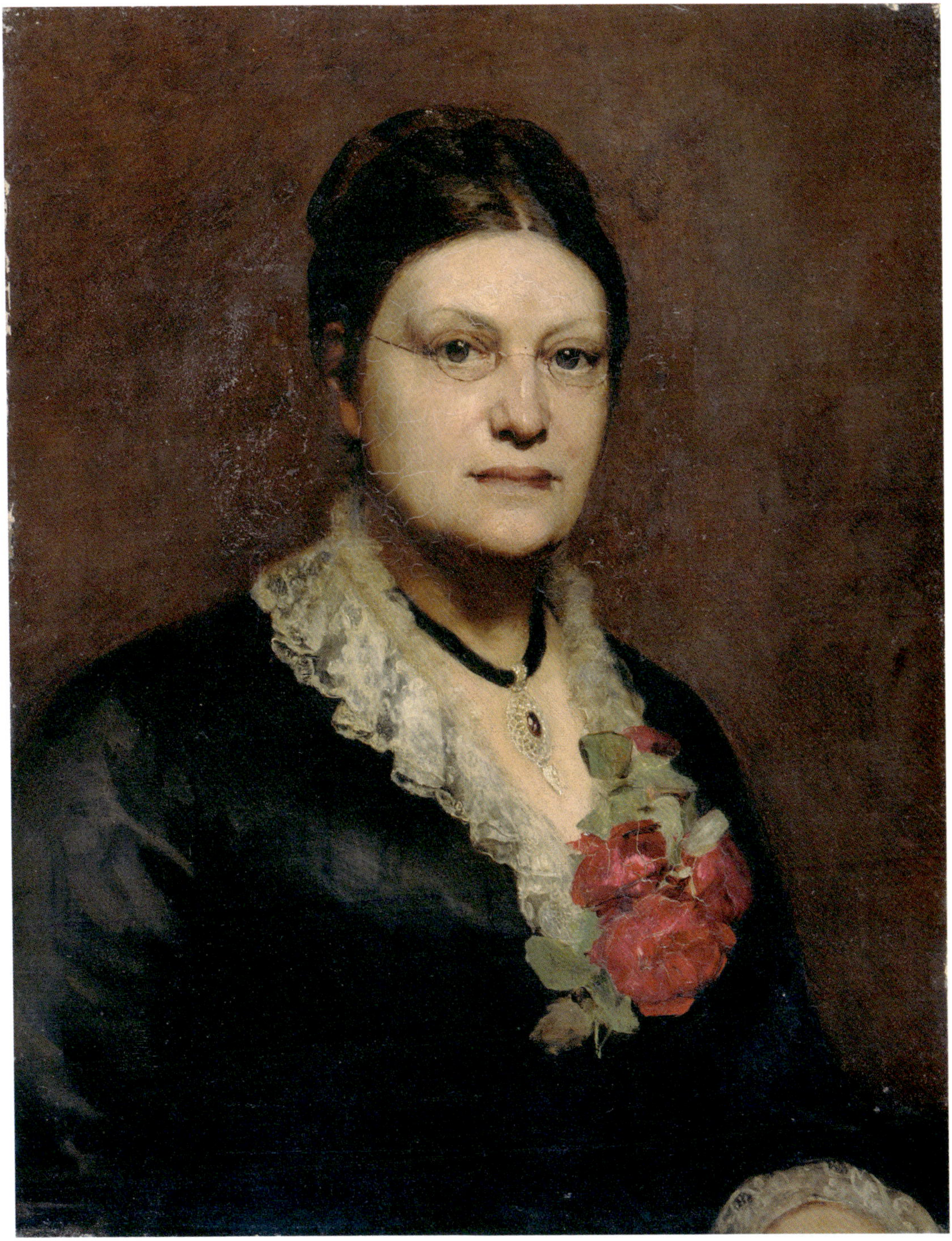

CAT 30 | *Dame Millicent Garrett Fawcett, CBE, LLD*
c.1899–1920

Oil on canvas, 82.5 x 74 cm
Tate. Presented by the Trustees of the Chantrey Bequest, 1930

Swynnerton's friendships with an extensive network of women influenced her artistic career. Her portrait of Dame Millicent Garrett Fawcett (1847–1929) demonstrates her connections to and involvement with prominent women's movement figures. Garrett Fawcett became Becker's successor as NUWSS leader in 1897 and her campaigning was instrumental in gaining British women over 30 the vote in 1918. She became a Dame in 1924 and was still alive, and present in Parliament, in 1928 to see the act passed that granted women equal franchise, bringing her life's work to fruition.

In this undated portrait, Garrett Fawcett wears the robes of the University of St Andrews, the institution that awarded her an Honorary Doctorate in Law (LL.D) for services to education in 1899. It was likely the portrait was painted to mark that achievement. The dark background and relatively sharp handling of paint, together with the apparent age of the sitter and similarity in appearance to photographs of her from the early 1900s, suggest that the portrait was painted close to the turn of the century. Surprisingly, considering Swynnerton's passion for depicting figures outdoors, in natural light, by this date, she shows Garrett Fawcett within a domestic interior. Daylight is blocked out by a large dark screen behind the sitter, but a strong shaft of light illuminates her face, the front of her doctoral hood and hands, creating a contrast between light and dark reminiscent of the traditional chiaroscuro technique Swynnerton perfected in her earliest known figurative paintings.

Swynnerton's remarkable faithfulness to the unadorned appearance of her middle-aged female sitters can be observed here. She built up and modelled layers of paint to replicate intimately the lines and creases that give Garrett Fawcett's face its individual character. The piece was well regarded enough during Swynnerton's lifetime to be included in the exhibition *Portraits of Distinguished Men and Women* at the Royal Academy of Arts in 1930, the year after Garrett Fawcett's death. An unnamed *Times* art critic duly remarked when this piece was shown in that exhibition, 'Swynnerton presents you to a real human being'.[1] The sitter's humanity, identity and achievements are foregrounded in this painting.

1 'The Royal Academy, Part I.', *The Times*, 3 May, 1930, 13, and also 'The Royal Academy, 1930', 10 May, 836–7.

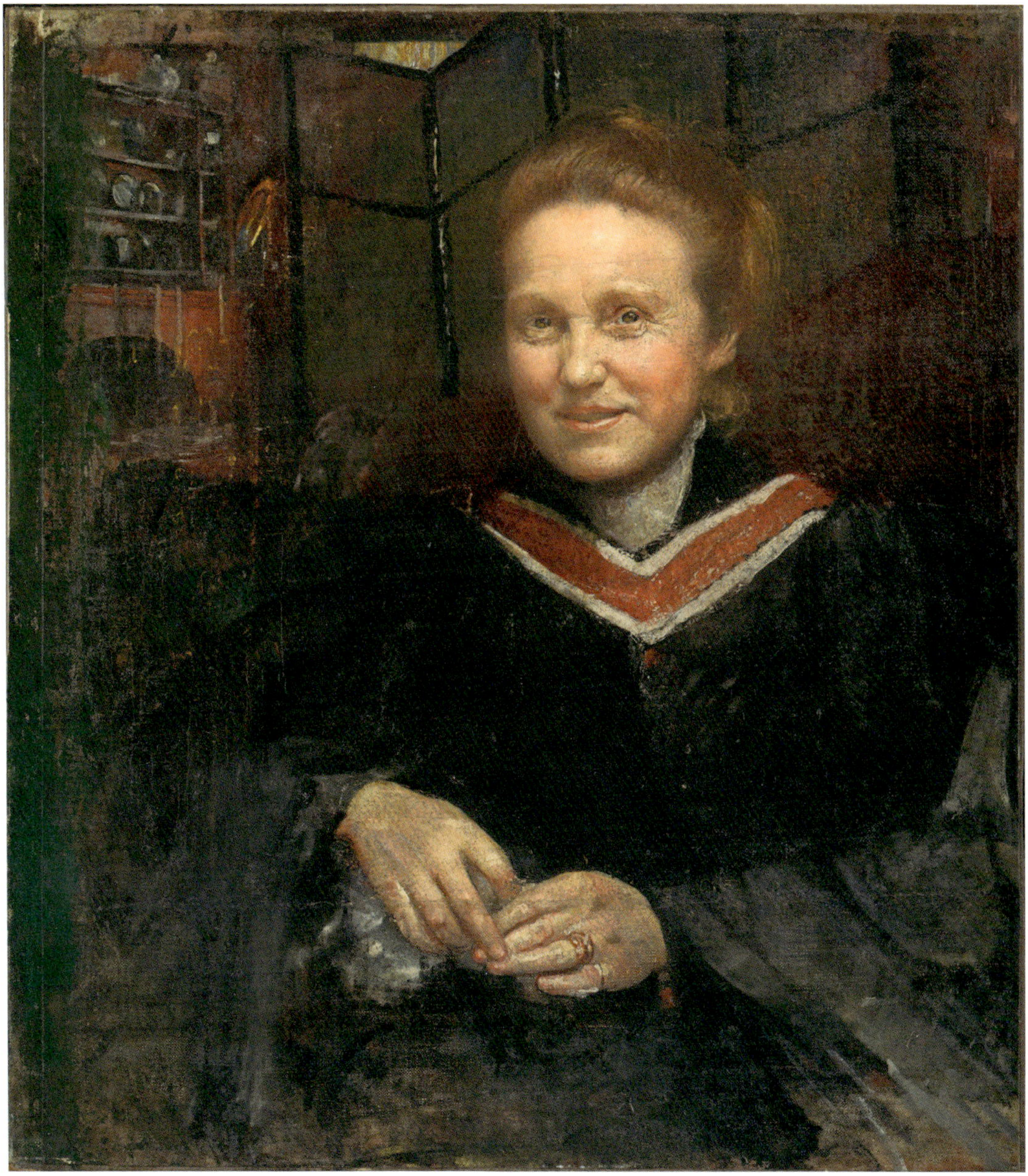

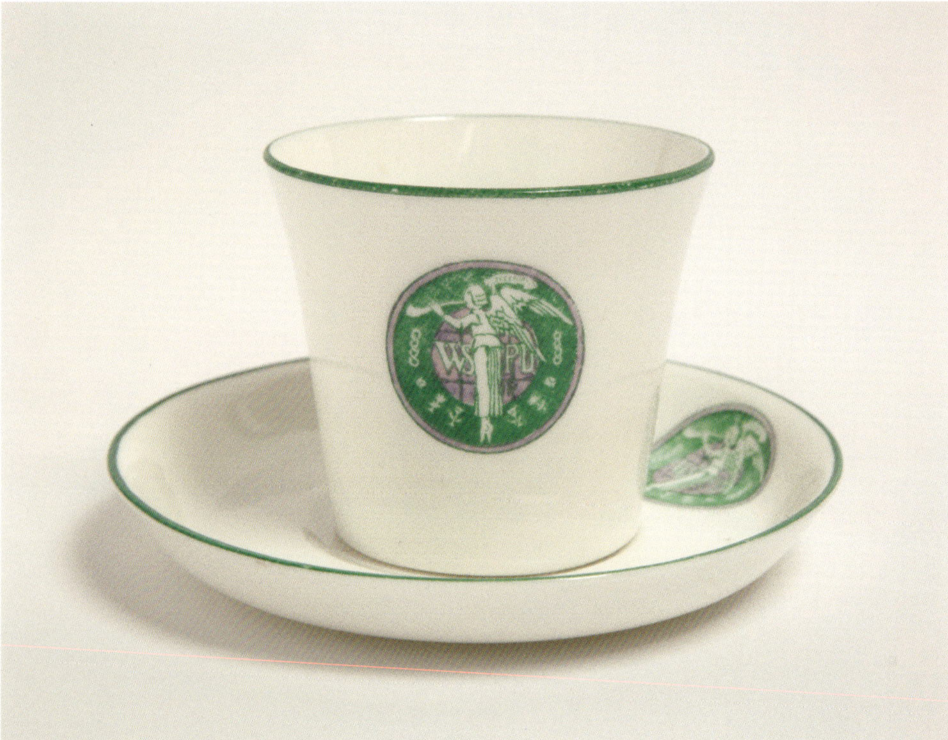

CAT 31 |

Suffrage tea service: tea cup and saucer 1909

Women's Social and Political Union (WSPU)
Sylvia Pankhurst 1882–1960 (designer)
H.M. Williamson & Sons (maker)
Bone china with printed logos
12.4 x 6.7 cm (saucer)
7 x 10 cm (cup)
Private Collection

This crockery, made for use at the 1909 Women's Exhibition at Prince's Skating Rink, London, bears a women's movement logo, the Angel of Freedom, depicting a winged female figure sounding the trumpet call for supporters. Individual pieces and whole sets were also sold to raise funds for the WSPU and the logo featured on publicity badges, banners and printed materials. Manchester artist and suffragette Sylvia Pankhurst designed this logo in 1908 for the WSPU, which she founded with her mother Emmeline and sister Christabel in 1903. Pankhurst trained at the Manchester School of Art and Royal College of Art, London. Her symbolic representations of the organisation's ideals and values made a key contribution to the early 20th-century women's movement. In 1912 she gave up art to found and devote herself to militant movement the East London Federation of Suffragettes. She is particularly known for her social realist-style gouache sketches, produced in 1907, that document the conditions of working women in Northern England and Scotland, which she reported on in an illustrated article 'Women Workers of England' published in the *London Magazine* in 1908.

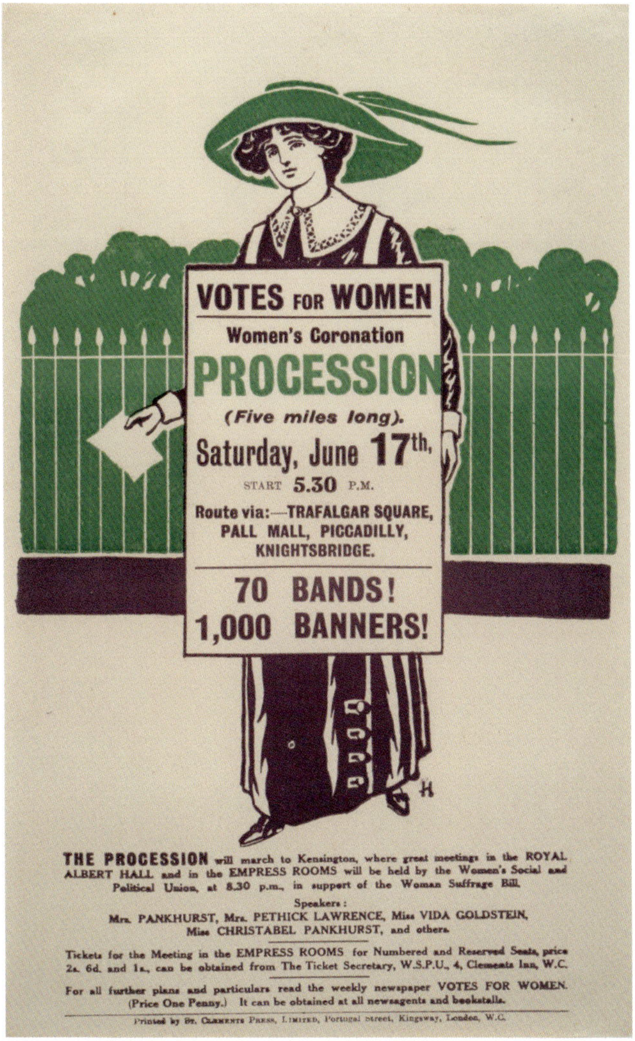

CAT 32 | **Handbill advertising the Women's Coronation Procession, 17 June 1911**

NUWSS, WSPU and other suffrage societies
Paper, 25.5 x 16 cm
Museum of London

The Women's Coronation Procession aimed to enlist King George V's support for the Conciliation Bill in favour of female suffrage. This handbill incorporates a suffrage movement colour scheme introduced by Emmeline Pethick-Lawrence in 1908. The colour scheme symbolised dignity, purity and hope.

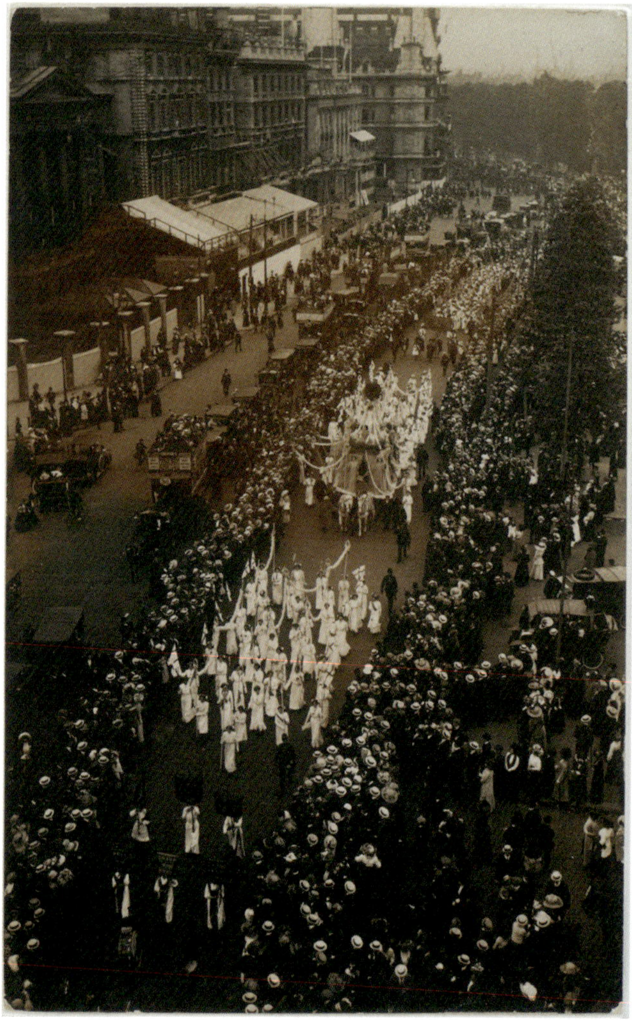

CAT 33 | **Postcard showing the Women's Coronation Procession, 17 June 1911**

NUWSS, WSPU and other suffrage societies; unknown photographer
Paper, 14 x 8.9 cm
Museum of London

The Women's Coronation Procession, involving approximately 40,000 women, was organised by 28 suffrage societies, including the WSPU and NUWSS. This postcard shows a section of the seven-mile line of marchers and floats that travelled from Embankment to the Albert Hall, London. The scale of the procession arguably provided a greater spectacle than George V's coronation.

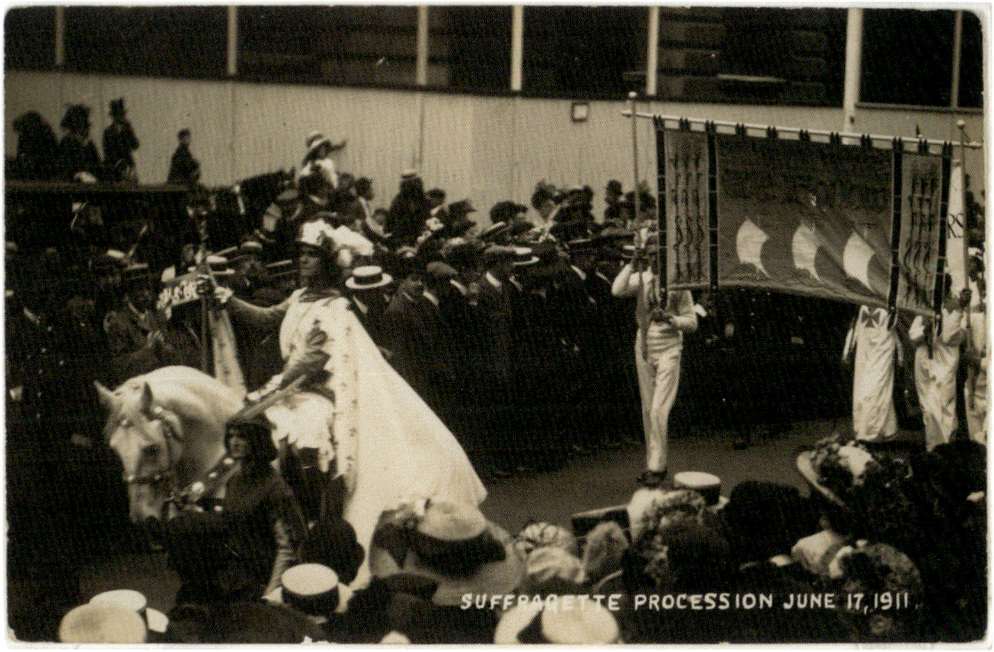

CAT 34 | **Postcard showing Marjorie Annan Bryce on horseback as Joan of Arc at the Women's Coronation Procession, 17 June 1911**

NUWSS, WSPU and other suffrage societies; unknown photographer
Paper, 8.7 x 13.8 cm
Museum of London

Suffragette Marjorie Annan Bryce led the procession, mounted on horseback and dressed as the movement's patron saint, Joan of Arc. The procession also included a 'Famous Women' pageant, in which suffragists dressed as other notable women from the past. (It is possible the woman guiding the horse is Marjorie's younger sister, suffragette Rosalind 'Tiny' Bryce.) Christabel Pankhurst adopted Joan of Arc as a symbol of a strong woman challenging authority and standing for a righteous cause while she was in France in 1912–13, avoiding arrest for militant activism in Britain.

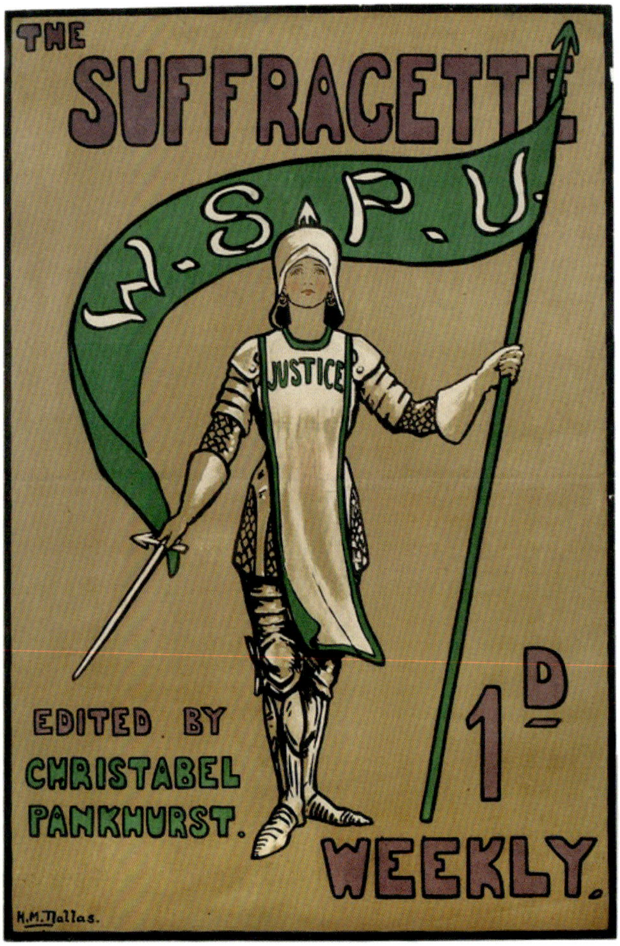

CAT 35 | **Woodblock printed poster promoting WSPU Magazine *The Suffragette*, edited by Christabel Pankhurst**

WSPU and Hilda Dallas 1878–1958 (designer)
Paper, 75.3 x 50.9 cm
Museum of London

This advertisement features an armoured Joan of Arc. Her strength and devotion to the cause is expressed by her ready sword and firm stance against a wind that causes the fabric of her tunic and WSPU flag to billow. The poster's designer, Hilda Dallas, joined the Suffrage Atelier formed in 1909 to promote 'the enfranchisement of women, by means of pictorial publication'. The Suffrage Atelier also trained non-professional artists in the low-cost, low-tech and easy-to-learn method of woodblock printing in order to help promote the cause.

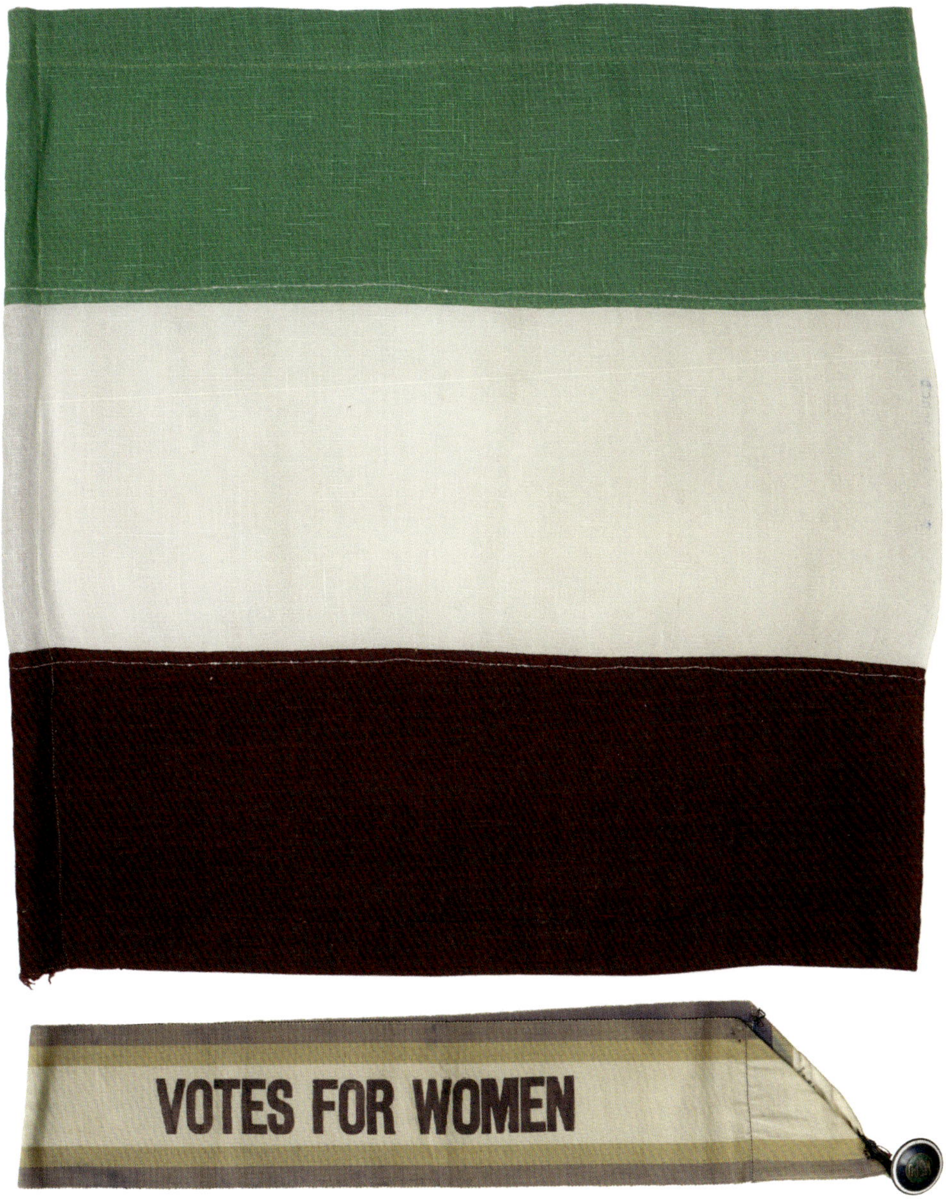

CAT 36–37 | **Suffrage flag and sash** c.1912–1914

Unknown makers, linen (flag); silk metal and enamel (sash)
Manchester Art Gallery. Dr C Willet Cunningham purchase 1947
and gift of Stella Newsome 1952

These items demonstrated allegiance to the suffrage cause. The flag and now-faded sash are comprised of purple, white and green fabric, according to the most commonly used suffrage colour scheme.

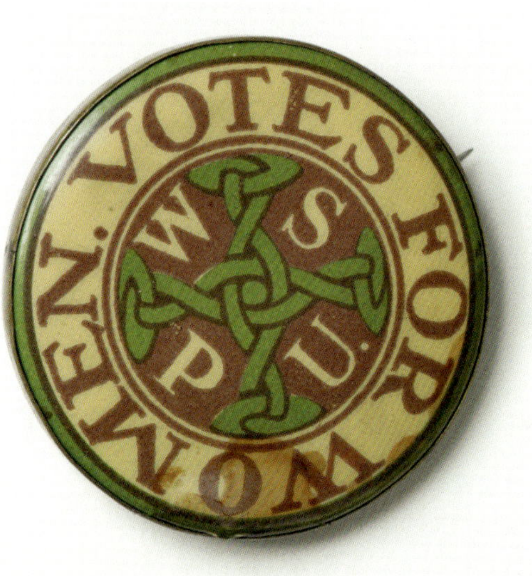

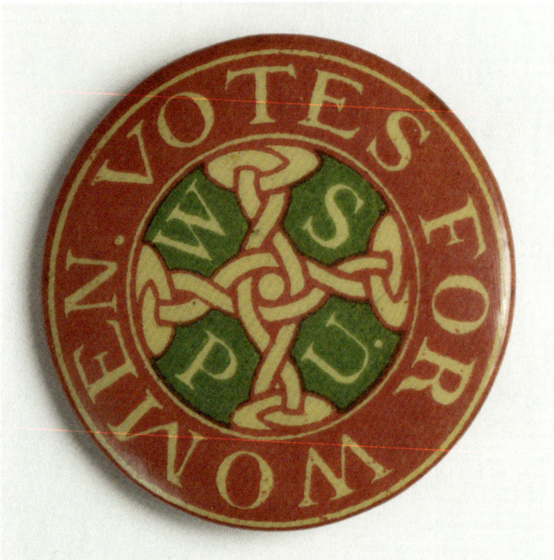

CAT 38–39 | **Pin badges** c.1912–1914

Merchants Portrait Co.
Metal and enamel
Manchester Art Gallery. Dr C Willet Cunnington purchase 1947
and gift of Stella Newsome 1952

These painted metal WSPU pin badges bear the words 'Votes for Women' and Celtic-inspired eternal knot imagery.

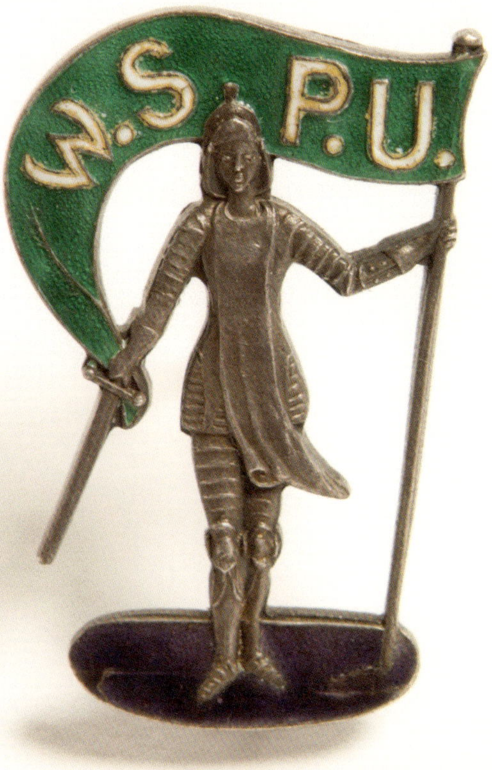

CAT 40 | **Joan of Arc brooch** 1912

Hilda Dallas 1878–1958 (designer)
Silver and enamel, 3 x 2.6 cm
Private collection

This silver brooch with purple, white and green enamel embellishment is based on Dallas's illustration of Joan of Arc carrying the WSPU flag. The increasingly militant tone of the latter stages of the suffrage campaign was reflected in the growing adoption of Joan of Arc as a patron saint by suffragettes and suffragists.

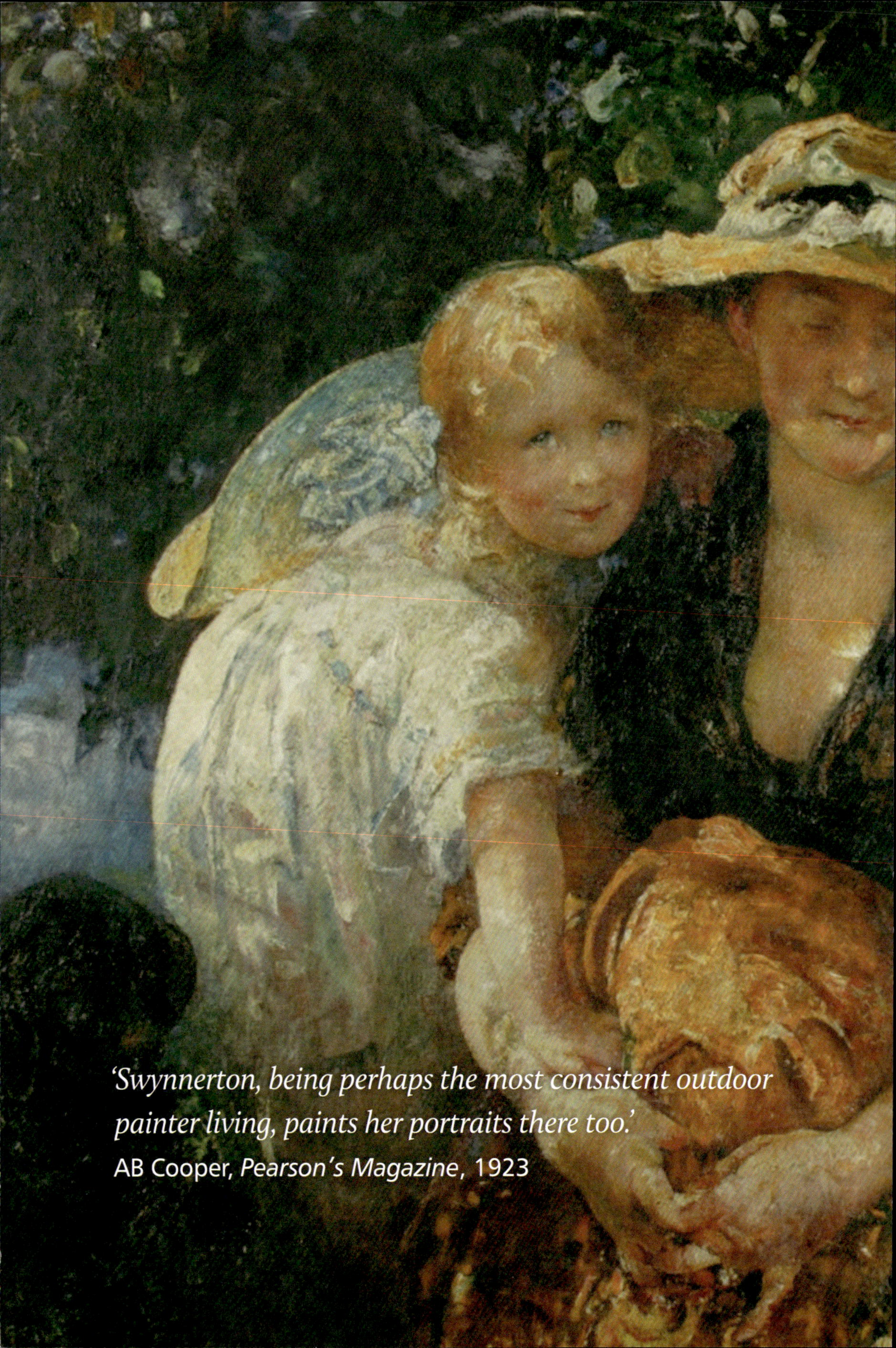

'Swynnerton, being perhaps the most consistent outdoor painter living, paints her portraits there too.'

AB Cooper, *Pearson's Magazine*, 1923

Portraiture, Individuality and the Outdoors

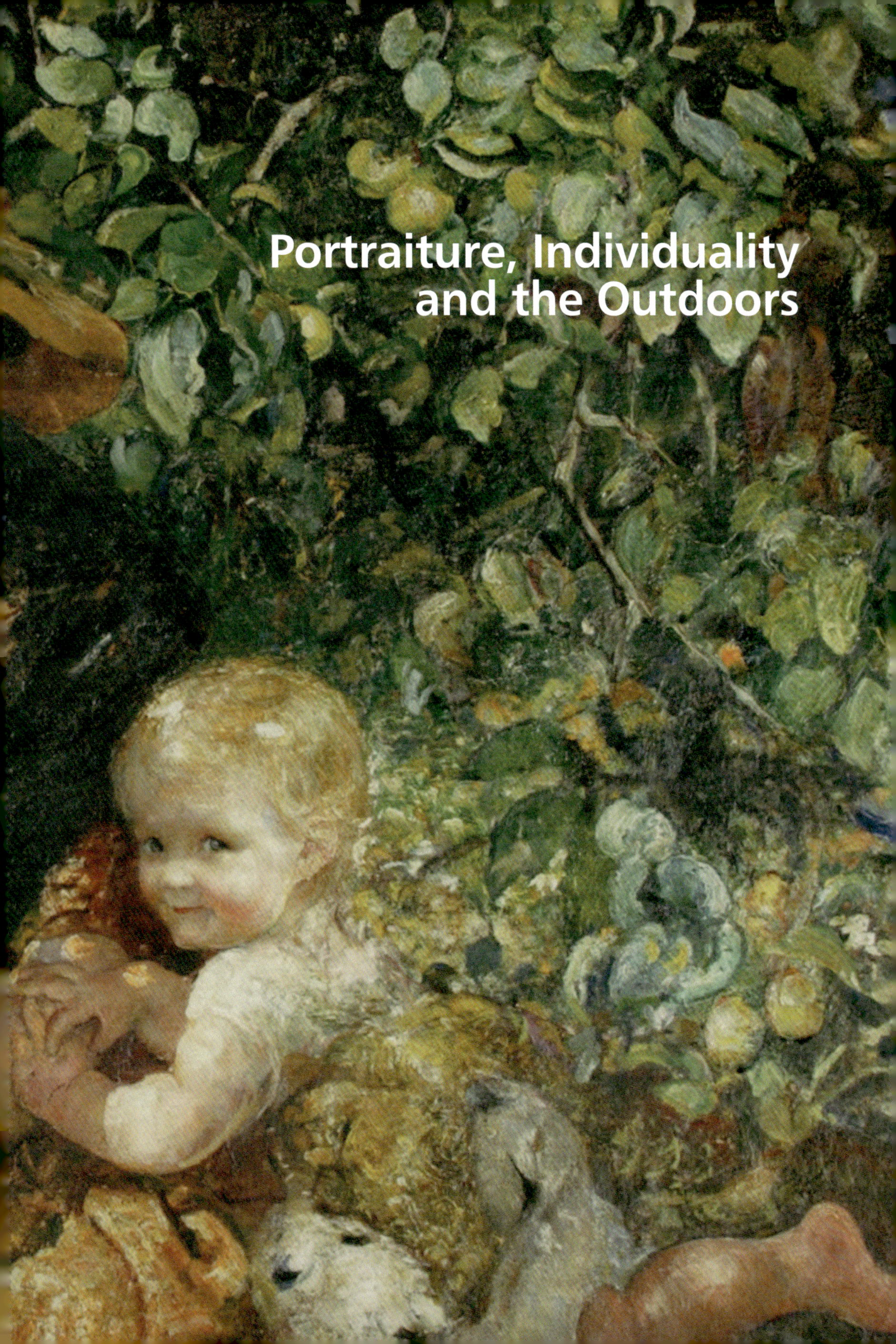

Portraiture, Individuality and the Outdoors

Swynnerton began her career painting portraits and portraiture remained an important part of her practice. In 1891 she became a member of the Society of Portrait Painters and, by the early 20th century, had become a prolific and esteemed portrait painter with many prominent patrons.[1] Her ambitions in this genre were timely, given that portraiture in late 19th- and early 20th-century Britain was experiencing a renaissance. This was largely driven by artists associated with the New English Art Club, of which Swynnerton was a member, and the patronage of families that had amassed great fortunes from expanding industrial and commercial activities. Such patrons preferred a painted likeness that was naturalistic and expressed a sense of an individual's identity rather than the documentary or idealised portrait styles that had been popular in the decades before the 1880s. Fellow artist John Singer Sargent played a pivotal role in introducing Swynnerton to such patrons and counted her amongst the greatest artists of their time.[2]

Swynnerton's mature portraits were an area in which she perfected a distinct approach. There is variety in her representation of sitters of different sexes and ages. Her devotion to depicting the individuality of each sitter without idealising their appearance is consistent and, in her portrayal of female sitters, reflects her women's movement politics. By the late 19th century her portraits were also as influenced by her passion for light and painting outdoors as her nudes and imaginative subject pictures. This is seen in her vivid colour palette, the landscape settings her sitters inhabit and the bold representation of natural light used innovatively to model form. These aspects sit at the heart of her originality in this genre, used as they were by Swynnerton to communicate the vitality of her sitters and the atmosphere and textures of their surroundings.

---

1 Society of Portrait Painters committee members Solomon J Solomon and James Jebusa Shannon were among the Royal Academicians who nominated Swynnerton to become an Associate of the Royal Academy. Louise Jopling and Anna Lea Meritt were contemporary female members of the society and Dame Laura Knight would later join.

2 It was probably Sargent who introduced Swynnerton to socialite Mrs Charles Hunter (née Mary Smyth), who became a key patron and friend. Both Swynnerton and Sargent painted portraits of her.

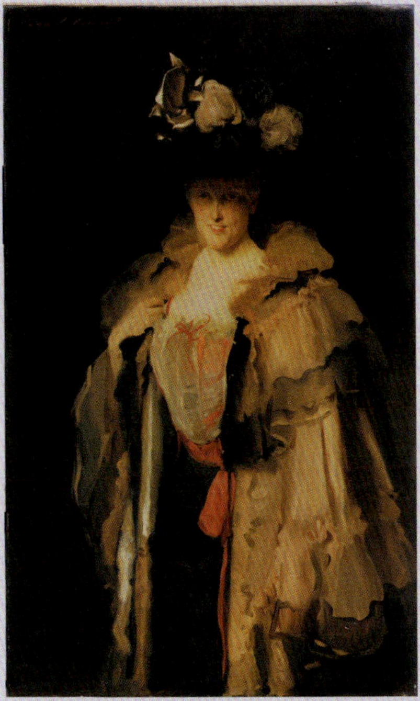

John Singer Sargent *Mrs Charles Hunter* 1898

In her later portrait career, Swynnerton achieved considerable renowned for her portraits of children. By the 19th century children had been given a new cultural status, becoming the centre of families and symbols of the continuation of family lines. This, together with the fragility of children's health, led to an expanding market for aesthetically pleasing likenesses of affluent families' children influenced by the earlier success in this genre of artists of the 17th and 18th centuries, Sir Anthony Van Dyck and Sir Joshua Reynolds. Swynnerton had a rapport with her young sitters. Her compositions show them in relaxed moments amidst playful pursuits that foreground their individual characters and energy. Evelyn Bellhouse, who was painted by Swynnerton as a child, explained, 'She was a splendid old lady and told me the most fascinating stories, hence my wide-eyed stare.'[3] What is more, Swynnerton took the painting of children seriously, an attitude she had in common with John Everett Millais, whose paintings of children, including *Autumn Leaves* (1856, Manchester Art Gallery), were similarly overlooked as kitsch and sentimental until the mid-2000s.

---

[3] Priscilla Hodgson, 'Myself When I was Young', *Cheshire Life*, October, 1982.

CAT 41 | ***The Debutant*** 1891

Oil on canvas, 122 x 72.5 cm
Richard Taylor Fine Art

It has been suggested that this portrait might depict Elizabeth 'Elsie' Ebsworth (later Swinton), who became a prominent society hostess and, unusually for her high social class, a singer. She was around 18 years old in 1891 and living in London. For her it 'was a time of hunts balls, concerts and plays, and visits to exhibitions.'[1] Ebsworth was painted by John Singer Sargent in 1897, so this painting may illustrate that Swynnerton not only gained patrons through Sargent's recommendation but also passed contacts on to him, in a reciprocal rather than one-way exchange.

In its format, plain backdrop and depiction of a fashionable sitter, the portrait declares an affiliation with the work of Sargent. It is also in keeping with the trend among young female sitters at the time to be portrayed in a more relaxed and spontaneous style, in contrast to the formality of earlier art. Swynnerton's independent focus on her female sitters as individuals is, nevertheless, apparent. Psychological depth was often sacrificed in portraits of this period in favour of the representation of status and social construction, however, Swynnerton strikes a balance between those elements. The underlying subject is the transition from adolescence to womanhood. The sitter, dressed in a full evening gown, seems to hold her skirt up in nervous anticipation of departure for a ball or other event in the world of adult society. Her flushed cheeks and the visible blue veins in her arms signal both her embodiment as a woman and her youthful fragility.

The many details of the young woman's black outfit, punctuated by her corsage of harmonious yellow flowers, set as it is against a plain backdrop, creates an aesthetically appealing effect. The limited palette employed by Swynnerton here reveals a further affiliation with the portrait oeuvre of Aesthetic painter James Abbott McNeill Whistler. The visual allure of the painting's surface is enhanced by Swynnerton's loose and thick application of paint.

1 Ebsworth's diaries do not cover this year but some information about her activities is provided by other documents; David Greer, *A Numerous and Fashionable Audience: The Story of Elsie Swinton* (London: Thames Publishing, 1997), 25.

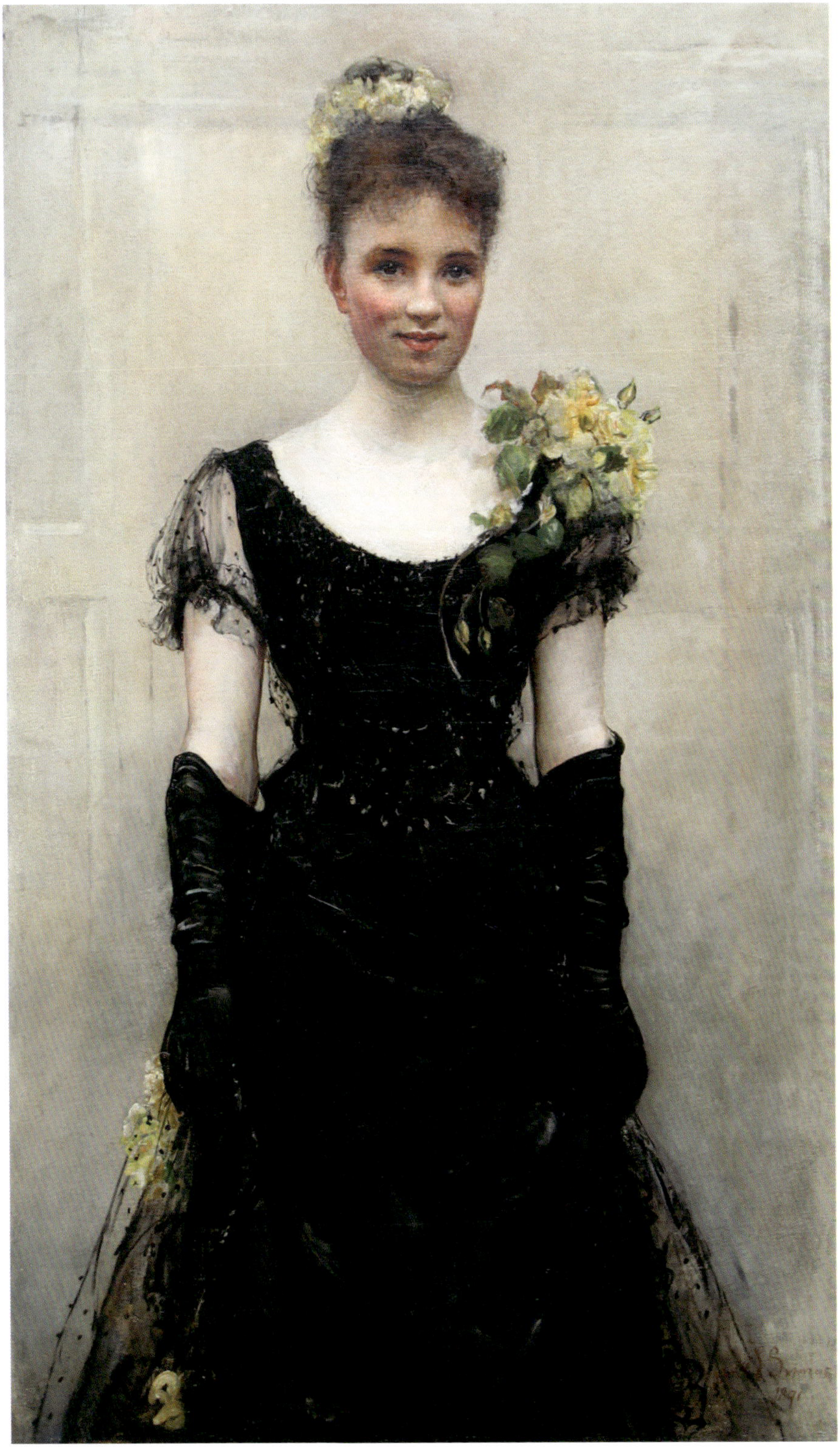

CAT 42 | *Geoffrey and Christopher Herringham* 1889

Oil on canvas, 91.5 x 91.5 cm
Royal Holloway, University of London

The two young boys depicted in this portrait were the sons of Christiana Herringham (née Powell). Like Swynnerton, she was an artist and, from the late 1880s onwards, a women's suffrage campaigner. She was in the fortunate position of being able to donate a significant amount of money to the cause and to be a patron of the arts.[1] She and Swynnerton likely met through their mutual friendship with women's movement leader Dame Millicent Garrett Fawcett and they, later, sat on suffrage committees together. This portrait commission underlines the positive impact of Swynnerton's political connections with a broad network of women throughout her career, which, in this case and others, led to patronage of her work.

During 1890 the painting was exhibited at the New Gallery and at the Liverpool Autumn Exhibition. It played a significant role in establishing the renown Swynnerton gained in the field of child portraiture during the 1890s.[2] In light of rising interest in the study of adolescence in the second half of the 19th century, the depiction of children in landscape settings enabled their physical and emotional changes to be expressed in relation to the cycles and changeability of nature.[3] This is nowhere more true than in Millais's *Autumn Leaves* (1856, Manchester Art Gallery), a work that Swynnerton knew and which is recalled by the twilight setting of the Herringham boys' portrait. The pink and yellow late afternoon sky above the blue hills in the background here is, however, strongly rooted in Swynnerton's own passion for and approach to landscape and light effects. Her use of light is bold in the boys' illuminated hair and faces, their heads being particularly well modelled. The effect of her attention to detail, in the glimmers of light that cling to their velvet costumes and her depiction of the natural world, is vivid and subtle like that of early Pre-Raphaelite landscape paintings.

1 Herringham also owned Swynnerton's *Oceanid* (Catalogue No. 25).

2 Henry Blackburn, *The New Gallery 1890: An Illustrated Catalogue of the Summer Exhibition* (London: Chatto & Windus, 1890), 66.

3 Barbara Dayer Gallati, *Children of the Gilded Era: Portraits by Sargent, Renoir, Cassatt and their Contemporaries* (London and New York: Merrell, 2004), 56.

John Everett Millais *Autumn Leaves* 1856

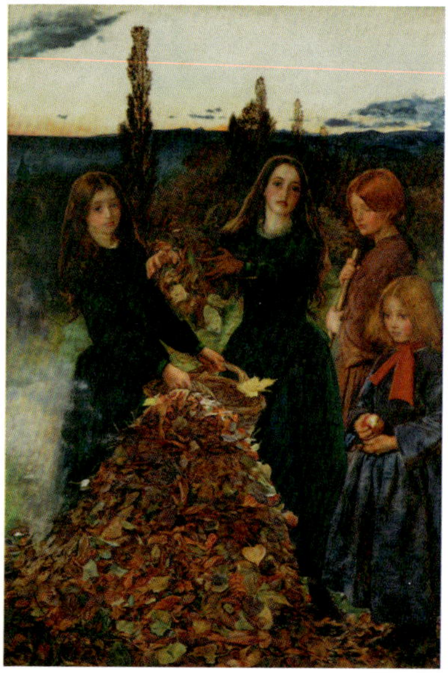

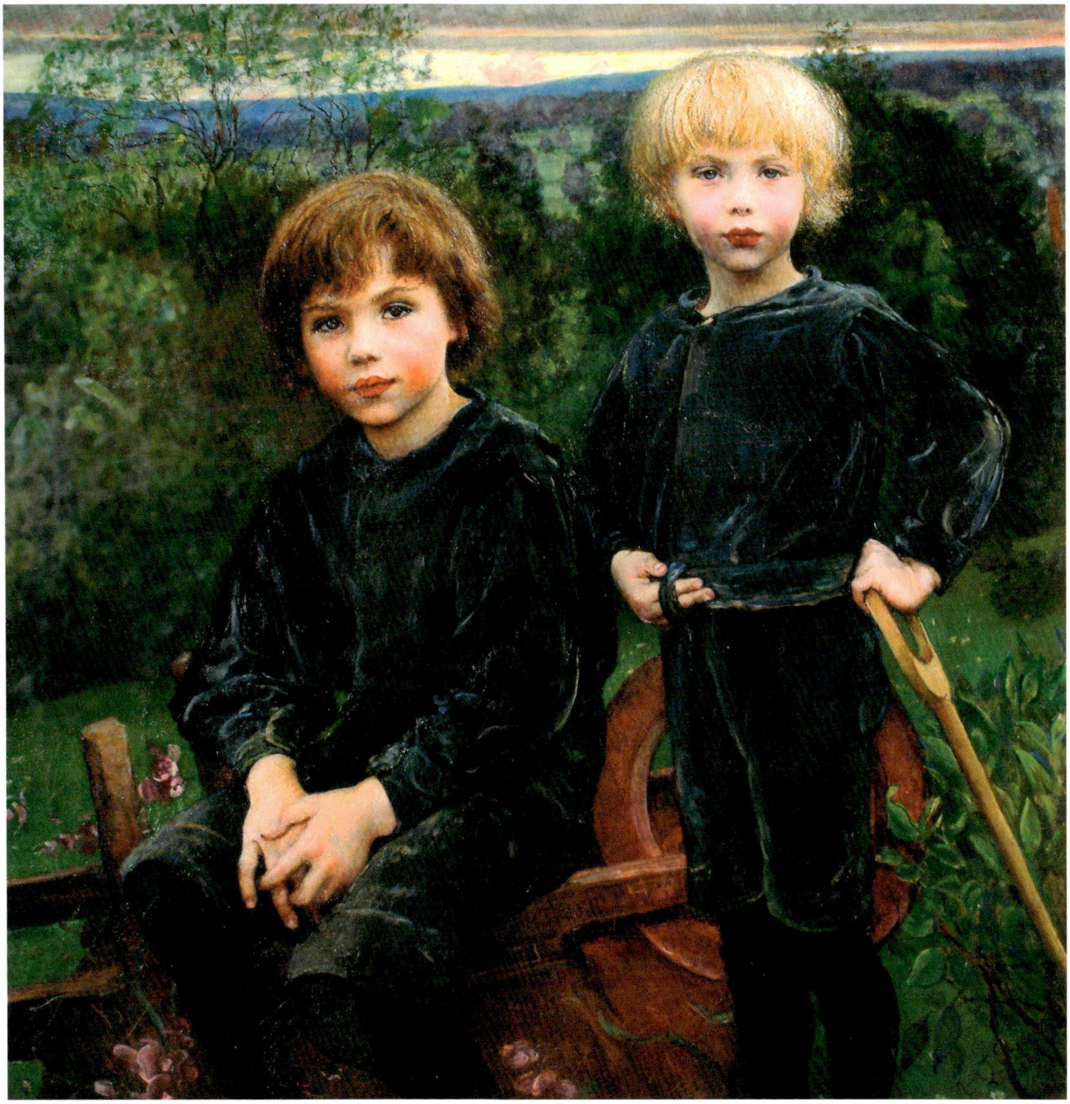

CAT 43 | *Count Zouboff* c.1908–9

Oil on canvas, 193.4 x 153.8 cm
Tate. Presented by Messrs Wallis and Son, 1932

This large-scale portrait painted at the spa town of Salsomaggiore Terme, in northern Italy, a popular destination for wealthy tourists in the 19th to early 20th centuries, illustrates Swynnerton's ambitions as a portrait painter. The sitter, Count Valentin Plantonowich Zouboff (1884–1969)[1] was a Russian intellectual and patron of the arts from a very wealthy and politically influential family; this status is symbolised in the painting by his prominent aristocratic ring. He studied in Germany and Italy, and spent the winter of 1908–9 based in Florence, trying to finish his doctoral thesis, which explains the book and crumpled papers beneath his chair. Later in life he became a well-known art historian and founder of the Russian State Institute of the History of Arts and Gatchini Museum, St Petersburg.

In this portrait Swynnerton clearly paid close attention to the sitter's individual appearance and character. His relaxed sinuous pose, reflective of his aristocratic status, dominates the picture and cuts across the strong uprights of the classic Doric columns in the background. The latter elements point both to his status and masculinity and reveal Swynnerton's knowledge and admiration of the work of esteemed 18th-century British portraitists Sir Thomas Lawrence and Thomas Gainsborough. Swynnerton painted other male sitters who held considerable status in the artistic and literary circles of late 19th- to early-20th century Europe, including the American-born British writer Henry James. However, *Count Zouboff* is the only such portrait held in a public collection.

Swynnerton's brushwork is loose and her use of bare canvas in the depiction of his fashionable attire is confident. He wears a relaxed, aesthetic-style velvet coat and waistcoat with shirt and necktie, an informal evening wear of the time. This reveals a modernity in her approach to painting, by this date, that is in common with contemporary painters associated with Impressionism. The prominent landscape backdrop makes similar associations, while simultaneously alluding to the financial and social mobility of the sitter. Gone are the dark backdrops of Swynnerton's early portraits of male sitters, such as *The Reverend William Gaskell* (Catalogue No. 3). The rugged hills, light, bright colour palette and layered application of paint in the backdrop recall her Italian landscape paintings of the same period and demonstrate the influence of the light and landscape of Italy on her mature portraiture.

1 Variously spelt Zubov, Zuboff and Zoubov.

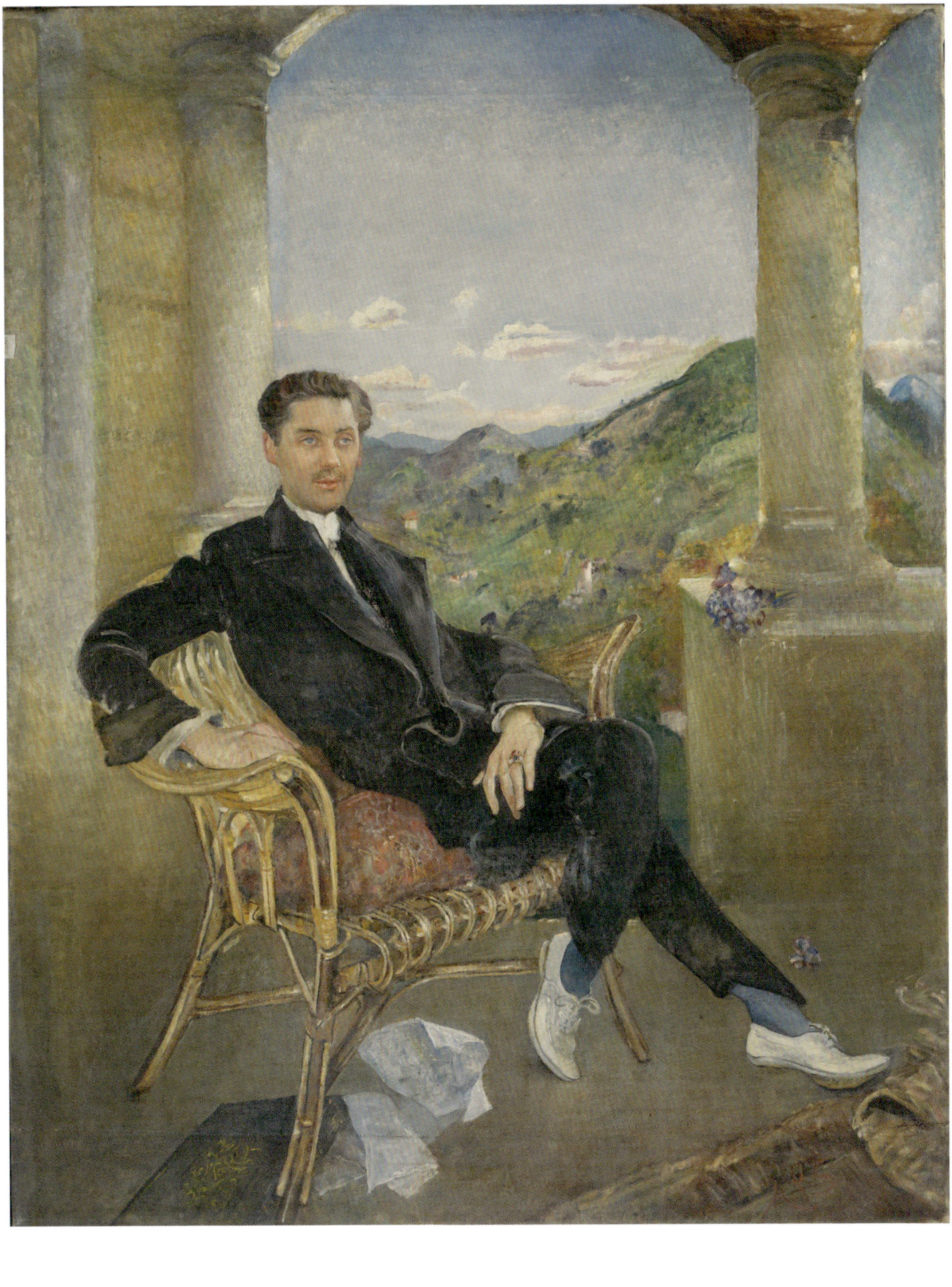

CAT 44 | ***Margaret and Chrystian Guthrie*** 1907

Oil on canvas, 131 cm (diameter)
The Wrathall Family

This portrait, exhibited at the Royal Academy in 1907, depicts the Guthrie sisters Margaret Ayliffe Elinor (1897–1948) (left) and Catherine Violet Chrystian (1900–1967). Little information is available about the sitters or the circumstances of this portrait's creation. Their father, David Charles Guthrie, was the 5th Baron of Craigie and, from 1892, of East Haddon Hall, Northamptonshire, the Georgian manor house where Swynnerton painted the girls. The identity of their mother, American-born Mary Guthrie (née Low), a women's rights campaigner who founded the Northamptonshire Ladies Linen League in 1910 is perhaps more significant.[1] Swynnerton may have met Mary Guthrie through her women's movement connections; she had already painted her portrait (now lost) in around 1891, shortly after her marriage.[2]

Swynnerton's work shows the girls sitting on a window seat with a view to the expansive East Haddon Hall gardens. They appear patient but restless, yet Swynnerton has skilfully captured their attention for a fleeting moment. Both children are torn between the desire to be outside and play, and sitting beautifully still, with their personalities coming though in their attitudes. The elder sitter tries hard to comply but the contortion of her right arm and leg shows that she is brimming with energy and the angle of her shoulders indicates her yearning motion towards the garden. However, her younger sister is less patient: she faces the window with her hands perched on the windowsill, indicating her interest in the sunny scene, as she turns her head back towards Swynnerton with a smile.

Swynnerton employed light effects to communicate her young sitters' restless energy, too. The light, coming from the window, represented by bold white highlights, falls strongly on the youngest sitter's face, hair and hands and creates an energetic dappling across the girls' white dresses, which recall Renoir's lively treatment of fabric, and casts playful shadows on the floor. The luminous glow of light on the girls' shoes also adds to the sense of their vitality. The broken brushwork Swynnerton employs here is typical of her handling of paint in this period. The shimmering yellows and greens and vivid blue of the backdrop, together with the rich deep pinks of the interior's curtains prompted an unnamed *Athenaeum* critic to remark that this painting has the 'colourist's enthusiasm'.[3]

1 Mary Low's mother, Mary Cowper Stiles, had founded the Women's Institute Savannah, Georgia.

2 Sargent painted Agnes Dorothea Anstruther-Thomson (1860-1941), sister of David Charles Guthrie, in 1900, evidencing the reciprocal exchange of patrons between him and Swynnerton.

3 'The Royal Academy', 25 May, 1907, 641.

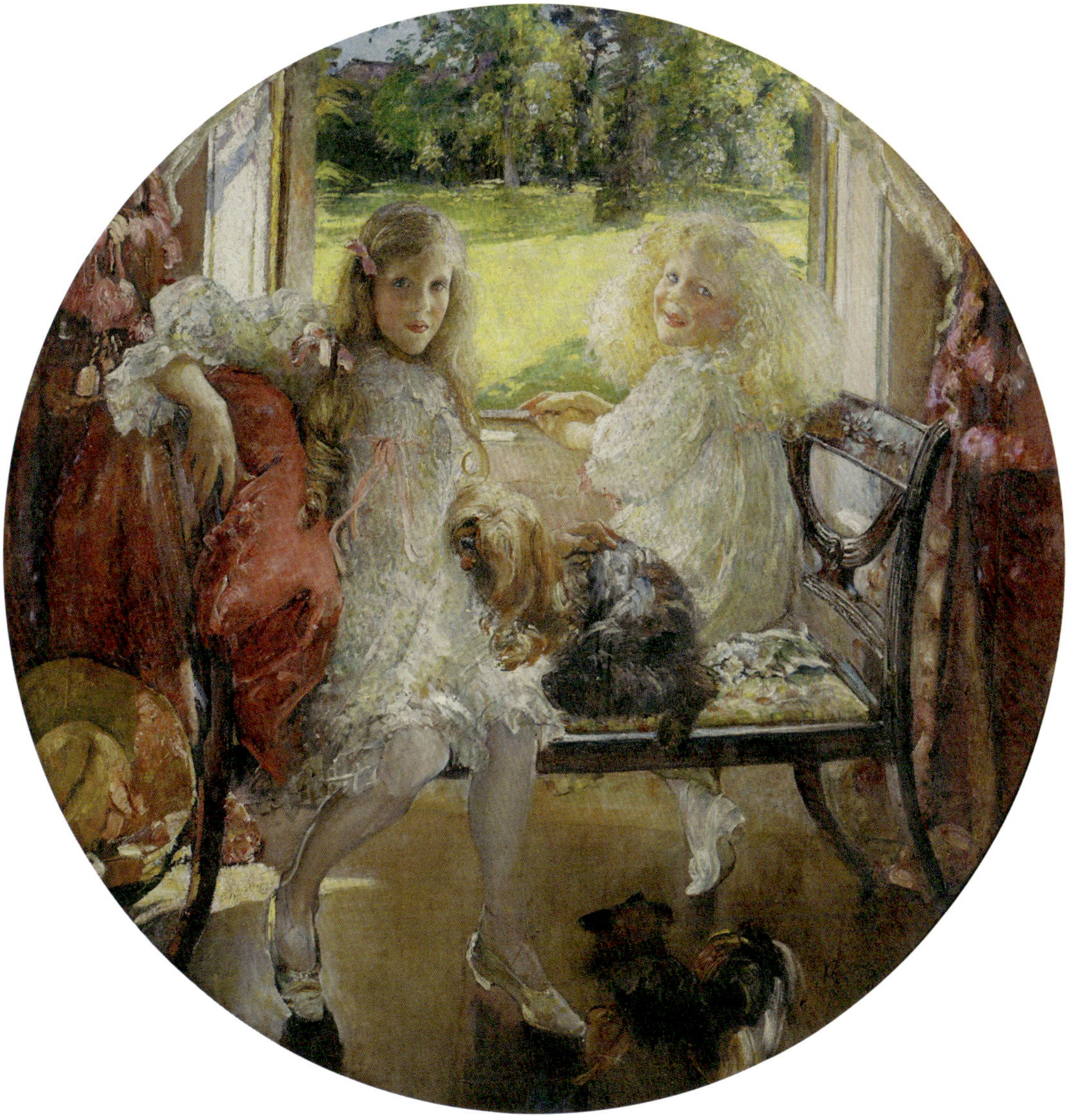

CAT 45 | ***Mrs A Scott-Elliot and Children*** 1912

Oil on canvas, 148.6 cm (diameter)
Manchester Art Gallery. Purchased from Marjorie A Scott-Elliot 1923.38

This portrait likely depicts Margaret Pirie Scott-Elliot (née Evans) (1868–1951), wife of Colonel Adam Scott-Elliot, and her two daughters Aline Margaret and Isabel Louisa. The family had homes in London and in Norfolk, where this portrait was painted. Isabel grew up to be one of a small number of women who became aviators in the first half of the 20th century. The group sit in a garden beneath a fruiting apple tree, which offers them shade from the bright sunlight. Their proximity to one another and the gentle touch of the children's hands against their mother's arms emphasise that this is a representation of a close family group, not a stately or reverent construction. The mother is in a relaxed pose with her eyes closed, an action which makes her seem self-effacing, a blank background to the personalities of her offspring. The white clothing of the two young children emphasises the innocence of childhood.

In the 1910s, mothers and children were commonly presented in official portraits in a style known as the Grand Manner. This style, seen in the work of Academic artists, including Solomon J Solomon and James J Shannon, was characterised by an idealised representation of sitters and their status, together with the formal arrangement and posing of figures. Swynnerton, however, combines grandeur with informality in this portrait.

The depiction of a mother with her children in this period, even in a secular image such as this portrait, was inescapably suggestive of images of the Christian Madonna and Child. In the context of Swynnerton's oeuvre, it also makes reference to her contemporary woman and child paintings of the 1880s. Furthermore, the triangular composition of the three figures and the circular canvas employed are reminiscent of Italian Renaissance religious paintings and sculptures showing the Madonna and Child with St John, by Raphael or Michelangelo, for instance. A striking frame, likely designed by Swynnerton, adds to the grandeur of the piece.[1]

1 The circular frame was made by Charles Mitchell May of CM May & Son, Golden Square, London, who produced frames in English and French styles and also carried out artists' own designs. He is also known to have worked for Whistler in the 1880s and Sargent from 1894 to 1922.

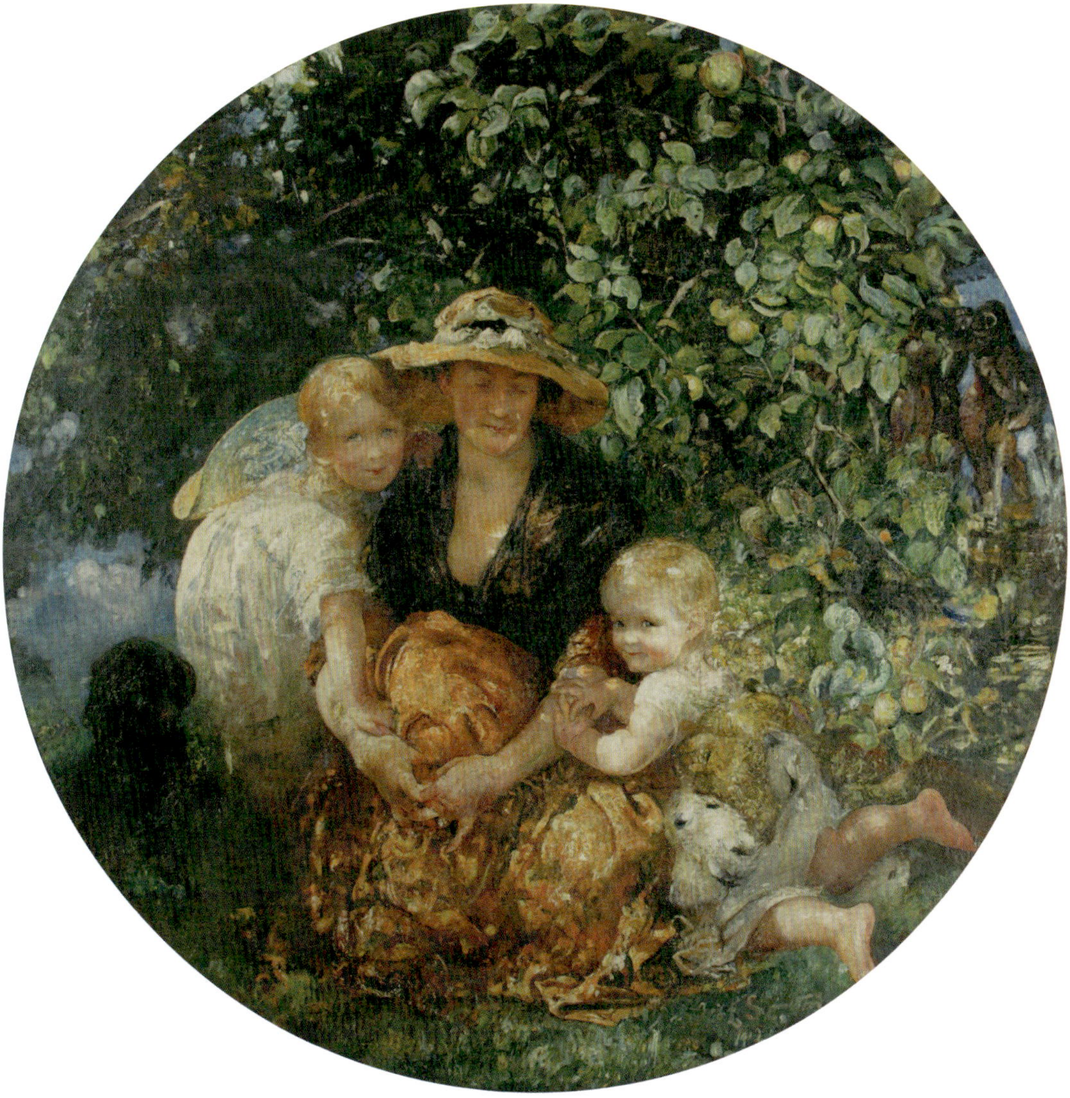

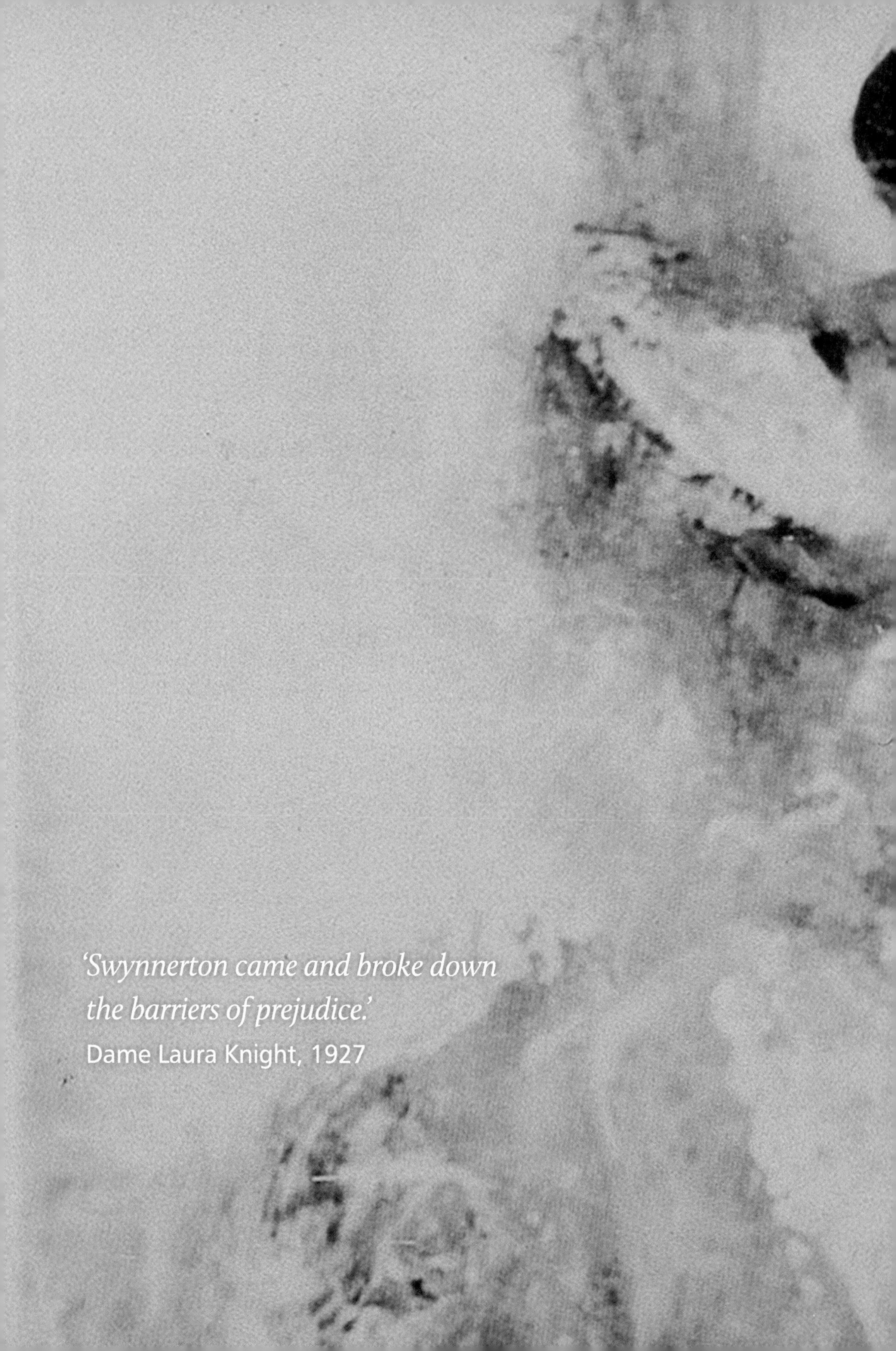

'Swynnerton came and broke down the barriers of prejudice.'

Dame Laura Knight, 1927

A Legacy

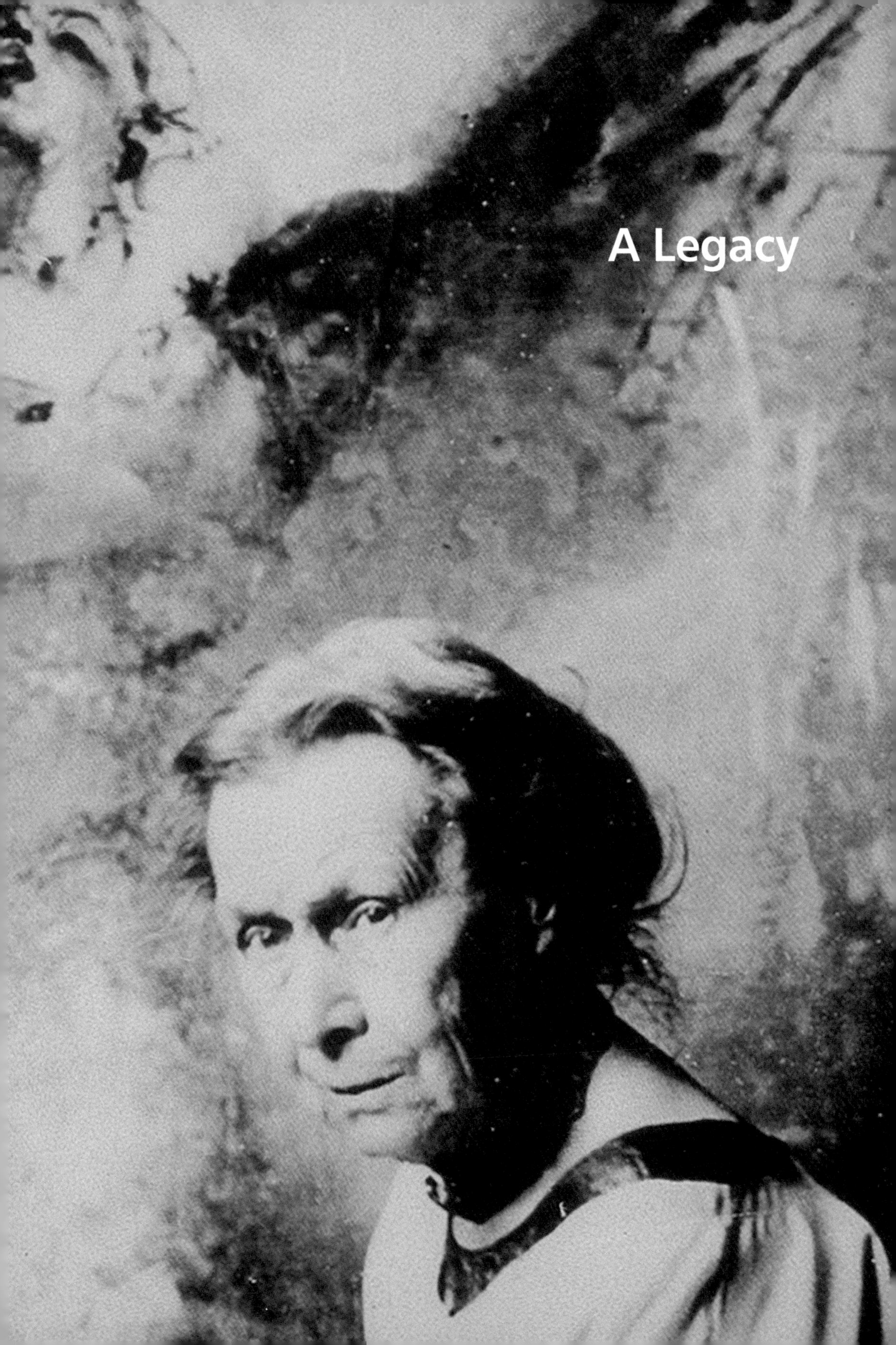

A Legacy

In 1922 Swynnerton was elected the first female Associate Member of the Royal Academy of Arts, London (ARA) since its foundation in 1768. This recognition was late for an artist who had maintained an international reputation from the 1890s onwards.[1] Members of that institution, which was a patriarchal stronghold of conservatism in the 19th century, had unsuccessfully nominated her twice before. Those who did so in 1914, including John Singer Sargent and George Clausen, appreciated her work due to their shared affiliation with the New English Art Club, a venue that nurtured Impressionistic styles of painting and was a stepping-stone to RA membership.[2] However, a continued resistance to women's involvement with the Academy, and factors including World War I as well as suffragette attacks on paintings at the 1914 RA exhibition, led six years to elapse before members supported her nomination again in 1920.[3]

Swynnerton was understandably ambivalent about her election. However, 'she gleefully sent many of her hitherto rejected works to the spring exhibitions',[4] and was proud to have achieved the ground-breaking accolade. It prompted a retrospective at Manchester Art Gallery (MAG) in 1923 and ensured a tangible legacy for her work. MAG, for instance, which by that date owned just one Swynnerton, *The Reverend William Gaskell* (Catalogue No. 3), acquired a further 15 after her election. Examples of her work now feature in more than ten British public collections and in international ones.

By 1923 Swynnerton's reputation was secure, leaving her confident and free to be bold in her artistic visions. Although her eyesight began to fail later in the 1920s, likely due to cataracts, that does not explain her strategy. She worked

---

1 Swynnerton's title of ARA, which would usually place an artist in line to become a full member of the Royal Academy (a Royal Academician or RA), was converted to Senior Associate a week after her election due to her being over the Academy's retirement age of 75, meaning that she was not eligible to become an RA. This goes some way towards explaining why her achievement has been overshadowed by that of the first woman RA, Dame Laura Knight.

2 Her other nominators in 1914 were Albert Julius Johann Olsson, James Jebusa Shannon and Solomon Joseph Solomon.

3 Clausen and Olsson supported her again in 1920, joined by Henry Scott Tuke, William Llewellyn, Charles Shannon, R. Bloomfield, Annerly Brown, David Young Cameron and Frank Dicksee.

4 Katey Dickens in Gladys Storey, *Dickens and Daughter* (1939; reprint New York: Haskell House, 1971), 201.

with an awareness of modernist trends of the early 20th century, which involved gestural painting and the simplification of form – particularly Post-Impressionism as championed by Cézanne, and the abstraction of form in landscapes and figurative paintings and sculptures by Matisse and Rodin. Her paintings from this period exhibit a looser, less built up and more gestural handing of paint than before, which becomes abstract in places, and, in the case of *The Soul's Journey: The Soul's Awakening* (c. 1925, Glasgow Museums), for example, displays the simplification of figurative form. Yet, they retain her characteristically robust modelling of figures, signature colour palette and passion for natural light. Although she suffered from a road accident and cancer, she continued to paint outdoors until her final months.

Women artists' struggles for equal access to education, exhibitions and accreditation were by no means over, but substantial progress had been made in her lifetime. Her achievements left a cultural legacy for women artists of the next generation, and those to follow. Dame Laura Knight, who, in 1936 became the first woman full member of the Royal Academy since its foundation, recognised her as someone who had paved the way for women to become professionals, declaring:

> *'We women who have the good fortune to be born later than Mrs. Swynnerton profit by her accomplishments. Any woman reaching the heights in the fine arts had been almost unknown until Mrs. Swynnerton came and broke down the barriers of prejudice...'*[5]

[5] Dame Laura Knight. *Oil Paint and Grease Paint*, Vol. 3 (London: Penguin, 1936), 326.

CAT 46 | ***Montagna Mia*** 1923

Oil on canvas, 112.3 x 183 cm
Manchester Art Gallery. Annie L Swynnerton bequest 1934.13

Swynnerton's conception of a robustly modelled female nude merged into a simplified, gesturally handled landscape illustrates the freedom in her artistic vision following her election as an ARA. A *Times* art critic remarked in 1923:

> *Montagna Mia ... is visionary but a little vague. There is an incongruity in the conception of a nude figure melting into a mountain which [Swynnerton] has not overcome by all her richness of colour and simplification of form.*[1]

Like her earlier allegorical and symbolic paintings, the meaning of this work is ambiguous. The title *Montagna Mia* (My Mountain) perhaps alludes to the struggles Swynnerton surmounted in the course of her career. It certainly reflects her intimate relationship with the Italian countryside – the mountain range and lake being reminiscent of her paintings of crater-lakes close to Rome – as well as a oneness between the depicted woman and landscape. The figure's right hipbone, breast and arm metamorphose into peaks, creating a sensual image, but the realistically depicted nude and the disappearance of her lower torso into the hanging mist denies any realisation of male sexual desire. The figure's truncation also alludes to Italian art, namely to a range of fragmented classical sculptures that Swynnerton would have seen in Italy, and the theory, often attributed to Michelangelo, that every block of stone contained a statue which the artist had only to reveal.[2] Such inspirations were something Swynnerton had in common with Rodin, whose modernist sculptures feature truncated figurative forms emerging from marble and who had praised her earlier, prize-winning female nude *Mater Triumphalis* (1892, Musée d'Orsay, Paris).

The closed eyes of the figure tell us that she is relaxed within the landscape that she dominates. Meanwhile, the 'melting' of her waterfall-like cascade of loosely painted yellow hair into the mountainside suggests she is undergoing a process of transformation. This is reminiscent of Swynnerton's late 19th-century allegorical and symbolic paintings of powerful female figures, who are mystically linked to the natural world, including *Oreads* (Catalogue No. 24), though no specific narrative is implicit here.

1 'Royal Academy – A Few Modernist Works: Conventional Styles', 5 May, 1923, 13.

2 The Swynnertons owned a vineyard at Carrara, the site famous for its stone quarry where Michelangelo and other sculptors sourced the best marble, a place that may have inspired *Montagna Mia*.

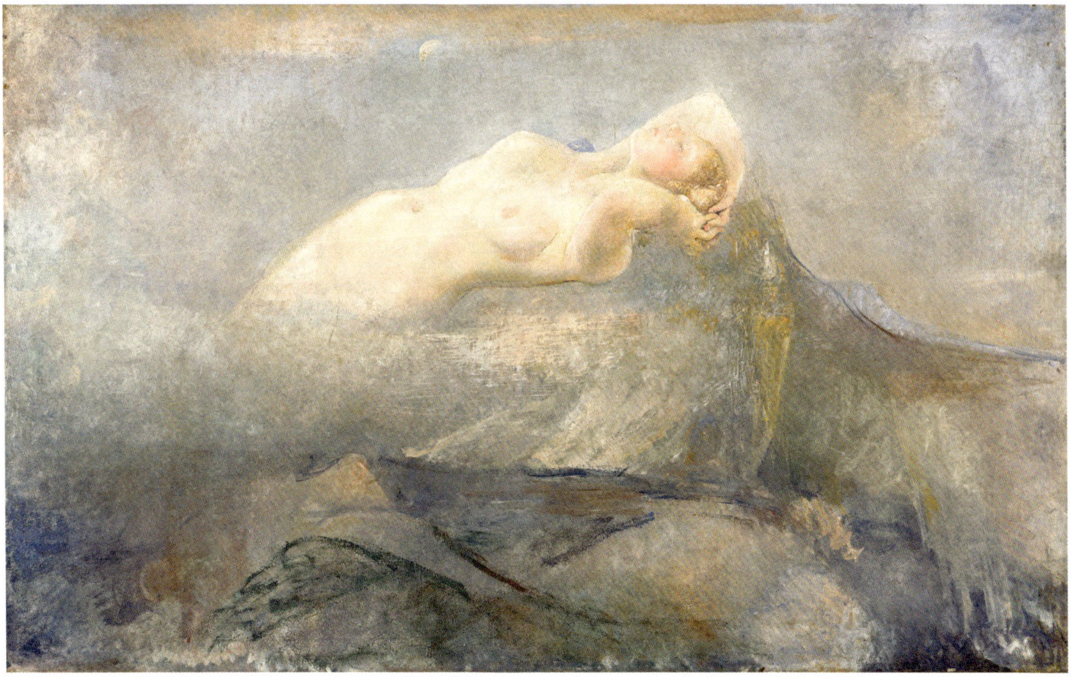

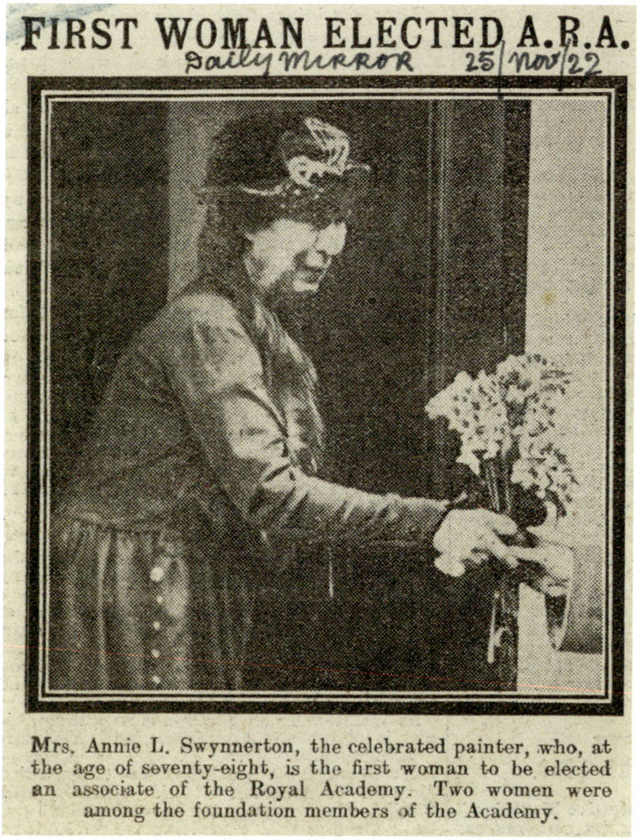

FIRST WOMAN ELECTED A.R.A.

Daily Mirror 25/Nov/22

Mrs. Annie L. Swynnerton, the celebrated painter, who, at the age of seventy-eight, is the first woman to be elected an associate of the Royal Academy. Two women were among the foundation members of the Academy.

CAT 47 |

'First Woman Elected A.R.A.', *Daily Mirror*, 25 November 1922

Newspaper article, 13 x 9 cm
Archive material compiled by David Brownlie (1880–1951).
The Executors of Christine Brownlie Allen (1953–2014)

The photograph included in this report shows Swynnerton being congratulated on the news of her election as an Associate Member of the Royal Academy of Arts. On first hearing the news she had remarked:

> *'My first thought is art. If I have been elected, I do not know if it will help women.'*[1]

1 Anon. *American Art News*, 1922, 3.

>

CAT 48 | **'The First Woman to be elected A.R.A.: Exclusive "Sphere" Pictures of Mrs. Annie Swynnerton', *The Sphere*, 9 December 1922**

Newspaper article, 36.5 x 22 cm
Archive material compiled by David Brownlie (1880–1951)
The Executors of Christine Brownlie Allen (1953–2014)

This article features a rare official photographic portrait of the artist. It also includes her, now lost, painting *The Dream of Italy*, a work that unites her passion for the sun and bold representation of the female nude.

A further photograph of her London studio contains an unidentified example of her equestrian portraits of children with their ponies, a genre she was renowned for.

THE FIRST WOMAN TO BE ELECTED A.R.A.

Exclusive "Sphere" Pictures of Mrs. Annie Swynnerton

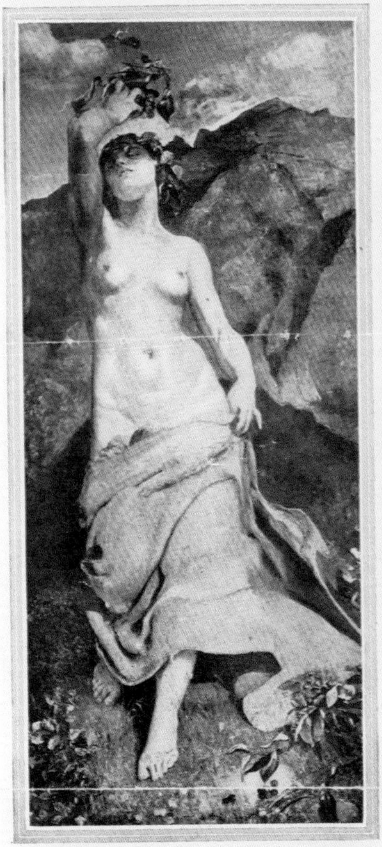

A Typical Example of Mrs. Swynnerton's Work

Mrs. Annie Swynnerton's work has long been admired by other eminent British artists. Among women she occupies an unique place. She has even been described as "one of the six inspired British painters living." Her work is of the most virile nature, as the few examples we reproduce here go to show

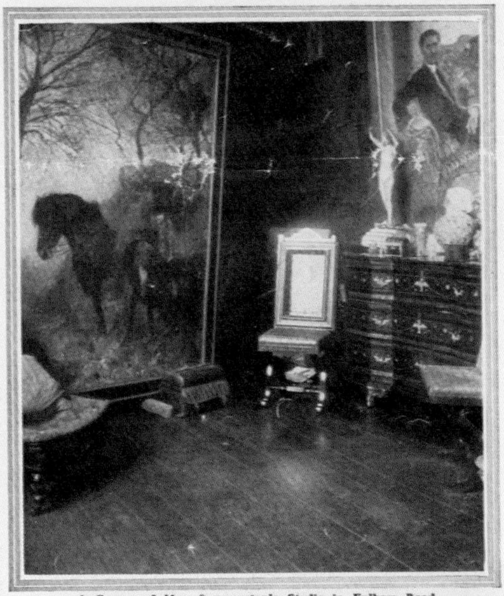

A Corner of Mrs. Swynnerton's Studio in Fulham Road

The new A.R.A. is the first woman since the foundation of the Royal Academy—the first woman, in fact, to be elected, the other two women members, Angelica Kauffman and Mary Moser, being foundation members over a century ago. At Mrs. Swynnerton's studio are many fine examples of her distinguished and virile art

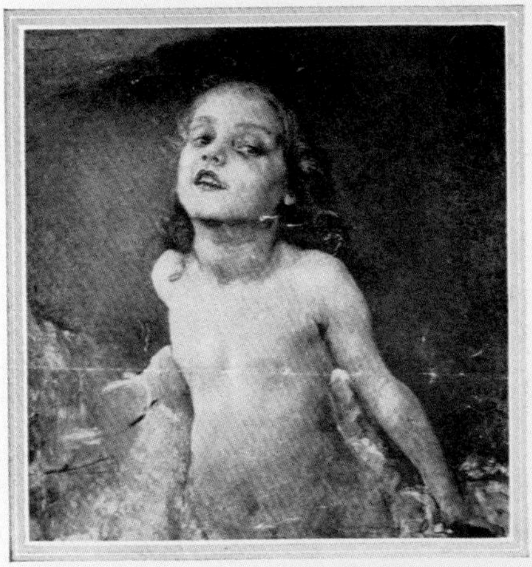

A Study of a Child by Mrs. Swynnerton

Pictures by Mrs. Swynnerton have been exhibited at the Academy for many years. One of them, the "Dryads," was recently presented to the nation by Mr. J. Sargent, R.A.

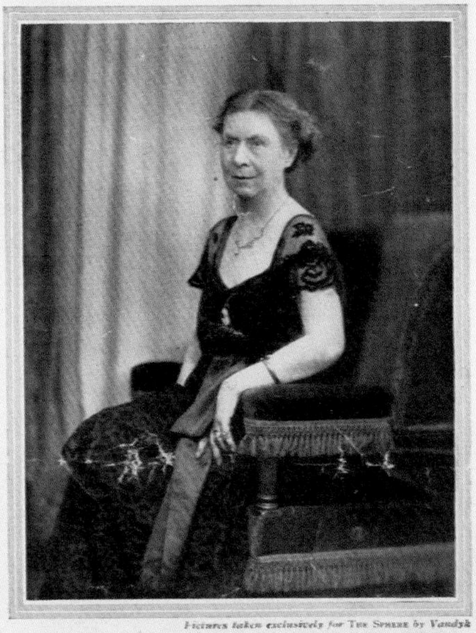

Pictures taken exclusively for THE SPHERE by Vandyk

Mrs. Annie L. Swynnerton, the First Elected Woman A.R.A.

The new A.R.A. is in her seventy-eighth year. She is the daughter of a Manchester lawyer, and learned the technique of her art in Manchester and at Rome

C

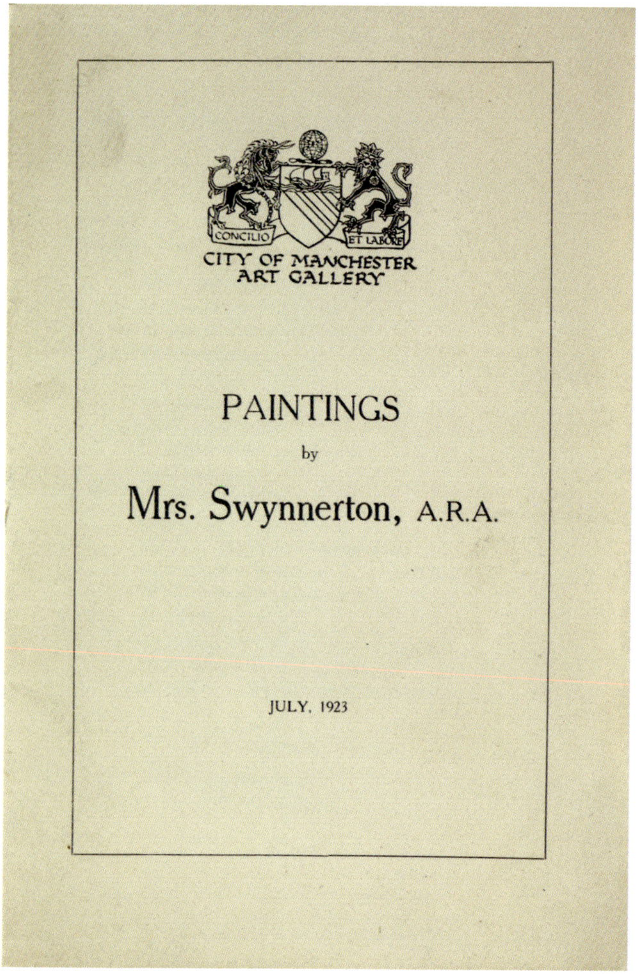

CAT 49 | **Exhibition catalogue**
Paintings by Mrs. Swynnerton, A.R.A., July 1923

Paper, 18.4 x 12.5 cm
Manchester Art Gallery Archive

Swynnerton's election as ARA prompted a major retrospective exhibition at Manchester Art Gallery, which she noted as an important event in her life in a biographical questionnaire she completed for the National Gallery in 1932. The show included 59 of her paintings; more than half of those are now untraced.

>

CAT 50 & 51 | **Photographs of the exhibition**
Paintings by Mrs. Swynnerton, A.R.A., July 1923

Unknown photographer, 15.9 x 21.6 cm
Manchester Art Gallery Archive

Occupying two large exhibition rooms, the 1923 exhibition adopted no thematic or chronological arrangement, owing likely to the complexity of Swynnerton's oeuvre. The paintings were organised, instead, by size and subject matter to form symmetrical displays. Works shown in the 2018 Manchester Art Gallery exhibition can be identified in these photographs.

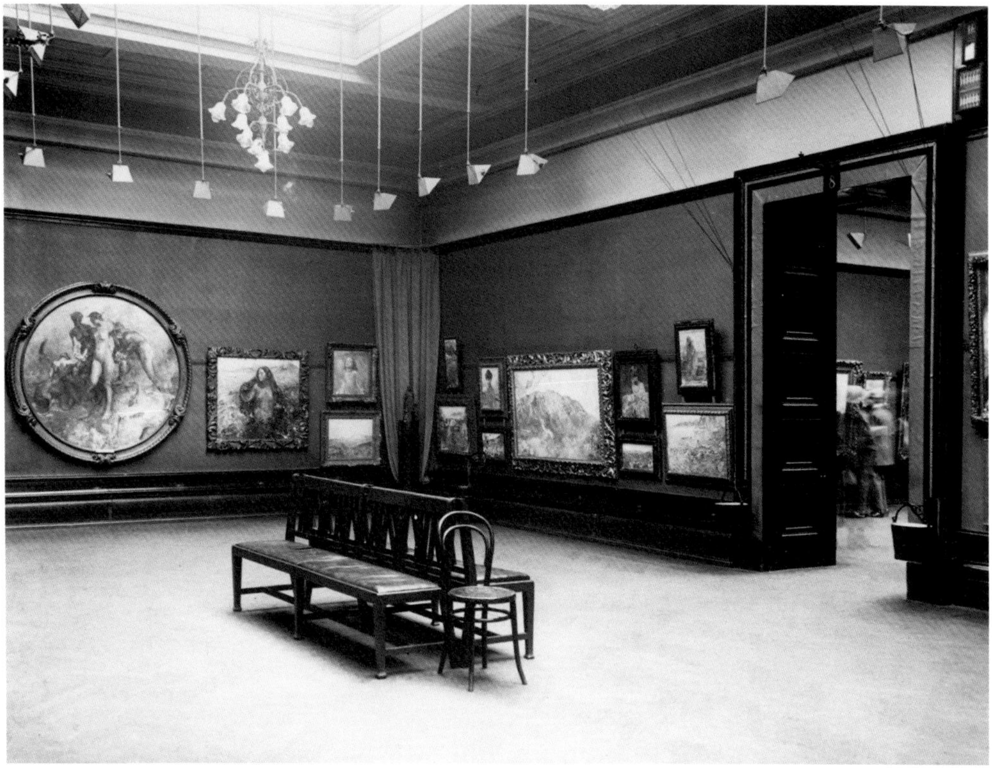

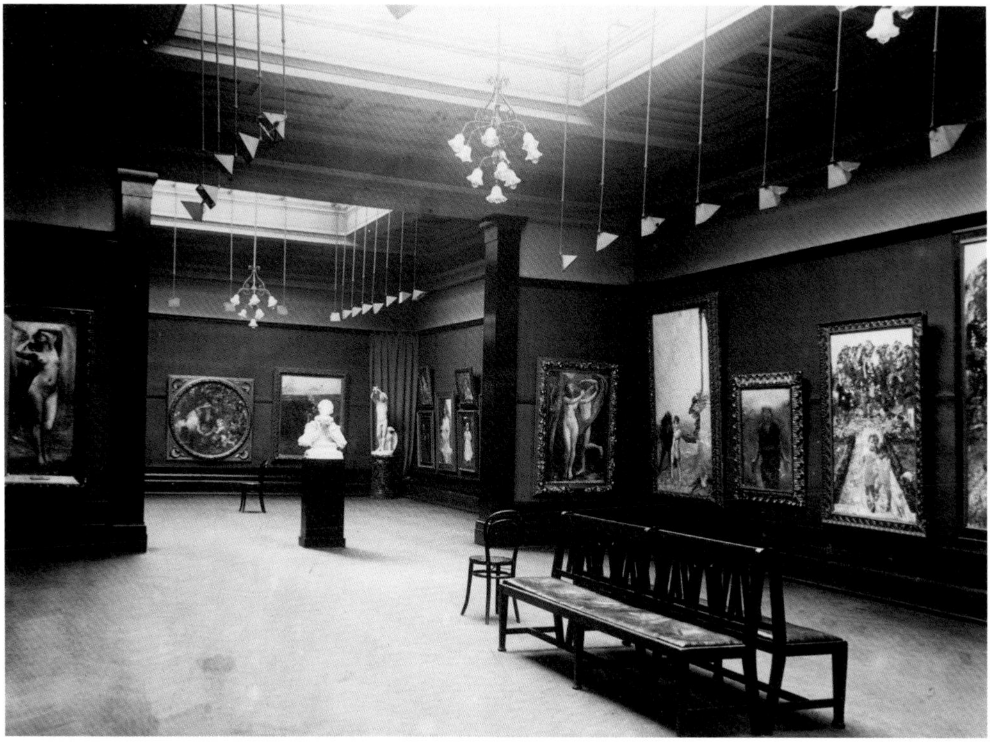

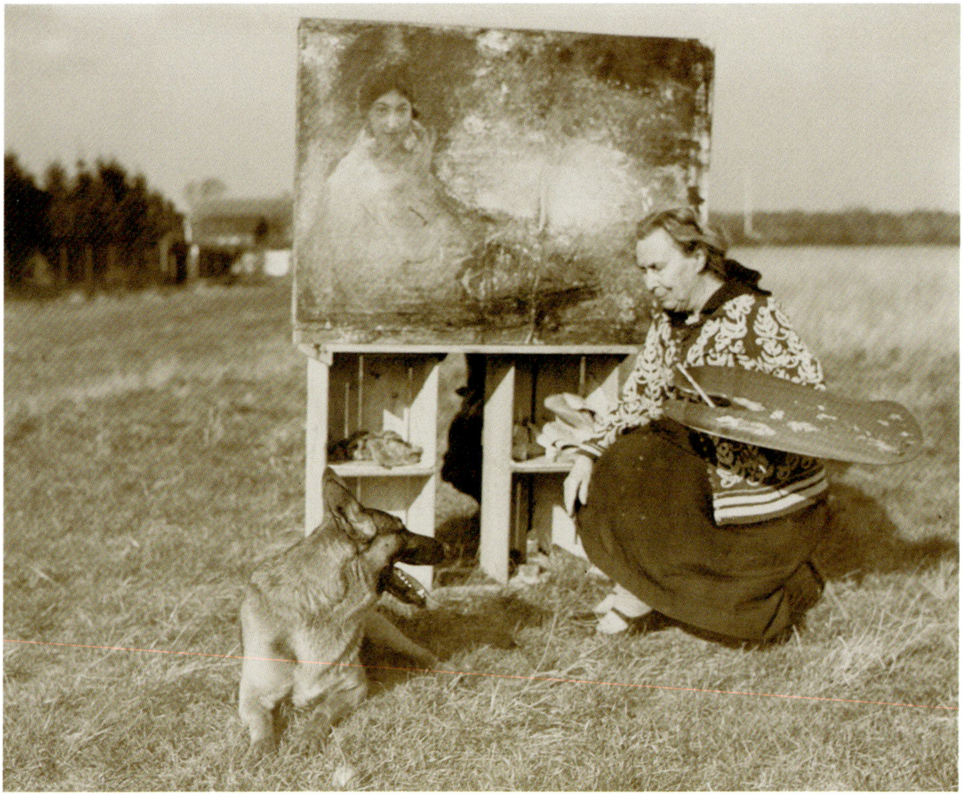

CAT 52 | **Swynnerton painting outdoors at Hayling Island** (date unknown)

Unknown photographer, photographic print, 26 x 20.2 cm
Archive material compiled by David Brownlie (1880–1951)
The Executors of Christine Brownlie Allen (1953–2014)

After her husband's death in 1911, Swynnerton continued to live between London and Rome until illness and a road accident left her unable to travel. Around 1931 she moved to Hayling Island, Hampshire, where she found the light better than in London and weather good enough to work outdoors almost every day until her death.

CAT 53 |

'First Woman A.R.A. for 150 Years Dies', *Daily Herald*, 25 October 1933

Newspaper article, 23 x 5.7 cm
Manchester Academy of Fine Arts Archive

Dozens of newspapers worldwide published reports of Swynnerton's passing, showing the extent of her renown. This one includes a characteristic photograph of the artist preparing to paint outdoors, seated with canvas and palette in hand. The reporter emphasises her well-known preference for painting 'in the open'.

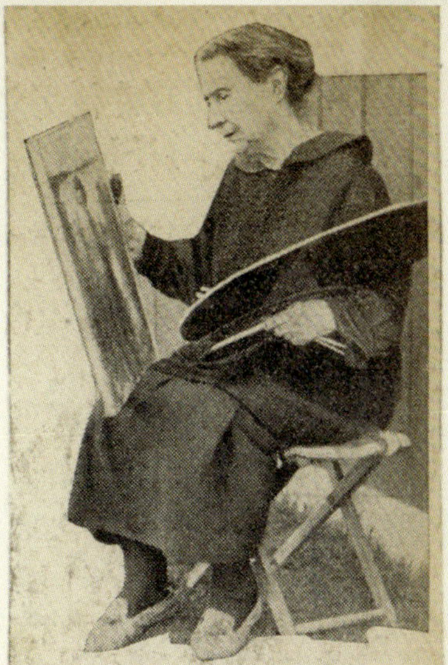

MRS. SWYNNERTON

FIRST WOMAN A.R.A. FOR 150 YEARS DIES

THE first woman A.R.A. to be appointed in 154 years, and apart from Dame Laura Knight, the only woman to hold the title, died at Hayling Island, Portsmouth, yesterday.

She was Mrs. Annie L. Swynnerton, aged 88, who was born in Manchester.

A few months ago her eyesight began to fail, but in spite of this handicap she continued to work until three weeks ago on a picture, "An Image of Desire," which is left unfinished.

On fine days, even until last month, she worked in the open, and otherwise worked in a garage which had been converted into a studio.

She was made an A.R.A. in 1922, the first woman thus honoured since Angelica Kauffman in 1768.

Most men relinquish their positions as A.R.A.s at the age of 75, yet Mrs. Swynnerton was 77 when elected.

For many years she exhibited in the Royal Academy, and her works are shown in several galleries throughout the country.

Her native city of Manchester gave her a civic reception a few years ago on the occasion of the Manchester Spring Show, at which she exhibited.

DAILY HERALD

OCTOBER 25, 1933

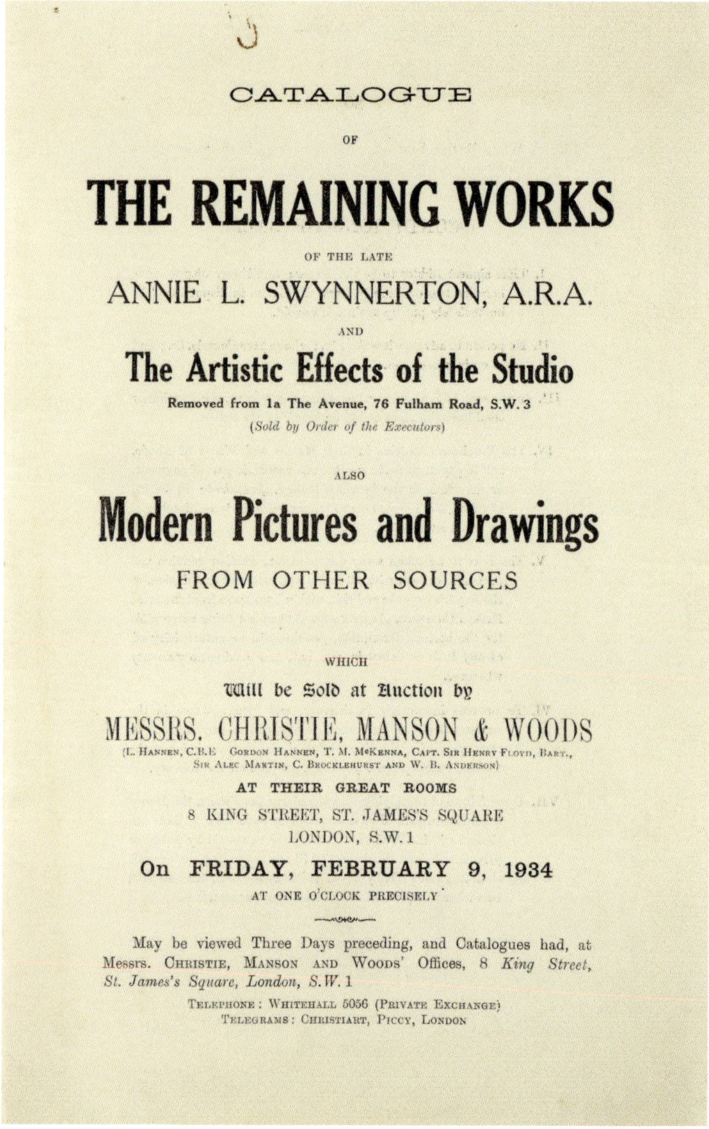

CATALOGUE

OF

THE REMAINING WORKS

OF THE LATE

ANNIE L. SWYNNERTON, A.R.A.

AND

The Artistic Effects of the Studio

Removed from 1a The Avenue, 76 Fulham Road, S.W. 3

(Sold by Order of the Executors)

ALSO

Modern Pictures and Drawings

FROM OTHER SOURCES

WHICH

Will be Sold at Auction by

MESSRS. CHRISTIE, MANSON & WOODS

(L. HANNEN, C.B.E. GORDON HANNEN, T. M. McKENNA, CAPT. SIR HENRY FLOYD, BART., SIR ALEC MARTIN, C. BROCKLEHURST AND W. B. ANDERSON)

AT THEIR GREAT ROOMS

8 KING STREET, ST. JAMES'S SQUARE

LONDON, S.W. 1

On FRIDAY, FEBRUARY 9, 1934

AT ONE O'CLOCK PRECISELY

May be viewed Three Days preceding, and Catalogues had, at Messrs. CHRISTIE, MANSON AND WOODS' Offices, 8 *King Street, St. James's Square, London, S.W.* 1

TELEPHONE: WHITEHALL 5056 (PRIVATE EXCHANGE)
TELEGRAMS: CHRISTIART, PICCY, LONDON

CAT 54 | **Auction catalogue, 9 February 1934**

Messers. Christie, Manson & Woods, paper, 25 x 15 cm
Archive material compiled by David Brownlie (1880–1951)
The Executors of Christine Brownlie Allen (1953–2014)

At the time of her death, 32 finished and 69 unfinished works, many of which were replicas and studies, remained in Swynnerton's London studio. Many were in poor condition due to her long absence from London. Nevertheless, it was at this auction that the Royal Academy acquired *The Letter* (Catalogue No. 7) for their collection.

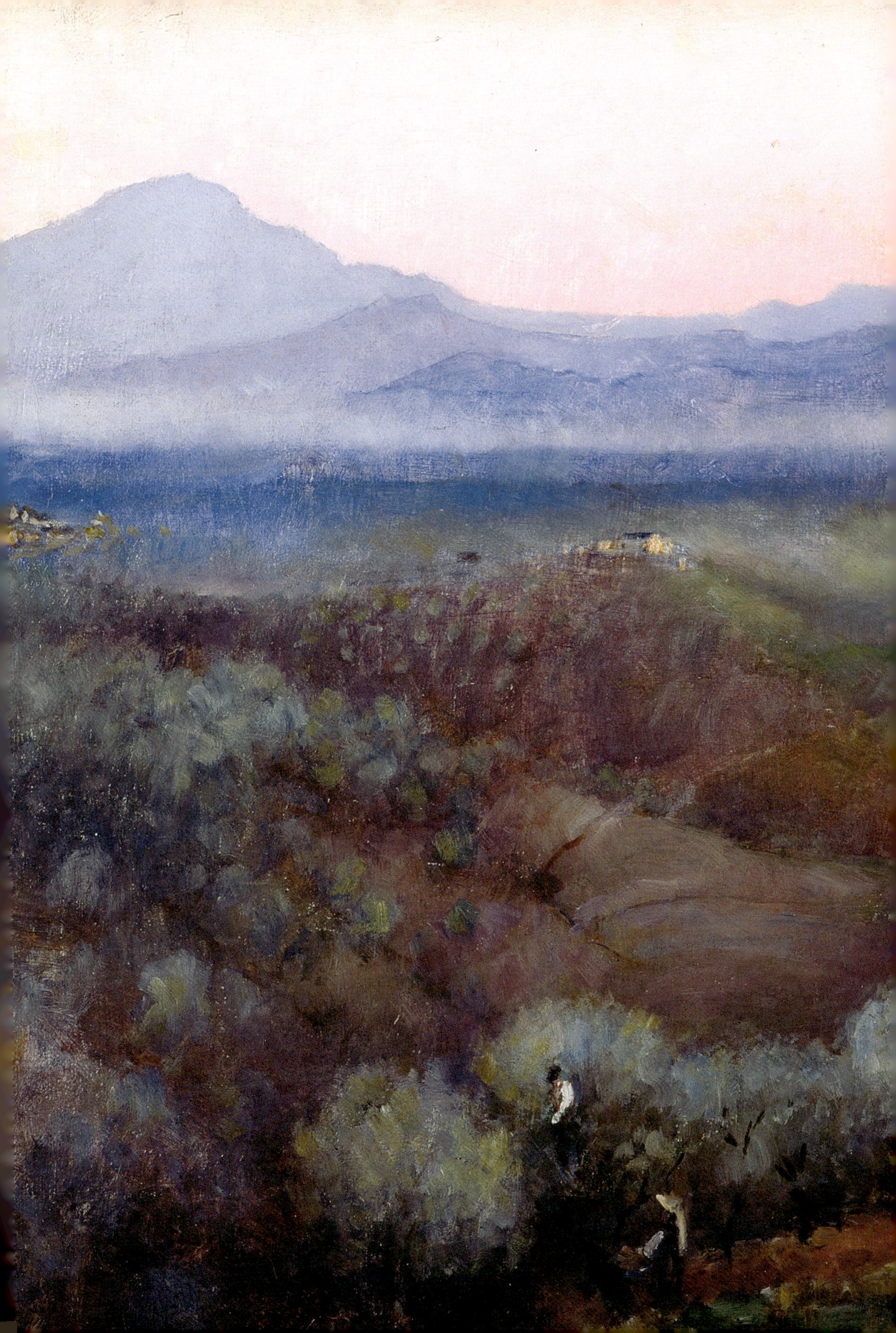

Further Reading

Archer, John H G, ed. *Art and Architecture in Victorian Manchester.* Manchester University Press, 1985.

Allen, Christine Brownlie and Penny Morris. *Annie Swynnerton: Painter and Pioneer The First Woman Associate of the Royal Academy.* Winchester: Sarsen Press, 2018.

Baile de Laperriére, Charles, ed. *A Dictionary of Artists and their Works in the Annual Exhibitions of the Society of Women Artists.* Wiltshire: Hillmarton Manor Press, 1996.

Barringer, Timothy. *Reading the Pre-Raphaelites.* New Haven, CT and London: Yale University Press, 1998; rpt. 2003.

Casteras, Susan P. and Colleen Denney, eds. *The Grosvenor Gallery: A Place of Art in Victorian England.* London: Yale University Press, 1996.

Casteras, Susan P. and Linda H. Peterson. *A Struggle for Fame: Victorian Women Artists and Authors*, exh. cat. New Haven, CT: Yale Center for British Art, 1994.

Chadwick, Whitney and Isabelle de Courtivron. *Significant Others: Creativity and Partnership.* London: Thames & Hudson, 1993.

Chadwick, Whitney. *Women, Art and Society.* London: Thames & Hudson, 1990.

Chapman, Alison and Jane Stabler, eds. *Unfolding the South: Nineteenth-century British Women Writers and Artists in Italy.* Manchester and New York: Manchester University Press and Palgrave, 2003.

Cherry, Deborah. *Painting Women: Victorian Women Artists.* London and New York: Routledge, 1993.

Crawford, Elizabeth. *The Women's Suffrage Movement: A Reference Guide, 1866-1928.* New York: Routledge, 2001.

Dakers, Caroline. *The Holland Park Circle: Artists and Victorian Society.* New Haven, CT and London: Yale University Press, 1999.

Deepwell, Katy. *Women Artists Between the Wars.* Manchester: Manchester University Press, 2010.

Dewsbury, Sheila. *The Story So Far: Manchester Academy of Fine Arts from 1859 to 2003.* Manchester: Manchester Academy of Fine Arts, 2003.

Fehrer, Catherine. 'Women at the Académie Julian in Paris', *The Burlington Magazine*, 136, no. 1100, (Nov 1994): 752-757.

Harris, Elree I. and Shirley R. Scott. *A Gallery of Her Own: an Annotated Bibliography of Women in Victorian Painting.* New York and London: Garland, 1997.

Harrison, Colin and Christopher Newall. *The Pre-Raphaelites and Italy.* Oxford: Ashmolean Museum of Art and Archaeology/University of Oxford, 2010.

Hutchison, Sidney. *The History of the Royal Academy 1878–1986.* London: Robert Royce Limited, 1968; rpt. 1986.

Kashley, Robert and Elizabeth Kashley. *The Julian Academy, Paris: 1868–1939*, exh. cat. New York: Shepherd Gallery, 1989.

Marsh, Jan and Pamela Gerrish Nunn. *Pre-Raphaelite Women Artists.* London: Thames & Hudson, 1997.

McConkey, Kenneth. *British Impressionism.* London: Phaidon, 1989; rpt. 1998.

Nead, Lynda. *The Female Nude: Art, Obscenity and Sexuality.* London and New York: Routledge, 1992.

Newall, Christopher and Allen Staley. *Pre-Raphaelite Vision: Truth to Nature.* London: Tate Publishing, 2004.

Newall, Christopher. *The Grosvenor Gallery Exhibitions: Change and Continuity in the Victorian Art World.* Cambridge: Cambridge University Press, 1995.

Orr, Clarissa Campbell, ed. *Women in the Victorian Art World.* Manchester: Manchester University Press, 1995.

Peters Corbett, David. *The World in Paint: Modern Art and Visuality in England, 1848-1914*. Manchester and New York: Manchester University Press, 2004.

Pointon, Marcia. *Naked Authority: The Body in Western Painting 1830–1908.* Cambridge: Cambridge University Press, 1990.

Prettejohn, Elizabeth. *Art for Art's Sake: Aestheticism in Victorian Painting.* New Haven, CT and London: Paul Mellon Centre for Studies in British Art and Yale University Press, 2007.

Prettejohn, Elizabeth. *Beauty and Art.* Oxford: Oxford University Press, 2005.

Sellars, Jane. *Women's Works.* Liverpool: National Museums and Galleries on Merseyside, 1988.

Staley, Allen. *The New Painting of the 1860s: Between the Pre-Raphaelites and the Aesthetic Movement*. New Haven: Yale University Press, 2011.

Storey, Gladys. *Dickens and Daughter*. London: Frederick Muller, 1939; rpt. New York 1971.

Thomson, Susan W. *Manchester's Victorian Art Scene and its Unrecognised Artists*. Manchester: Manchester Art Press, 2007.

Weisberg, Gabriel P. and Jane R. Becker, eds. *Overcoming All Obstacles: The Women of the Académie Julian*, exh. cat. New Brunswick, NJ and London: The Dahesh Museum New York, 1999.

Curators' Biographies

Dr Katie Jane Tyreman Herrington is a Non-Stipend Affiliated Postdoctoral Researcher in the Department of History of Art, University of York, who works as a freelance researcher/curator. She is principally a historian of 19th- and early 20th-century British and European art, and has a particular specialism in the work of women artists. In 2013 she undertook an AHRC-funded postdoctoral Cultural Engagement Fellowship entitled *Three Graces: Victorian women, visual art and exchange*, the chief outcome of which was an online exhibition: http://hoaportal.york.ac.uk/hoaportal/threegraces.jsp. She has led the Tate British Art Specialist Network Sub Group 'British Women Artists 1750 to 1950' since 2015.

Rebecca Milner is a Curator of Fine Art at Manchester Art Gallery where she specialises in British and European art pre-1900. She has organised numerous exhibitions and displays including *Ford Madox Brown: Pre-Raphaelite Pioneer* in 2011 and *Artists in the Frame: Self-portraits by Van Dyck and Others* in 2015. She has previously worked as a curator at the V&A, London and the National Trust.

Acknowledgements

A great many people have been involved in the realisation of this important exhibition and our greatest thanks are due to the lenders whose cooperation and kindness have made it possible. We are particularly indebted to the private collectors who have agreed to lend works for a whole year. We also acknowledge the generosity of the following institutions: Museums and Galleries, City of Bradford MDC; Dublin City Gallery, The Hugh Lane; Museum of London; National Museums Liverpool/Walker Art Gallery; Nottingham City Museums & Galleries; Gallery Oldham; Royal Academy of Arts, London; Royal Holloway, University of London; Salford Museum & Art Gallery and Tate.

The curators Rebecca Milner and Katie JT Herrington have worked closely to bring about the exhibition and catalogue. I would like to make special mention of Herrington's PhD scholarship on Swynnerton and the further research she has done which sheds new light on many of the artist's works. Thanks go to the Paul Mellon Centre for Studies in British Art, who funded a Research Support Grant that enabled Herrington to view works in public and private collections in the UK and Europe. I would also like to thank the team at Manchester Art Gallery for their diligence and professionalism in realising the exhibition and catalogue.

We are grateful to the Art Fund for providing a grant towards the exhibition catalogue and other activities associated with the exhibition. This supports our participation in a nationwide programme of in-conversations, exhibitions and events with Art Fund support to celebrate the 250th anniversary of the Royal Academy of Arts.

Alistair Hudson
Director, Manchester Art Gallery

Curators' Acknowledgements

We would like to thank the many individuals and institutions that have helped make this exhibition and catalogue possible. In particular we gratefully acknowledge Melva Croal (former Curator of Fine Art at Manchester Art Gallery) who long sought a Swynnerton retrospective and whose work to that end has been of great help to us and Prof Jason Edwards (University of York), Dr Sarah Monks (University of East Anglia), Alison Smith (Chief Curator, National Portrait Gallery) and Carol Jacobi (Curator British Art 1850-1915, Tate) for their advice and support. We also thank Penny Morris and Nicholas Allen for their help and encouragement, and Danny Morrell, Lauren Turner and Michael Kirkbride, whose research enhanced our knowledge of select paintings and Swynnerton's early life. Special acknowledgement goes to Christine Brownlie Allen (1953–2014), whose biographical research on Swynnerton with Penny Morris is about to be published. We are indebted to our catalogue editor Lindsay Porter for her expertise and enthusiasm and to the catalogue designer Alan Ward. We would also like to thank the following staff and teams at Manchester Art Gallery for their help delivering the exhibition: Adam Butler, Shamus Dawes, Claire Grundy, Bev Hogg, Natasha Howes, Julia Jackson, Sian Millar, Catriona Morgan, Chris Russell, Art Technicians, Audience Development, Learning Team and Visitor Services. Finally we thank our families for their support throughout this project.

Katie JT Herrington & Rebecca Milner